Inception
and Philosophy

Popular Culture and Philosophy® Series Editor: George A. Reisch

For full details of all Popular Culture and Philosophy® books, visit www.opencourtbooks.com.

Popular Culture and Philosophy®

Inception and Philosophy

Ideas to Die For

Edited by
THORSTEN BOTZ-BORNSTEIN

OPEN COURT
Chicago and LaSalle, Illinois

Volume 62 in the series, Popular Culture and Philosophy ®, edited by George A. Reisch

To order books from Open Court, call toll-free 1-800-815-2280, or visit our website at www.opencourtbooks.com.

Open Court Publishing Company is a division of Carus Publishing Company.

Printed and bound in the United States of America.

Library of Congress Cataloging-in-Publication Data

Inception and philosophy : ideas to die for / edited by Thorsten Botz-Bornstein.
     p. cm.—(Popular culture and philosophy ; v. 62)
    Includes bibliographical references (p.   ) and index.
    ISBN 978-0-8126-9733-9 (trade paper : alk. paper)
    1. Inception (Motion picture) I. Botz-Bornstein, Thorsten.
    PN1997.2.I62I58 2011
    791.43—dc23

                                         2011031893

Contents

Who's Putting Ideas in Your Head?

Two and a half thousand years ago Plato asked: How exactly can we explain our perceptions of reality? The top has been spinning ever since.

Dreams are the original virtual reality. For thousands of years dreams have been ransacked for hidden memories, messages, desires, fears, and secrets.

Dreams are generally weird and sometimes seem absurd, but they don't usually feel weird when we're in them. When we wake up from a dream, we're surprised to find that in the dream we accepted as real many things we now automatically reject as preposterous. But maybe we're now accepting other things we would find equally preposterous if we could wake up from what we call waking life.

Dreams are often tremendously intricate and detailed. If the world of the dream isn't real, who made it up? We know that we most certainly didn't. So where does this world come from? Although strange things can happen in a dream, not anything can happen. We have only limited control over what goes on in our dreams. They have strict laws of their own. Dreams possess a deadly, implacable logic, which may sometimes frustrate or terrify us.

Many viewers enjoy *Inception* as a story while telling themselves that nothing like this thrilling tale could happen in real life. But (as Chapters 1 and 2 of this book explain) modern neuroscience and philosophy of mind have been showing that most of what occurs in *Inception* could become hard reality very soon. We almost have the technology to perform inception by way of shared dreams.

To watch *Inception* is to get into endless discussions about what's really going on in the movie. Various theories are kicked around in this book. At one extreme, there's the theory that the entire movie is just a single dream: Cobb's dream on the long airline flight. This theory appeals to psychoanalysts and takes care of a lot of troublesome problems with the story: it's expounded by Nicolas Floury in Chapter 17. We guarantee that once you've read Nicolas's chapter, you'll never again be able to watch *Inception* without finding one confirmation after another of the single-dream theory.

A very different—but equally ingenious and equally haunting—interpretation is given by Randall Auxier in Chapter 21. Randy proposes a theory that explains most of the difficult or apparently inconsistent points in the story, but which many fans of the movie will find quite startling.

Matthew Brophy takes a different tack in Chapter 14, arguing that the dreams in which Cobb and his team navigate are actually electronic dreams. They don't exist in the individuals' brains but on a server. This is why, for Cobb, Mal has become Mal-ware. Technology has made shared dreaming possible: computer users regularly jack in and populate worlds created by programming architects. Forty-three percent of residents of virtual worlds such as *Second Life* report that they feel at least as strongly about their virtual community as they feel about the real world. Are they walking away from the real world just as Dom Cobb did? Or are they simply walking from one reality to another? For some people, one reality just isn't enough.

Three and a half centuries ago, René Descartes pointed out that, logically, we can never be sure we're not dreaming. Yet while Descartes called into question the reality of our experience, he did not doubt that our thoughts are our own. This claim is contested in *Inception*. And strangely enough, recent findings in neuroscience apparently show that our thoughts *cannot possibly* be our own (as Janet Testerman explains in Chapter 5)—because we act upon them before we become aware of them!

Inception is not the first movie to develop the theme of "implanted ideas." In *Blade Runner* (1982), Rachael plays piano for Deckard in his apartment and remarks that she remembers having had piano lessons. She's not sure if she actually learned to play, or if her piano-playing abilities are the result of neural implants. In *Inception*, however, ideas are implanted into the minds of humans, not replicants. And not by chemical means (as in *Dark City*), but by stealthily breaking and entering people's subconscious minds via their dreams.

Some people feel bad about what happens in their dreams, though if the dream is purely their own creation, and all the other people in the dream are just imaginary, then why feel bad? Shooting and killing people in dreams can't be wrong, as they're not really people. All this changes if we can get into other people's dreams and share their dream worlds.

We all agree that inception—implanting an idea in someone's mind—would most often be morally wrong, though we may not agree on exactly why it's wrong or *how* wrong it is. Most folks would probably think that inception is not *very* bad, that it's a bit like telling fibs. In Chapter 7 Marcus Schulzke points out that implanting an idea in a person's mind is a clear violation of autonomy. Inception is a sort of 'thought manipulation' similar to propaganda, peer pressure, or advertising. In more severe cases it can be like brainwashing or non-consensual hypnosis.

Chapters 7 and 8 look at some of these ethical problems. But, as Daniel Malloy argues in Chapter 6, *Inception* is fundamentally a tale from the business world. The major players are not real persons but those subconscious projections called corporations.

What about the authenticity of ideas? We live in a world where it has become difficult to tell real from fake, and where the rights of the 'original creator' have become a fiercely contentious issue. In *Inception* we learn, sadly, that even *true inspiration* may have been faked.

You just have to go deeper. We all know that *Inception* is about myth and religion. In Chapter 16 Indalecio Garcia looks at some of the views of timelessness and eternity which have fed into *Inception*, while in Chapter 9 Thomas Kapper contemplates the maze of myth with the help of the original clue-giver—Ariadne, of course. In Chapter 10, Randy Auxier tells us why dreams need architects, and what this has to do with mythic consciousness.

How will *Inception* change your thinking? You can't imagine. How will *Inception and Philosophy* change your life? You simply have no idea.

Level 1

Come Back to Reality, Please

1

How to Keep Track of Reality

Sylvia Wenmackers

At first sight, *Inception* has a happy ending: Cobb manages to return to his home country without problems and finally sees his children again. But the spinning top makes you wonder: is Cobb really seeing his children or is he still inside a dream? *Inception* may also make you wonder about your own life. Can you ever be certain that it's real? How do you know that you're really reading this book now, instead of dreaming that you are? Skeptical philosophy claims that, ultimately, you can never be sure of this.

Inception's Dream Theory

Let's first look at some dream basics. During our sleep, we go through several sleep cycles, each consisting of a number of phases. The sleeping phase in which we dream is characterized by rapid eye movements, hence the name 'REM sleep'.

Diagrams of Reality

The content of a dream is supposed to originate from a subconscious part of the sleeper's brain. 'Sub' means 'below'. Therefore, a dream is referred to as a 'deeper' level than reality in *Inception*. Figure 1.1 depicts the experience of a dream: the full line keeps track of which level the subject is aware of and the horizontal direction marks the passing of time. The downward arrow indicates that the subject enters the dream, the upward arrow that he stops dreaming. A similar diagram can be used to represent other 'virtual' experiences such as being absorbed in a game, or having a hallucination. It could even be you, as you were watching *Inception*, completely forgetting the actual world around you.

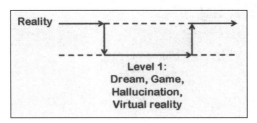

Figure 1.1. When we dream, we experience a virtual reality. The diagram represents this as a lower level of reality.

Throughout this chapter, I'm going to use this type of diagram. At first, you might think it would be more natural to visualize the worlds-within-worlds as built upward rather than downward. In the case of a computer-generated world, like *The Matrix* or *The Thirteenth Floor*, the base level of reality is required to host the computer infrastructure which runs the simulation. This suggests that the virtual level is built on top of reality. However, since the dream world of *Inception* is what we're most interested in, I'll always depict the virtual worlds as *below* the actual world.

A Dream Shared by Soldiers, Architects, and Thieves

You may have experienced a dream in which you suddenly realized that you were dreaming: a lucid dream. You may even be among those who try to enter this dream state on purpose. If so, you probably keep a dream diary and ask yourself critically 'Am I awake or am I dreaming?' several times a day. When this has become a habit, the same thought may occur to you during a dream. Then, you may become aware that you're in a dream, ringing in a lucid episode. When that happens, you can actively influence the plot and the scenery of your own dream. You are then ready to become the star in the movie that's screening inside your own skull. Some people claim that lucid dreams can be used to train you in certain skills, such as skiing.

In *Inception*, the military has developed a technology to allow soldiers to share lucid dreams, in which they can practice their fighting skills on each other without harming anyone. Drugs are used to control the depth of their sleep and architects are hired to design the dreams. One of them, Stephen Miles, a professor of architecture in Paris, started using shared dreams as a new way of creating buildings and showing them to other people. He introduced the technique to his daughter Mal and her partner Cobb, both students of architecture.

After Mal's death, Cobb starts using shared dreams for extraction and inception: stealing information from someone's unconsciousness or implanting a new idea into it, while the victim—the mark—is participating in a shared dream unknowingly. Miles also introduces Cobb to one of his current students, Ariadne. Arthur teaches her to design maze-like levels and to include paradoxical architecture: short-cuts based on Escher-like optical illusions, such as the Penrose steps.

Dreaming in the Classroom

If the possibility of sharing a dream is ever realized, it may be of great value as a team building or brain storming activity, or simply for entertainment. As a physicist, I also believe it would be a great tool for physics education: imagine that instead of doing paper exercises, you could do hands-on experiments on gravity by going to the Moon or to Mars. You could test how fast you could ride on a bike if there was no air friction. You could see how the color of the sky changes by adjusting the composition of the atmosphere. If such a technology existed, instead of penalizing students for day-dreaming, teachers would actually encourage sleeping in the class room!

Novel technologies bring new opportunities as well as new threats. This has been true since the Stone Age. If you have fire, you can cook a meal or burn down a village. *Inception* shows how thieves can take advantage of the technology of shared dreaming. And of course, it's possible to want too much of a good thing: sharing the dream turns out to be highly addictive! We learn that Cobb and Mal spent too much time in the world they built from their imagination and we see a group of addicts, who come to share the dream every day, at Yusuf's place.

Dreams-within-Dreams

While in a dream, it's possible to invoke a new shared dream. In that case, the dreamer of the initial dream level stays behind. Whereas extraction can be performed in a first-level or second-level dream, inception is supposed to be much harder, requiring at least a third-level dream. Dreams-within-dreams are unstable and therefore require stronger sedatives.

At a time before the story of *Inception* begins, Cobb and Mal experimented with dreams-within-dreams. Figure 1.2 depicts some of their dream experiments. Together, they also discovered a very deep dream level—nobody knows how deep exactly—Limbo.

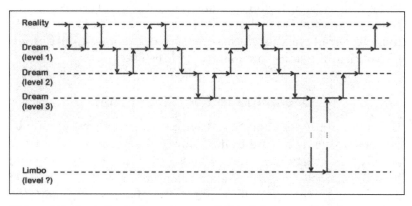

Figure 1.2. *Inception* features the possibility of dreams-within-dreams.

Wake Me Up Before You Go-Go

I've had some spontaneous lucid dreams, but instead of going on an adventure, I found the experience rather claustrophobic. I tried to feel the position of my sleeping body or to open my eyes, but realized that I had no access to any of my senses. Trying to wake up by jumping up and down (within the dream) failed. Later, I learned a better way to wake from a lucid dream, based on the fact that dreams occur during REM sleep: just keep your eyes fixed on something—that should do the trick.

A shared dream ends when the drugs run out. To warn the dreamers, musical count-down is used. To wake a dreamer earlier, he can be given a kick: a period of free fall followed by suddenly hitting a surface. When the inner ear registers this discrepancy between the actual and the dream state, the person wakes up. This also works under sedation, provided that the inner ear isn't affected by the drugs. If someone dies in a dream, he wakes up, but this does not work under sedation! When a person dies in a dream but is too sedated in the actual world to wake up, he enters Limbo instead: he washes up on the shore of his unconsciousness. Nothing exists there, except for what's been constructed by any of the team members who've been there before.

A Matter of Time

In a dream, we may have the impression that a lot of time has passed, much longer than the actual duration of our sleep. Arthur explains to Ariadne that an hour in the dream corresponds to five minutes in the real world. So for every minute of reality, there are twelve minutes in the dream. Yusuf provides the team with a stronger version of the compounds, which make the time spent in a dream increase by a factor of twenty, not twelve—supposedly by speeding up brain function. In each deeper dream level, time goes faster by the same factor.

This is a strange premise: after all, there are no additional drugs administered to the dreamer's body at the level of reality. How is his brain supposed to keep up with creating the environment of dreams-within-dreams? I guess, in dreams some things just don't add up . . . So, let's accept the premise and calculate the time. In the third level, the factor is twenty times twenty times twenty, or eight thousand. Ariadne realizes that the ten-hour flight of Sydney to LA will take eighty thousand hours or about ten years at the third level, but Eames reassures her that they won't have to spend more than a couple of days at the deepest level.

Because the time factor is multiplied each level down, time increases exponentially. This means that a short time span at the level of reality appears as an enormous time down in Limbo: enough time for Cobb and Mal to grow old together, and enough time for Saito to forget where he is, until Cobb comes back to remind him.

Keeping Track of Reality

It's the possibility of dreams-within-dreams that leaves the viewer puzzled at the end: it's a genuine possibility that Cobb is still in a dream and that we haven't had so much as a glimpse of the real world in the whole movie. This disturbing thought relates well to skepticism. Skepticism is a branch of philosophy with an attitude: an attitude of questioning the obvious, of doubting what most people assume to be unshakable truths. Now, we're going to explore skeptical questions and apply them to make sense of *Inception*'s ending.

Are Dreams Less Real than Waking Life?

The world that surrounds us appears real to us. It has predictable properties which seem to be consistent over time. In the West, dreams are traditionally considered to be less real than the world we experience while we're awake. This wasn't the case for all times and cultures.

The Butterfly Who Dreamt He Was a Philosopher

As Cobb points out, dreams also appear real to us while we're in them. It's only when we wake up that we realize things were strange. This observation brings us to our first skeptical question:

> Are we justified in considering the experiences we have while we're awake as more real than the ones we have while dreaming?

Zhuangzi, a Chinese scholar in the fourth century B.C., was one of the first skeptical philosophers. In a famous poem, he stated that he did not know whether he was Zhuangzi who had dreamt that he was a butterfly, or a butterfly dreaming that he was Zhuangzi. This poem can be made into a diagram with two levels, as in Figure 1.3: one level contains a man, the other level contains a butterfly, but it's not clear which one's at the top (more real) level. Or maybe both are equally real?

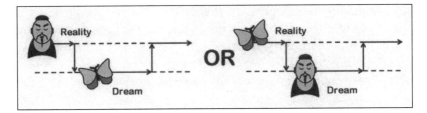

Figure 1.3. Zhuangzi dreams he's a butterfly. Or is it the other way around?

The dreamer addicts at Yusuf's place are said to come to be woken up; dream has become their reality. The idea that there's another world which is more real than the one we normally experience is also present in Aboriginal mythology: the Dreaming is a spiritual world in which the soul of each person exists eternally (in cyclical time). Only some persons are able to have contact with this spiritual world (for instance, by entering a dream or state of trance).

(How) Can We Know When We're Dreaming?

Keeping track of what's real and what's not, becomes even more urgent when you live in a world where several people can enter the same dream and you may be lured into such a dream by criminals who want to steal your secrets, or—worse still—implant foreign ideas into your mind. Cobb and his team are practical people. They have little time for pondering whether their dreams are more real than their waking life. A question that does matter to them is:

How Can We Establish Whether We're Awake or Dreaming?

This is a skeptical question, too: probably you take for granted that you're reading this book while being awake, rather than dreaming it up, but how can you be so sure? As a side note, another movie that combines the theme of lucid dreaming and existentialist questions is Richard Linklater's *Waking Life* from 2001.

Asking yourself 'Am I awake or not?' until it becomes a habit isn't the only way of making yourself aware that you're dreaming. After all, when it comes to it, you may still fool yourself into believing that you're awake. A trick to realize that it's a dream is to check light switches: supposedly, in a dream they won't function properly. Because our dreams occur during REM sleep, trying to read a text or looking at the details of something will usually not work in a dream and discovering this, may also start a lucid episode.

The Stolen Totem

The main characters of *Inception* have a 'totem'. This is a personal object with a certain weight distribution, which is supposed to be known only by the owner. If someone doesn't know the exact properties of your totem, it may still figure in his dream, but the totem will react differently from normal. The idea is that you, the owner, can use the totem to establish whether you're in someone else's dream or not.

There are at least two strange things about Cobb's totem. One of the rules is that you should never allow someone else to touch your totem, but Cobb has taken Mal's. This doesn't mean that he can't use this spinning top as a reliable way of keeping track of reality, just that he ruined it as such a tool for his wife. We see him with her totem, which she had locked in a doll house (to forget that they were deep down in Limbo rather than awake), but in order to get her totem, he should take it in reality. We didn't see that happen, but he may have taken it after she died (although he did have to leave in a rush). The fact that Cobb's totem was actually Mal's and we didn't see how he got it helps to make the movie's ending so dubious. This is a good thing.

Now a point of criticism. The way this particular totem is supposed to work—it keeps spinning when in a dream—just doesn't make sense. Everybody knows that in the real world, a top doesn't keep spinning, due to friction. As Ariadne demonstrates, the dreamer may influence the laws of physics in a dream in dramatic ways. So, removing friction should be peanuts, but why would any dreamer who tries to fool someone else into mistaking his dream for real life, make such an obvious mistake? In that respect, the red die of Arthur, which is loaded but in an unknown way, and the chess piece of Ariadne, a bishop in which she drilled a hole to influence its tipping point, seem far more credible as reality-tracking devices.

Follow the Red Thread

Ariadne does justice to her Greek name: not only does she design maze-like dream levels for Cobb; she also leads him out of his own labyrinth. She helps Cobb to resolve the perforating guilt which feeds his projection of Mal, making her appear like a monster much like the Minotaur, jeopardizing the operation of his entire team. While watching the movie, I was hoping that Ariadne would also help us, the viewers, to determine whether or not the floor level of the movie is real—Ariadne would've made a very elegant device for keeping track of reality! —but I wasn't able to spot any such clue, except maybe for the very fact that she belongs to the level Cobb assumes to be reality.

(How) Can We Know whether Our World Is Real?

Totems won't help us with our following question:

> How (if at all) can we know whether the world we experience while we're awake is real or not?

Since we don't have totems, we have to find some other method of inquiry. The Greek word for 'inquiry' is 'skepsis'. Inquiry often leads to doubt. As such, skepticism can be interpreted as the philosophical school of doubt.

Cave Men

'Plato's Cave' is a story written by Plato, who attributes it to his teacher Socrates. The story deals with a group of prisoners who have lived their entire life in a cave. They're chained, with their heads fixed, and all they can see are shadows on a wall. The prisoners are unaware that the shadows are produced by people holding objects in front of a great fire, because all of this happens behind their backs. For all the prisoners know, the shadows in front of them are the only reality.

In the story, a single prisoner is freed. He's allowed to see how the shadows are produced and even what the world outside the cave looks like. It must be very hard for such a man to understand what he sees: he has never seen color or depth and has no words to describe those sensations. All the words he knows refer to shadow forms, rather than the real objects surrounding him now. Given some time, however, he may start to make sense of it all. He'll realize that shadows aren't objects, that they're merely projections of real objects. Figure 1.4 is a diagram of his experience.

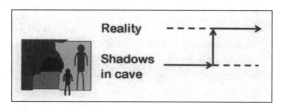

Figure 1.4. A prisoner is freed from Plato's Cave.

Suppose then that the man has to return to his fellow prisoners. He claims that the world they see isn't real, but he can't provide any explanation for this wild claim, at least not in any terms that they'd understand. They lack the words and the concepts for color and depth, and, unlike the man who was freed, they aren't able to learn them from experience. They're unable to understand his stories about the fire behind them and the world outside the cave. They'll call him crazy. When he offers them the chance of going out into the world, they'll refuse, afraid to spoil their own eyes the way he has spoiled his.

Shadows of Ideas

The prisoners simply can't imagine a world different from the two-dimensional dark-and-bright appearances in front of them. Are we like the prisoners? True, we can distinguish between shadows and real objects, but how real are the objects we consider to be real? Are they figments of someone's imagination, someone whose dream we're sharing? Are they merely projections of a higher reality?

Plato claims that the ever-changing objects in the material world that we perceive are really projections of eternal 'Ideas' or 'Forms' that exist in some higher level of reality. Hence, Plato's philosophy is called idealism. So, the original meaning of 'idealism' isn't a fight for higher goals, but the belief that there exists a level of reality that's to be considered as 'more real' than what we usually consider to be real. This world of eternal Ideas is similar to the Dreaming in Aboriginal mythology.

Figure 1.5 shows us Plato's two-step reasoning. In Step 1, he realizes that some people may confuse shadows with reality. In Step 2, he applies this idea to what we take to be reality and concludes that our reality may be a 'shadow' of some higher level of reality, too. We'll soon see that the diagram for the world of *Inception* has a structure similar to that of Figure 1.5.

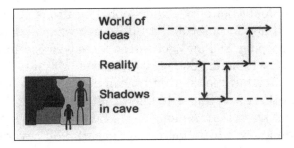

Figure 1.5. By considering the illusory nature of what the lifelong prisoners of a cave would consider reality, Plato concludes that our world may also be an illusion.

Job Description for Philosophers

The story of the cave is intended to make us doubt about our world, but also as a job description for philosophers: like the prisoner who was freed, philosophers have to enlighten other people about the reality beyond the things they can see directly.

Unlike the prisoner who was freed, however, philosophers have no means to access any other level of reality than the one they and everybody else experiences every day. They're as much prisoners with limited senses as everybody else. They have no clue as to whether we're in someone's dream—maybe the (shared) dream of god(s)?—in a projection from a higher-dimensional world, or something else entirely. In my opinion, nobody, not even a philosopher, can tell what the ultimate level of reality is like. The task of a philosopher is rather to make people realize that we can't know this. Even if we were to find out that our life is a dream, the problem would pop up again: we wouldn't be able to establish whether the level of reality at which the dreamer lives is itself a dream or a projection. And if we were to establish this . . . You see where we're going. This profound uncertainty is the basis of skeptical philosophy.

Know that You Know Nothing

Philosophy is a discipline about questions rather than answers. It's a tribute to doubt. According to Socrates, true wisdom comes to us only when we realize how little we understand about life, ourselves, and the world around us. If *Inception* made you doubt not only about Cobb, but also about your own life, even if just for a second, it fulfilled the core task of a skeptical philosopher. You may consider this to be a pessimistic outcome: we try to determine on which level of reality Cobb is or where we are, but realize that we can never be sure how many levels 'up' there are. But if we know that we can't establish this, we at least know *that*. As long as we know that we know nothing, we do know a little more than people who never question the reality of their everyday world. Socrates would've been proud of us.

I Doubt, therefore I Am

Another champion of doubt was René Descartes. His 'cogito ergo sum'—I think therefore I am—is one of the most famous philosophical quotes. Although it sounds firm and certain, the very thought was born from doubt. Like most people, Descartes doubted some things, but then he reasoned: the very fact that I have doubts about something shows that I doubt, which shows that there's a subject (someone who does the doubting: me), therefore I exist. In other words: I doubt, therefore I am. Although Descartes's philosophy starts from doubt, it leads him to certainty. In that sense, he's not a skeptical philosopher, because the conclusion of his reasoning is that the existence of the world is certain.

So we no longer need to doubt our own existence. Phew! The certainty of our own private existence does, however, not prove that there's a material world. The world we experience could still be a dream. We could be the victim of a demon who makes us believe that all of this is real. All it takes is a con man, like Cobb. (In particular, all other people may be projections—a position known as 'solipsism'.) How did Descartes deal with this? Well, he provided a proof for the existence of god and relied on god's good nature to rule out this demonic possibility.

Nowadays, Descartes's conclusions, which he was so certain about, aren't regarded as valid anymore. In particular, it's no longer believed that religious matters can be settled in any definitive way. Without his god, Descartes is unable to help us with interpreting *Inception*: whether or not Cobb is fooling himself into believing he's home, can't be settled. Cobb, the con man, may be fooled by Descartes's evil genius, who tricks us into taking an imaginary world for reality.

Dreams and Other Forms of Virtual Reality

One observation that may lead to skepticism is this:

In our life, we have dreams.

When we're dreaming, we usually don't realize that it's a dream.

Therefore, all our life may be a dream without our knowing.

But there are other ways of imagining that our life isn't real, for instance Plato's Cave story:

In our world, there are shadows.

We can imagine people who confuse shadows with reality.

Therefore, our world may be some sort of shadow, too.

Let's now consider a third possibility, which is more up-to-date with our current technology:

In our world, we have realistic computer simulations.

We might be in a world simulated by a supercomputer, without knowing it.

These ideas offer great opportunities for movie makers: dream worlds and virtual realities allow for fantastic events to happen, which would be unbelievable when set in the real world.

Suggesting that 'the real world' is or might be unreal, adds a sense of uneasiness, that may stick with the audience as the end titles roll up the screen, and possibly longer still. Therefore, the worlds-within-worlds theme is popular in science fiction and horror, as well as in skeptic philosophy.

Filmosophy

Let's look at three movies from before *Inception*, whose plots can be understood as updated versions of Plato's cave story: *The Matrix*, *The Thirteenth Floor*, and *eXistenZ*—all three released in 1999. The premise of *The Matrix* (written and directed by Andy and Lana Wachowski) was this: what we consider to be the real world is actually a simulation, which runs in a world we've never seen. In the movie, this world looks different from ours, but our bodies appear there much as how they appear here.

Figure 1.6 shows the diagram for Neo, the protagonist of *The Matrix*. If you compare it to Figure 1.4, you'll see that Neo's experience matches that of the prisoner who's freed from Plato's Cave. Only the nature of the lower level is different: shadows in Plato's case, computer simulations in Neo's case.

Like Plato's Cave, *The Matrix* suggests that we can question the existence of our world: Is it real or simulated? Can we ever know this? And, does it matter?

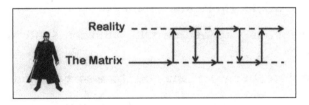

Figure 1.6. Neo escapes from *The Matrix* . . .

The Thirteenth Floor (directed by Josef Rusnak) features Descartes's 'I think therefore I am' as its motto. The movie explores the possibility that computer simulations become realistic enough to allow the simulated entities in it to become conscious. Douglas Hall discovers that our world is also a simulation. Figure 1.7 shows the diagram of his story, which has exactly the same structure as Figure 1.5: the existence of lower levels of reality prompts the discovery of higher ones.

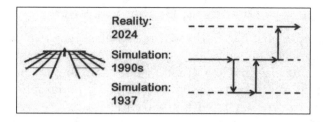

Figure 1.7. Douglas Hall discovers his world isn't real in *The Thirteenth Floor*.

The beginning of *eXistenZ* (written and directed by David Cronenberg) is set in a world where people play games by connecting a piece of technology called a 'pod' (see left-hand side of Figure 1.8) to a 'bioport' in their spine. Multiple players can enter the same game and there are games-within-games—much like the dreams in *Inception*.

It turns out that the launch of the game 'eXistenZ' shown at the start of the film, doesn't take place in the actual world, but is itself part of a game called 'tranCendenZ'. Figure 1.8 shows the most straightforward interpretation for the main character, Allegra Geller, which looks like an elaborate version of Plato's idealism of Figure 1.5. At the end of the movie, the participants seem uncertain as to whether they're still inside some game or not, leaving the viewers utterly confused. The possibility that there are higher levels of reality is also indicated in Figure 1.8. The multiple sub-levels and the open ending make this diagram the most similar to the one we will draw for *Inception*.

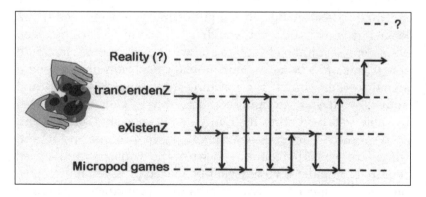

Figure 1.8. Allegra Geller's realities in *eXistenZ*.

Dreaming Brains-in-a-Vat

In *Inception*, just like in these three movies, people appear with the same body on each level. (Only Eames can present himself as someone else inside a dream; we see him impersonate Peter Browning and a blonde woman.) In 1982, philosopher Hilary Putnam confronted us with a scarier skeptical scenario: at the highest level of reality, we may consist of nothing more than a brain, a dreaming brain in a vat filled with nutrients.

In a way, your mental image of the world is some sort of virtual reality, even when your brain really *is* inside your body. Your brain can only interact with your body (and thus with the rest of the world) via electrochemical signals. Specific nerves carry information from your sense organs to your brain: they send it pulses to evoke visual and auditory sensations, smells and tastes, feelings of pressure, heat and pain. Other nerves carry signals from the brain to your muscles to make you move. So, at least in principle, it should be possible to disconnect the brain from the body, keep it alive in a vat, and connect its nerve endings to a supercomputer, which is able to compute the virtual reality as experienced by all the brains connected to it, simultaneously and in real time.

This brings us to a new phrasing of one of our skeptical questions:

Is it possible that our brain isn't in our skull, but in a vat?

Well, wait a minute, you might say: I know that I'm not a brain-in-a-vat, for I can see my own hands and move them. The skeptical philosopher won't be convinced by your argument: if the machine is fast enough to compute what you would see if you looked at your hands, you couldn't tell the difference between what your real hands look like and what a brain-in-a-vat would see. If you want to move your hands, your brain has to send a signal to them, but if the machine intercepts this signal and adjusts what you see (and feel) accordingly, your brain is still not able to tell whether it's really inside your skull or in a vat.

As a second attempt, you might try this counterargument: there are no supercomputers with the capacity and speed required to render a virtual reality shared by seven billion people, and brain-computer interfaces aren't advanced enough to make such a connection work for even a single brain. Again, the skeptic won't be impressed. If we're brains-in-a-vat, all we know is this virtual reality. We've never seen anything of the real word in which our brains reside. The technology may be more evolved there, or the entire world may be entirely different from ours, with a different physics, allowing possibilities unknown to us.

The Virtue of Curiosity

The possibility of spending our whole life in a simulated environment brings up ethical concerns: Would it be wrong to deprive a person of knowing the truth about the world, even if we offer him a better though simulated world? Would you agree to leave the world behind completely, to live in a more exciting game world, or to avoid ever feeling pain again? These questions were posed by Robert Nozick back in 1974: he called his thought experiment 'the experience machine'. If you could live a more pleasant life in Limbo, what's wrong with that?

As long as there are hints about a higher level of reality, it's only human to try and learn as much as possible about this higher level. This incurable curiosity has driven our science and technology. Some physicists hypothesize that elementary particles are vibrations of higher dimensional strings, or that our universe is a hologram.

The situation is different, however, when there are no hints which point into the direction of further, higher levels of reality. Then we have to accept our existence on the level we happen to be at, in the knowledge that we can't know its ultimate status.

Maybe We Don't Really Exist?

Suppose that we appear in someone's dream as a projection, but have no independent existence of our own outside this dream. Or, suppose that we figure in a simulation, but that there's no counterpart of us in the world that runs the simulation. We may be conscious on that level, but when the dreamer wakes up, or when someone shuts off his computer, we'd simply disappear. It seems like we would still like to claim that we exist, although the dreamer or programmer may deny this. Maybe, in so far as there are different levels of dreams, there are also different levels of 'existence'? (The projection of) Mal says that Cobb doesn't believe in one reality anymore.

The way our brain works allows us to keep track of only one level of reality at a time. So, from our subjective point of view, reality is a relative concept: our mental experiences are equally real on each level we have access to. In other words, the subjective versions of the diagrams in this chapter would all be straight lines: the logic of our environment may change over time, but our experiences feel equally real.

Damn You, Nolan!

I should've known better than to go and see *Inception*. I'd seen Christopher Nolan's *The Prestige* and thinking through its consequences kept me up all night. Same story with *Memento*: I just had to see that one again until it all made sense.

No, I don't like open endings. You sit there, pondering and trying to remember if the top really did become slightly more wobbly just before the closing scene was cut, or you just imagined that. The credits roll up the screen and you put on your coat. And what do you hear as you leave the movie theatre? It's Edith Piaf's *Non, je ne regrette rien*, as if you're being woken up by your own team members operating from your real life, just one level up. The song even slows down near the end and the cold chill of doubt rolls down your spine.

Damn You, Plato!

The more philosophy we apply, the more open-ended *Inception* becomes: Cobb may be awake or in a dream, but even when he's really awake, reality itself may be a projection or some kind of a dream. Figure 1.9 shows the diagram for Cobb during his failed extraction in Saito (left) and during his final assignment (right): the inception of Robert Fischer is planned at the third dream level, but Cobb ends up in Limbo with Saito. The diagram gives a chronological account of Cobb's story, not the order of the narrative in the movie, which starts with a scene from Limbo.

The main diagram in Figure 1.9 takes *Inception* at face value, with a happy ending. The most tantalizing alternative interpretation is that Cobb ends at the level where he started the job, but that his level of reality is actually a dream. If his reality is a dream, it could be a shared one (similar to brains-in-a-vat), or all the other characters (including Arthur, Ariadne, Saito, Yusuf, Eames, and Fischer) may be projections from an unconscious part of Cobb's own brain. So far, we've learned that we may never know what the ultimate, highest level of reality is.

The diagram for the prisoner who was freed from Plato's cave (Figure 1.4) shows a step function: the prisoner becomes aware of a higher level of reality. We've seen that a movie like *The Matrix* has the same underlying structure (Figure 1.6). The diagram for *Inception* in Figure 1.9, however, doesn't show such a step function. Now, remember how Plato's Cave was intended to have a certain effect on its audience: to make them aware of (the possibility of) a higher level of reality, as depicted in Figure 1.5. This is precisely what *Inception* does to its viewers, too.

And so, Christopher Nolan pulled off a masterly piece of inception himself. Making a movie is a great way of getting

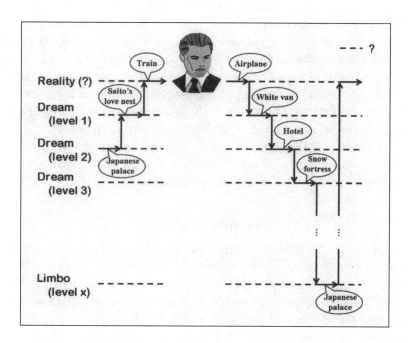

Figure 1.9. Dom Cobb attempts extraction in Saito (left) and inception in Fischer (right).

ideas into people's heads . . . If you take into account the fact that Cobb is a fictional character in a movie, his top can never tell him this. And even if it would, he can never transit from his level of reality to ours: he can't step from the screen into the movie theater, can he? That's a good reason not to show whether or not the top stopped spinning: in an absolute sense, Cobb is certainly not at the highest level of reality, but relative to his story in the movie, he may be.

Why I Won't Commit Suicide (and You Shouldn't Either)

One of the premises of *Inception* is that if this life is all a dream, we may wake up by killing ourselves. But if we're wrong about being in a dream, we'll just end up being dead instead of awake. . . . This motive may remind us of cult suicides: some people in sects believe that by dying they will 'wake up' into a supposedly better afterlife. Within this delusion, committing suicide is just a way of speeding up the process.

As far as I know, nobody killed himself after seeing *Inception*. Phew! But doesn't this mean that the viewers don't take its philosophical message seriously? No, it doesn't. One good reason is that, unlike in the movie, there are no strong hints in our environment that we can enter into the kind of dream experience that is so convincing and consistent over the long term. But also without clues, life may be a dream or a simulated experience of some kind. Shouldn't we wake up from it?

However, if the assumption of the movie is right, and time goes faster in a dream, then if we're in doubt, we should *not* end our current life experience by committing suicide.

Happy Ending

Suppose that Cobb does make the terrible mistake of turning to a dream-version of his children. The longer he stays in the dream, the older his children will be when he returns to the real world. Suppose he never realizes. In the worst case, he lives a whole life in this dream world. But even if he stays until he dies of old age, time will have passed slower in the actual world. He will still have plenty of time to pass with his real children. And tell them great stories of what happened to him while he was 'out'. So, we see that a little philosophy can even rescue the happy ending.

If you happen to be a projection in someone else's dream, this is as real as it gets for you. From the subjective point of view, reality is a relative concept and existence feels equally real on each level. When in doubt, make the best of where you are, even if it's not real in an absolute sense. Know that you don't know whether you're at the top level of reality or not. That you *can't* know it.

Even if you happen to have a spinning top, or some other elegant device that's supposed to keep track of reality, know that it can't be trusted. Like Cobb, turn away and don't look at the top.

2
The Mad Neuroscience of *Inception*

BERIT BROGAARD

Christopher Nolan's *Inception* is about mind thieves who hack into people's dreams to steal their secret ideas. One of these mind thieves, Dom Cobb (played by Leonardo DiCaprio), is given the task of doing something much more difficult: planting a new idea in someone's mind. Planting an idea is called 'inception'. Cobb's assignment is to plant the idea in the mind of Robert Fischer, heir to the gigantic Fischer Morrow Energy Conglomerate, that he ought to break up this business empire.

The reason planting a new idea is much more difficult than stealing ideas is because people will know that the idea isn't theirs and will fail to believe it. As mind thief Arthur says to Saito, the man who hires them to do the job: "The subject's mind can always trace the genesis of the idea. True inspiration is impossible to fake." Cobb responds "No, it isn't."

Cobb comes up with the plan of hacking into Robert Fischer's subconcious's subconcious's subconscious and planting an emotional idea about his father, in order to make him draw the conclusion, on his own, that he should break up his father's business empire. But what idea would make Fischer draw this conclusion?

Fischer has spent his life thinking his father wanted him to keep the conglomerate going. Their relationship is tense. After some back and forth with assistant thief and forger Eames, Cobb hits on the notion of planting the idea: "MY FATHER DOESN'T WANT ME TO BE HIM."

The motive behind the intended inception is self-interested on Saito's part, but apparently not especially malign. As Saito says, "Fischer Morrow has the regulators in their pockets. We're the last company standing between them and total energy dominance and we can no longer compete. Soon they'll control the energy supply of half the world. They'll be able to blackmail governments, dictate policy. In effect, they become a new superpower. The world needs Robert Fischer to change his mind."

One tiny problem: Cobb can no longer design dreams, because his ex-wife, Mal, appears in his dreams and attempts to violently stop him. Cobb therefore hires the young Ariadne from the École d'architecture in Paris to design the dream.

The team succeeds. Everyone is happy. But is this science-fiction adventure possible science or nothing more than impossible fiction? Can you plant an idea in someone's mind? If you read this chapter, I'm going to plant in your mind the idea that the method of inception in *Inception* isn't completely outrageous but is in fact quite consistent with recent results in neuroscience and the philosophy of mind.

The method of inception? What's that? Good question.

The movie doesn't explicitly tell us what the method is. It just sprinkles a dozen references to the psychoanalyst Jung and then has the characters enter technologically advanced dream machines and take an unspecified drug called "Somnacin," to quickly enter and prolong their dream states. However, the characters in the movie make a lot of implicit references to the method of inception, so we can say something about it.

In the movie we have the power to hack into other people's dreams and gain access to their subconscious, to control the course of the dream and to plant ideas into their subconscious while they are dreaming. I will look at whether any current scientific methods could be used to plant ideas in human beings like us in a world like ours with the physical laws that constrain it. As we'll see, the story of *Inception* is more realistic than you might have supposed.

The Dream Narrative

ARIADNE: But are you trying to fool him that the dream is actually real life?

COBB: (*nodding*) While we're in there, we don't want him to realize he's dreaming.

An apparently innocent idea in *Inception* is that of a dream that has a 'plot' or 'narrative' that is logical enough to seem real. This idea, however, isn't as innocent as it may at first seem. Dreams often seem very wacky, bizarre narratives that string together people and events from waken life in a bizarre order. Impossible things can occur. As mind thief Arthur puts it, "In a dream, you can cheat architecture into impossible shapes. That lets you create closed loops, like the Penrose Steps. The infinite staircase."

Harvard Psychiatrist J. Allan Hobson, who in the 1970s famously argued against Freud's theory of dreams as symbols of hidden wishes and desires, originally argued that we experience dreams as wacky because our dream experiences are a "patch job." They're meaningless narratives patched together to make sense of basic automatic responses, such as biochemical changes (such as a drop in serotonin and an increase in acetylcholine levels) and spontaneous electric pulses, coming from the brain stem.

While our brains eventually create these narratives, the narratives don't mean anything, says Hobson. The narratives enter the scene only once biochemical and pulse changes have occurred in the deep parts of the brain, and we enter a state in which we can use language- and logic-regions of the brain to make a story out of the electrical signals and the chemicals. Dreaming is merely an epiphenomenon of rapid eye movement (REM) sleep, Hobson says.

Tuft philosopher Daniel Dennett has defended a similar theory of dreams (*Brainstorms*, MIT Press, 1978). Dennett thinks dream experiences are queer narratives we create as we wake up from the REM sleep and our cognitive function returns to normal.

Hobson first proposed this theory, also known as the 'activation-synthesis model', when he discovered REM sleep. Sleep occurs in ninety-minute cycles each of which have eighty minutes of non-REM sleep and ten minutes of REM sleep. REM sleep is the final state of the sleep cycle. It's also the state after which we wake up when we're done sleeping. The discovery of REM sleep and the observation that REM sleep often is followed by reports of dreams led Hobson to suggest that the neural correlate of REM sleep and dreams is the same: the brain stem.

But as the brain stem has no cognitive or emotional function, dreams can't be symbols for wishes, desires or emotions. So, Hobson happily concluded, Freud's theory that dreams are symbols standing in for deeper wishes and desires is probably wrong! This was essentially his argument against Freud. He later went on to say (in the journal *Neuropsychoanalysis* in 1999), that dreams are produced by random activation in the forebrain, thus leaving his criticism of Freud considerably weakened.

Hobson's original reasoning, however, is flawed in several ways. First, it assumes that if dreams only occur during REM sleep, then REM sleep and dreams must be matched with the same goings-on in the brain. This assumption is mistaken. My experiences of seeing things always occur during times when I'm breathing, but it doesn't follow that the parts of the brain responsible for my breathing are also responsible for my visual experiences.

Second, Hobson's reasoning assumes that because we report dreams after waking up from an REM state, dreams only occur during REM sleep. This, too, is mistaken. We only report yesterday's experiences when we have a hippocampus that is working well (the hippocampus is the seahorse-shaped area in the limbic regions of the temporal lobe that is the main area of the brain responsible for storing memories). It doesn't follow that amnesiacs who can't report yesterday's experiences because they don't remember yesterday did not have experiences yesterday (the point of Christopher Nolan's *Memento*).

Dreams are not coded in the hippocampus in quite the same way as wide-awake conscious experiences, so it could be that people have dreams during other states of sleep but just can't remember their dreams from those states because they don't wake up until after the last state of REM sleep. In the airport scene after the team has carried out their mission Fischer merely glances at Cobb as if thinking maybe he should know him and then moves on, despite having just spent hours with him in a shared dream.

Empirical findings now support the idea that dreams don't originate in the pons, the part of the brain stem that is responsible for REM sleep. As neuroscientists David Foulkes and John Antrobus, have argued, narrative dreams with bizarre elements can happen in non-REM states. For example, it has been found that patients with lesions (injuries) on their ponses do not have REM sleep—but they do still have dreams. There's no qualitative difference between dreamers' reports of dreams during REM sleep and reports during non-REM sleep. The REM dream reports just tend to be longer.

Patients who have suffered damage to the ventromesial quadrant of the frontal lobe (this is the part of the brain responsible for motivation, the part that initiates goal-oriented behavior) do have REM sleep, but have lost both the ability to dream and the motivation to do anything.

The ventromesial quadrant contains the dopamine pathway that transmits the neurotransmitter dopamine from the middle of the brain to higher areas. Dopamine is a reward chemical required for motivation. Without dopamine people don't do anything on their own, even though they can do almost anything you ask them to do. Mark Solms ("The Interpretation of Dreams and the Neurosciences," 1997) noticed that the two areas of the brain that underlie dreams are both in the cerebral cortex, one (as just mentioned) is responsible for goal-directed behavior and the other is responsible for spatial cognition.

Further evidence that dreams don't originate in the pons: People who are given dopamine or other drugs that stimulate the dopamine pathway (such as the drug L-DOPA used for people with Parkinson's disease) have more vivid and more frequent dreams. But these drugs have no effect on REM sleep!

A drug containing a dopamine stimulant together with a sedative and an REM-sleep inducer such as Acetylcholine may work just like *Inception*'s Somnacin.

If the frequency and intensity of dreams is unusually high, dreams can be brought closer to normal by using anti-psychotic drugs that prevents the transmission of dopamine. Or the dopamine pathway can be severed by surgery, as happened with the prefrontal leucotomies of the 1950s and 1960s. This type of brain surgery reduced the symptoms of psychosis but it also led to a lack of dreams and motivation, as illustrated by the memorable book and movie *One Flew over the Cuckoo's Nest*.

All this supports the view that the areas of the brain responsible for REM sleep and dreams are separate both in location and function. While dreams often are very wacky, we don't have to assume that they must be, as they are generated by higher areas of the brain responsible for goal-seeking behavior, spatial cognition, motivation and complex emotions. So, the mostly-streamlined dreams of *Inception* can't be ruled out.

Dream and Reality Are Not Symmetrical

ARIADNE: We were only asleep for five minutes? We talked for an hour at least. . . .

COBB: When you dream, your mind functions more quickly, so time seems to pass more slowly.

In *Inception*, there are tons of references to the asymmetry between how time is perceived in reality and in dreams. This idea is something we all know about. We sometimes enjoy (or endure) a party lasting for hours during the ten minutes of REM sleep left in the dream cycle just before we wake up.

But does the mind really function more quickly during dreams or does it just skip boring scenes the way a film does, making it seem like an hour has passed when in reality only five minutes has gone by? To answer this question it's helpful to take a look at the subconscious of the minds of savants.

Savants are people with extraordinary mathematical or creative abilities following a brain injury or abnormality. Many of them suffer from autism, though not in a way that prevents high performance. Others have no disabilities in addition to their superhuman abilities. Daniel Tammet, a famous savant, has amazing mathematical abilities. He can make calculations faster in his head than you can on a calculator. Tammet has a special condition called 'synesthesia' that allows him to do that.

In synesthesia, stimulation along one dimension of your mind gives rise to experiences along another dimension. One of the most common forms of synesthesia is grapheme-color synesthesia in which people see numbers or letters as colored.

What makes Daniel Tammet so unique is that he has a distinct color, shape, and texture for every number he can think of. When he multiplies two numbers the shape that fits in between the two numbers when they are placed next to each other is the result of the multiplication. Daniel can see the numbers he's multiplying and he can see the result but he's unconscious of the calculations. His brain simply performs them super-fast, below the level of conscious awareness.

Jason Padgett is another synesthetic savant with special mathematical abilities. Jason Padgett acquired his superhuman abilities in a mugging incident. He now sees curved or spiraling objects, numbers, and formulas as mathematical fractals. The images are so vivid that Padgett can hand-draw what he sees with amazing precision. He can also predict the vectors for prime numbers. The translation of objects, formulas, and numbers into mathematical fractals occurs below the level of consciousness.

While people like Daniel Tammet and Jason Padgett have special super-human abilities, their abilities suggest that the human brain has the capacity to perform mathematical calculations very fast.

Dreams sometimes are the place where problem solving takes place. Many famous and influential ideas originate in dreams. The Danish physicist Niels Bohr hit upon his famous model of the atom during a dream, Albert Einstein thought of the speed of light as a constant after dreaming that he was riding at the speed of light, the Spanish painter Salvador Dali's melted clock painting called "The Persistence of Memory" came from a dream, and the German chemist Friedrich August Kekulé discovered the benzene ring in a dream about the molecules taking the form of a snake biting its own tail.

Our minds might indeed be functioning more efficiently during dreams than in real life. In dreams our minds might be more like Tammet's and Padgett's, perhaps allowing more of the complicated calculations and attention to details to take place below the level of conscious awareness. As Cobb puts it, "They say we only use a fraction of the true potential of our brains . . . but they're talking about when we're awake. While we dream, the mind performs wonders."

Manipulating the Content of Dreams

Saito: But in my dream, we really ought to be playing by my rules . . .

Nash: Ah, yes, but you see, Mr. Saito

Saito turns to Nash.

Cobb: We're not in your dream

Saito turns back to Cobb, but Cobb has vanished.

NASH: We're in mine

Efficient dreams with a sensible narrative don't quite give us what *Inception* gives us. What we need in addition to that is a way for us to manipulate dream content. At first glance, a scenario in which one manipulates one's own dream content seems as far removed from the actual world as could be. But if we look closer at the different kinds of dreaming that exist, manipulating the content of one's dreams may be possible, even today. What we would want, though, isn't ordinary dreaming but lucid dreaming.

According to Hobson, lucid dreaming is a hybrid state characterized by both waking and dream consciousness. Lucid dreaming is biochemically similar to ordinary dreaming. They both are cholinergic (characterized by high levels of acetylcholine). They are also phenomenally similar. They both involve internally-generated visual imagery. But consciousness accompanying lucid dreams lies in the higher frequency range (around 40 Hz) in the frontal areas of the brain. This is also a feature of very vivid and active states of waking consciousness.

Psychophysiologist Stephen Laberge, the founder of the Lucidity Institute, is famous for having invented several devices to help people enter lucid dream states, among others, the lucid dream mask. The lucid dream mask uses infrared technology to detect the rapid eye movements that occur during REM sleep. It then flashes lights that enter your eyelids and makes sounds that you can pick up and integrate into your dreams. The lights and sounds from the outside world are supposed to help you 1. stay in the lucid hybrid state and 2. manipulate dream content.

There are several ways the lucid dream mask can help you manipulate the content of your dreams. Differences in the lights and auditory stimuli will lead to a difference in interpretation. But the constancy of the interpretations in response to the stimuli can also serve as a cue for you to enter your lucid dream and control the content.

Or so the manufacturers of the lucid dream mask claim. Laberge has offered some evidence of dream control. An experimenter and a subject would agree on an eye movement during

REM as a signal that they were in conscious control of the dream. During their lucid dream phases, they could then signal to the experimenter. Positive results of the experiment were allegedly found in eight subjects <http://spiritwatch.ca/alan_worsley.htm>.

There are other well-known tricks you can use to gain control of your dreams. You can't bring a totem into a dream the way Cobb, Mal, and Ariadne did it—because we don't quite know how they did it. But you can identify totems in dreams. In dreams, clocks are usually blank or flicker through time. There are other totems, too. Try to read the same sentence twice or turn on the television in the room. I bet you can't do it. If you think about how clocks appear in dreams before you go to sleep, you may be able to remember this in the dream. Even better: Make a habit out of always checking whether clocks and watches are blank or flicker through time. If you always do that in real life, you'll be more likely to do it in dreams too. When you identify a clock or a watch that is blank or flickers through time, you know you're in a dream. You then attempt to manipulate the dream content by deciding what you want to do from there. With a little practice, this works splendidly! And it's the coolest thing ever!

Entering Other Peoples' Dreams

ARIADNE: Who are the people?

COBB: They're projections of my subconscious.

ARIADNE: Yours?

COBB: Sure, you are the dreamer, I am the subject. My subconscious populates your world. That's one way we get at a subject's thoughts—his mind creates the people, so we can literally talk to his subconscious.

Even if the lucid dreaming techniques are successful and there are ways for us to manipulate dream content, we still haven't gotten what *Inception* gives us. We will also need a way of entering other peoples' dreams and controlling the content of their dreams.

In *Inception*, the chemist Yusuf says: "The compound we'll be using to share the dream is an advanced Somnacin derivative. It creates a very clear connection between dreamers, whilst actually accelerating brain function." So, the team is using a drug, a so-called Somnacin derivative, to enhance the connection between them in the dream.

But just taking a drug isn't going to make you enter other people's dreams. We will need a way for our brains to interact with each other. One person must be the dreamer, the one with the cognitive power, and the other must be the dream recipient whose subconscious we're scrutinizing and manipulating.

What would it take to connect people and create a division of labor like this? Split-brain syndrome offers a partial answer. Split-brain surgery, or corpus callosotomy, is a drastic way of lowering the severity and frequency of epileptic seizures. It involves cutting the corpus callosum, the region of the brain that connects the left and right hemispheres. When a patient has had a split-brain surgery performed, his left and right hemispheres don't communicate as effectively as before. This can give rise to split brain syndrome.

Michael Gazzaniga and Roger W. Sperry, the first to study split brains in humans, found that most patients who had undergone a complete callosotomy suffered temporarily from split-brain syndrome ("The Split Brain Revisited," 1998). In patients with split-brain syndrome the right hemisphere, which controls the left hand and foot, acts independently of the left hemisphere and the conscious intentions of the person. This gives rise to a kind of split personality, in which the left hemisphere issues demands that reflect conscious intentions, whereas the right hemisphere issues conflicting demands that reflect hidden preferences.

Sperry and Gazzaniga's split-brain experiments are now legendary. One of their patients, Paul S., had developed a language center in both hemispheres. This allowed the researchers to interview each hemisphere. When they asked the right side what Paul S. wanted to be, he replied "an automobile racer," and when they asked the left, he replied "a draftsman." Another patient tried to pull up his pants with the right hand and pull them down with the left. Another time, this same patient's left hand tried to strike his wife as his right hand grabbed it to stop it.

To enter other people's dreams we don't need to perform split brain surgery on them. It will be enough if we can temporarily deactivate the subject's left hemispheres, the hemisphere that appears to issue demands that reflect conscious intentions.

Neuroscientists like Tony Ro from CUNY are already using transcranial magnetic stimulation applied over the visual cortex to make people temporarily blind. Magnetically stimulating the visual cortex can temporarily set it out of function. It isn't too far-fetched to think that magnetic stimulation can be used to temporarily disable people's left hemisphere. If it can, then we have direct access to the disabled subject's unconscious preferences.

But how do we enter a subject's right hemisphere? To do that we will need to design an electric wire that can function as an artificial corpus collosum between our own brains and the recipient's right hemisphere. This wire will transfer signals across hemispheres and guarantee access to our subject's right hemisphere.

Once we have connected our hemispheres, our recipient's unconscious preferences are going to surface in pictorial form in our shared dream. Planting an idea in someone mind the way Cobb planted an idea in Mal's mind and the way the team planted an idea in Fischer's mind is now straightforward. We simply take control of the dream content in the shared dream and create a scenario like the one the team created in the dream they shared with Robert Fischer.

But there are complications. In *Inception*, Robert Fischer has a way of preventing his two brain halves from being completely separate. As Arthur puts it, "Fischer's had an extractor teach his mind to defend itself. His subconscious is militarized. It should've shown on the research." Additionally, our own subconscious may surface in the dream, the way Cobb's subconscious guilt suffices in the shared dream during the team's mission.

Embedded Dreams

COBB: We need you there to tailor compounds to our particular requirements.

YUSUF: Which are?

COBB: Great depth.

YUSUF: A dream within a dream? Two levels?

COBB: Three.

The most suspicious element in *Inception* isn't the science it displays but the notion of an embedded dream. We can dream that we go to sleep and dream that we dream but that wouldn't constitute an embedded dream in the sense portrayed in *Inception*. As Ariadne puts it: "Each level relates to the part of the subject's subconscious we're trying to access. I'm making the bottom level a hospital, so that Fischer will bring his father there."

For the notion of an embedded dream to be believable, the brain would have to store information in different places. Some of the information will be more difficult to get to and it will also be less penetrable by our brains' cortical control centers. This by itself seems to correspond well enough to how our brains function. We store memories in the hippocampus for the short term and medium term but the memories stored for the super-long term are stored in the outer layers of the brain (the cerebral cortex), and our emotional memories are partially stored in the amygdala (the brain center for fear processing).

But how would dreaming that we inject each other with Somnacin-derivatives and get connected via an electric wire make us enter a different layer of the recipient's memory? In the film, there's another way to go down deeper: Dying. But how does dreaming that we die make us enter a different layer of the recipient's memory?

The scene in which Cobb convinces Fischer that he's in a dream may shed some light on this. Fischer suddenly remembers something from his extraction exercises.

FISCHER: If this is a dream, I have to kill myself and wake up.

Fischer raises the gun towards his head.

COBB: I wouldn't do that—they've probably got you sedated. If you pull that trigger, you might not wake up. You might drop into a lower dream state.

Cobb then convinces Fischer to join their team and enter a deeper level of his own subconscious.

This suggests that it's the subject's own beliefs that cause him to let his guard down. Pulling the trigger or entering the dream machine in the dream causes the subject to allow further memories to surface in the shared dream. So, there's just one dream that represents other dream layers.

This still leaves open the question of how the team manages to "enter deeper layers" when the subject isn't in on it. One possibility is that the sedative itself is a time release drug. But that doesn't quite correspond to the freedom the team has in deciding when to go deeper.

Legal and Not So Legal Forms of Inception

COBB: An idea. Resilient, highly contagious. Once an idea's taken hold in the brain it's almost impossible to eradicate. A person can cover it up, ignore it but it stays there.

Even if we have the technology to perform inception via shared dreams (and we actually do), we still need to manufacture the devices, and get the officials' approval or do it illegally. Darn.

Are there legal or simpler forms of inception? Well, one would have thought that parents, teachers, therapists, counselors, coaches, and priests plant ideas in people's minds all the time. The characters of *Inception* are skeptical about this suggestion.

In the scene where Saito initially wants to hire Arthur and Cobb to plant an idea in Fischer's mind, Saito asks: "If you can steal an idea from someone's mind, why can't you plant one there instead?" Arthur replies "Okay, here's planting an idea: I say to you, "Don't think about elephants. What are you thinking about". Saito: "Elephants . . . " Arthur replies "Right. But it's not your idea because you know I gave it to you." Saito suggests planting it subconsciously, but Arthur dismisses this idea: "The subject's mind can always trace the genesis of the idea. True inspiration is impossible to fake."

Arthur's last remark seems like a slight exaggeration. Our beliefs and desires are probably partially formed by the people who taught us about the world. But the team in *Inception* is under time constraints. They need to plant an idea fast.

A faster and more subtle way of planting an idea in someone's mind is through mind control techniques. Mind control requires having a good theory of mind. A theory of mind is a theory about how people think, feel and behave in response to certain kinds of stimuli. For example, if you're trying to sell your old car for more than it's really worth, you want to make it seem like the car is worth that much. One way to do this is to make it seem hard for your potential buyers to get the car. There may be other (fake) buyers calling you while your real buyers are looking at it. Or you could pretend to be hesitant about selling it. If other people want the car or you're thinking about keeping it, then the car suddenly seems more valuable. So, you can plant the idea in people's mind that your car is more valuable than it actually is by doing and saying the right things.

If mind control seems out of your league and you, like me, are a bit of a neuroscience geek, then you might prefer a more sleazy way of planting ideas in people's minds. Fear conditioning has always worked well. You could ask CUNY professor Tony Ro if he will help you temporarily deactivate your subject's hippocampus, the seahorse-shaped part of the brain that stores memories. While the subject's hippocampus is deactivated, show him scary pictures portraying his current preferences. If need be, apply an appropriate amount of pain to him while he looks at the pictures. When you're done with him, he won't remember a thing but he'll make the right choice.

3

Inception and Deception

NATHAN ANDERSEN

At first blush, the movie *Inception* seems to deliver a thrilling new illustration of Descartes' dream argument, that it's impossible ever to be sure you're not dreaming. In fact, it raises a deeper problem.

While Descartes called into question the reality of experience, he held that our thoughts, at least, are our own. Even if I'm dreaming up the content of my experience, it's up to me how to think about that content. That's what makes genuine knowledge possible. I can resolve to think carefully and critically, to reject the opinions of others, testing all my conceptions for myself, and accept only those I'm unable to doubt. *Inception*, however, raises the possibility that this autonomy of mind could be subverted from without, and my thoughts become subject to a core conception it never occurs to me to question.

At the heart of modern skepticism, as presented forcefully by seventeenth-century philosopher René Descartes, is the basic problem that I can never be sure my experience reflects accurately a reality outside myself. *Inception* poses a deeper problem: that I can't even be sure of myself, that the convictions that inform my understanding of experience and the desires that drive me to respond, could in fact originate elsewhere. In fact, it's Christopher Nolan's preoccupation with just this issue, and its implications for how to think about personal identity and moral responsibility, that seem to serve as a guiding thread through all his work as a filmmaker.

Chris Nolan's Obsessions

Nolan has always taken an interest in depicting alterations of ordinary experience, that call into question its reliability. *Memento* depicts what the world would be like without long-term memories to sustain its continuity. *Insomnia* explores the effects on experience of a haunting guilt combined with lack of sleep in a world of constant daylight. The most memorable moments in *Batman Begins* are those in which ordinary perception is altered by a drug-induced fear.

Inception exploits the capacity of the cinematic cut to bridge gaps across time and through space, in order to deliver the experience of dreaming, where we suddenly find ourselves in a situation and it makes some kind of sense, but we can't say how or why we arrived there. Perhaps more central to his work from the very beginning, however, is a preoccupation with the theme that serves as central motif in *Inception*. What appears to intrigue him most is the extent to which our thoughts and self-conceptions can be manipulated deliberately through misdirection.

Nolan's first feature film, *Following*, tells the story of an aspiring young writer, obsessed with tracking random strangers to see where they go and what they do. He runs into another man—incidentally named Cobb, like Leonardo DiCaprio's character in *Inception*—who gives him the idea of going further, of breaking into people's houses, stealing their secrets, and introducing uncertainty by rearranging objects. With his beautiful accomplice, Cobb manipulates the writer into deciding he should break in and steal incriminating photos from a mafioso's secret safe.

A similar scheme takes place in *Memento*, when Natalie manipulates the memory-impaired Leonard Shelby into attacking Dodd, a man she owes money. Later, Leonard deliberately decides to provide himself with clues he knows will mislead him into thinking that the conniving cop Teddy is in fact the man who killed his wife.

The film *Prestige*, about rival nineteenth-century magicians, gets its titular focus from the strategy that magicians employ to misdirect and mislead their audience. Al Pacino's aging detective in *Insomnia* solves crimes similarly, crossing lines of legality to mislead suspects into revealing more of themselves than they should, until he meets a suspect who's able to play him the same way. That's also what makes *The Dark Knight* so unsettling—that Heath Ledger's Joker achieves his twisted aims through deception, by playing upon the motives of his victims in ways that lead them to do his work for him. Batman is born of Bruce Wayne's realization that as a man he is weak, but as a terrifying idea induced into the minds of his enemies, he has enormous power. As Ducard puts it to him in *Batman Begins*: "Theatricality and deception are powerful weapons . . . You must become more than a man in the minds of your opponents . . . You must become an idea."

Given that backdrop, it's no surprise that when the enormous success of *The Dark Knight* gave Nolan the chance to create a passion project on a big budget studio scale, he turned to a special-effects driven blockbuster narrative that explores once again the idea of implanting ideas into the minds of others by playing upon their basic emotions. In *Inception*, Nolan reflects directly on a theme that plays a pivotal role in all of his films to this point, the question whether it's possible to co-opt thoughts through suggestion.

The movie suggests that what shapes identity is the overarching conception, or obsession, that provides direction and meaning for our actions. It's just this kind of guiding theme, and not some trivial notion, that the dream spies attempt to induce into the mind of the hapless Robert Fischer. If that's so, to achieve "inception" is in fact to co-opt the identity of another—not merely to steal secrets, or implant ideas, but to subjugate subjectivity.

At the same time, perhaps the most significant lesson of *Inception* is that the proper response to this risk of self-loss isn't to question everything and everyone, as Descartes recommends in light of the possibility he's dreaming. It's, rather, to make the leap of trust. Other people aren't merely sources of deception, but are essential to the development of a healthy self-conception. In *Inception* the key to waking up and coming back to reality is to be found in releasing doubts, turning away from the spinning top, and beginning to trust in, and become responsible to, the reality of other people.

Whose Thoughts Are These Anyway?

It's not easy to say where my thoughts come from. Some ideas just come to me, apparently unbidden. Others I inherit, from parents and siblings and friends and neighbors. What is often repeated by others, whether or not it's true, I tend to repeat to myself. Some thoughts arrive filtered, through film and television, radio and culture, and from people around me. In the course of education, or as a result of reading, I develop strategies for assessing and rejecting ideas, but also internalize textbook notions about the world at large that I later take for granted as if obvious.

Are these my own thoughts? In one sense, yes, since I happen to think them. They occur to me unawares and I can call them to mind when called upon to consider the subjects that surround them. On the other hand, ideas acquired indiscriminately tend to be lacking in the kind of unity and coherence that allows them to belong together, much less belong to myself. Thoughts absorbed as if by osmosis tend to evaporate into thin air when they are challenged, when I consider others of my own thoughts that give me reason to doubt them.

The seventeenth-century philosopher and mathematician René Descartes proposed to doubt ideas directly, suggesting we reject in advance all those thoughts that could later be found inconsistent with more basic ideas or discoveries. The one thought he couldn't doubt is the idea of the thinker, so the ultimate test for any idea became whether that idea belonged necessarily to the thinking of any rational being, including God, or at least whether, given our evidence, any rational being would be led to the same conclusion. In other words, I shouldn't accept as my own any thoughts except those which all rational beings must accept by virtue of being rational. Math and logic, therefore, are acceptable, and physics and other disciplines are fine insofar as the experimental data they rest on is accepted only provisionally, with the understanding it could later be refuted by future evidence. This standard, now known as the rationalist criterion of knowledge, has seemed perhaps too strict for subsequent philosophers, while others argue that even Descartes himself didn't always adhere to it.

Still, Descartes was certainly right to say that we're in dubious possession of thoughts whose origins we're unsure of. Also, thoughts can't be mine to the extent they're inconsistent, incapable of being thought together at once by one and the same thinker. I can't suppose both I'm dreaming and I'm not, or that Arthur is both married and a bachelor. Still, there's something more than rationality or theoretical coherence at stake in saying a thought belongs to me. My thoughts need not only be internally consistent from the standpoint of theory, but should also be consistent with practice, with what I'm willing to say and what I'm going to do.

I can consider all kinds of thoughts, but I don't possess them except to the extent I am possessed by them. Only those thoughts can truly be said to be mine that I can't shake off, those thoughts that shape and define me. When, in *Inception*, Saito first proposes that Dominic Cobb take on the job, his point man Arthur responds that it's impossible. Saito asks why, if you can steal an idea, you can't plant one instead. "Okay," responds Arthur, "here's me planting an idea. I say 'don't think of an elephant.' What are you thinking about?" The answer is, of course, "an elephant." There is, however, an obvious difference between entertaining an idea and owning it. Someone who claims not to be racist but behaves like a bigot in dealings with people of different ethnic background is either lying or self-deceived. Ideas are my own only to the extent that they inform my activity, and thoughts without impact on my actions are not truly my thoughts, even if I may happen to think them. In the case of the elephant, Arthur points out, it's easy to see that the thought originates elsewhere and that Saito's consideration of it doesn't make it his own.

Inception 101: How to Deliver Ideas

The point is, it's easy enough to deliver ideas. It's done all the time, and without need for any specialized dream heist technology. Just words and willing ears. To make them stick requires either indoctrination through repetition and persuasion or the long and painstaking process of education, where there can be no guarantees.

In the case of Robert Fischer, however, both requirements are lacking. There isn't much time, and he's not willing to listen. If forced to listen, he'd surely reject what he hears. So the real task of inception isn't just to deliver ideas, but to deliver them surreptitiously to an unwilling recipient. Further, he must adopt these ideas as his own, as a basis for action, and as if he'd arrived at them himself and without intervention.

The solution is through dreams. Cobb's dream team plans to give Fischer the idea he should break up his father's company through a series of suggestions, delivered one at a time in a set of tiered dream states, dreams within dreams. On the one hand the dream state is ideal for the elaborate con because in dreams we tend to take a great deal for granted, and it wouldn't occur to Fischer to question how he arrived into the setting they'd designed to entrap him. In dreams we just tend to accept as real what may be utterly implausible or uncharacteristic, as long as it feels more or less right.

Dreams are essential for inception because what the dream team needs isn't merely for Fischer to consider an intriguing proposition but for him to adopt it as his own theme and live by it. He needs not only to think, but to feel this idea as something essential, as what defines him. The idea to be delivered through inception is akin to a deep conviction, a feeling for what really matters most. In this case, a feeling that his overall worth isn't to be measured based on whether he lived up to his father's legacy, but whether he can create his own, beginning by dismantling the inherited empire that might otherwise serve as a crutch.

In the end this new conception amounts to little more than a shift in how Fischer interprets his father's final word: "disappointed." Fischer took this as a final statement of rejection, that his father's dying act was to put into words what he'd apparently made clear in the past through silence, that his son never lived up to his high expectations. The idea implanted in him inverts this interpretation, reading his father as disappointed instead that in his effort to measure up to his father's accomplishments Robert never had the opportunity to pursue his own plans. The core idea that defines him and the new idea that will redefine him are really just self-assessments rooted in an interpretation of how he is considered by his most significant other.

Dreams are critical for inception because in dreams, above all, we encounter the significant persons in our lives and work through in sometimes bizarre ways the issues that define us in relation to these others. What that means for

Cobb and his dream team is that they can readily deliver simulations of the people who matter in the life of their victim, and allow him to experience the emotional catharsis that comes from reconciliation.

Self and Others

That Nolan always has his lead characters obsessed by unsettled memories of significant others shows he's not primarily interested in the problem how the purely rational Cartesian self can achieve certainty about the world outside. It's rather the question of self-certainty, of how we define ourselves in relation to others, that appears to matter most in Nolan's films. What's at stake isn't so much getting things right about the world, but being right and responsible in one's relationships with others, and Nolan tends to focus on characters who are damaged because they have been betrayed or abandoned, or have betrayed others and can't find solace in themselves.

Descartes held that what defines us is our thinking, and that we think best in isolation from the influence of others. The first task of philosophy, for Descartes, is to doubt everything, and especially what is learned from other people, so that we can begin to think for ourselves. This isolation in thought, however, is achieved only as an idea or in theory. In practice it's not so simple. Even in dreams we're never alone, since we bring with us a sense of self that is informed by our relationships with others. Cobb, for example, can never leave Mal behind. She, or at least the projection of his memories of her, will always be there with him in dreams to sabotage his plans because he has defined himself in terms of the guilt he feels over her death.

We can, of course, be wrong or irresponsible in our assessments of ourselves, as much as we can be wrong in our interpretation of the world outside of us. In *Memento*, the memory-impaired Leonard Shelby defines himself as on a quest for vengeance, to take the life of the man who killed his wife and robbed him of his memory. Various clues in the film, however, suggest that his wife may have survived the attack, and that he may have been the one to kill her, accidentally by giving her too much insulin. What's worse, it begins to look as though he's already killed "John G," the man on whom he'd pinned her death, and that he's willing to forget this in order that he might still have something to live for, and still consider himself to be a wronged man in search of justice.

In Shelby's case, it isn't so much that he can't know the truth about himself but that he resists that knowledge. He refuses to consider the evidence from others that would require him to change his most basic beliefs, and abandon the revenge quest that defines him. His problem isn't, as Descartes would have it, that he's insufficiently skeptical of the world around him and the ideas of others. Rather, his problem is that he has defined himself in isolation from others, and he's unwilling to allow their input to change his self-assessment.

Shelby does have reason to doubt what others say, since others do take advantage of his memory problems to manipulate him. Still, at pivotal moments he's able to see something about himself through his interactions with others. While he's clearly unsettled by such self-revelations, his problem is that he refuses to remember them by writing them down, thereby refusing to allow them to impact his long term sense of self.

Doubt versus Trust

Descartes is right to insist we be cautious, and not always trust either our senses or the opinions of others, but what he overlooks is that one's identity as a person is always defined in relation to other people. The self is more than merely an isolated ego, constituted solely by its consideration of abstract ideas. To be a self is above all to be an agent, which means to have an identity defined through action, and it's only through our experiences with other people who validate and challenge us that we come to identify for ourselves what is important to accomplish.

Descartes's philosophy attempts to root a knowledge of the world in our knowledge of ourselves, but the self knowledge that can be attained in isolation from other people is a rudimentary and merely formal sense of self. All that I can know of myself with certainty on my own is that I am, and that I am aware of a world around me comprised of interacting people and things. As soon as I go beyond this merely formal self awareness, I am confronted by the limits of my point of view, that I see things only from one side and interpreted in light of assumptions I can't be sure of. The most significant limitation on the knowledge of the world I can acquire on my own is that I can't see myself by myself. I can't experience my limits on my own, and can't learn what it is to be a self except through interaction with others whose perspectives differ from mine.

Skepticism is no longer healthy when it leads to suspicion and paranoia, and when it means I am unwilling to allow that others may have something to teach me. Questioning everything and everyone isn't, as might appear, the highest accomplishment of reason, but rather manages to cut one off from the kind of feedback through dialogue and interaction that makes possible self-criticism and growth. It places one effectively in Limbo, a world unhooked from reality, populated with objects of imagination alone. This is the true sleep, and the dream from which it's impossible to wake unaided. This is what it means to lose oneself. Healthy skepticism is warranted, but without trust, and without risk, there can be no legitimate self-knowledge and you're in jeopardy of losing your grip on reality altogether. This problem is illustrated quite effectively in the stories of both Cobb and Mal in *Inception*.

Cobb and Mal in Limbo

In their quest to see how deep they could go inside of a dream, Mal and Dom Cobb ended up in Limbo, an inner world of unconstructed dream space, where they were free to create their own reality as they pleased. As Cobb relates, it was wonderful for a time, but the sense that none of it was real nagged at him until he was ready to wake up and return to reality. Mal, however, was perfectly content in their shared imaginary world, unwilling to admit it wasn't real. She'd hidden the truth from herself, deliberately chosen to forget about the test she'd designed to check whether or not she was awake. Like Leonard in *Memento*, she'd decided to conceal conclusive evidence from herself, because it was easier to believe in the lie.

To convince Mal, Cobb had to find her totem, the top she used to test reality, and set it spinning again. Its ceaseless rotation finally managed to shake her conviction in the reality of the dream world they'd constructed for themselves. She took the leap of faith required to return to reality, by killing herself in the dream.

The problem was that when she woke up after what was nearly the equivalent of an entire lifetime in Limbo, reality was no longer satisfying. The seeds of doubt that Cobb had planted in her mind in order to bring her back, only continued to grow after they'd returned, and she began to believe that this too was a dream from which she could wake only by taking her own life again. This time she had to convince Cobb to come with her, and he was unwilling. She attempted coercion, but only managed to leave him behind broken, accused by the law of killing her directly but holding himself personally responsible for having planted the idea that led to her killing herself. He had managed to achieve inception, by infecting her mind with Cartesian doubt; but doubt turned out to be a philosophy it was impossible to live by and whose impact was devastating.

As his team begins planning later for their inception job on Fischer, Cobb suggests that to be effective the idea they plant should take a positive rather than negative spin. Rather than consider breaking up the company as an act of rebellion against a domineering dad, the plan should appear to originate from the father himself, as indication he accepts his son's need to make his own way. As reason for this preference, Cobb claims that positive emotions always trump negative, but it's hard not to detect in his insistence a memory of the impact on his own wife of accepting a negative ideal, a skeptical orientation towards the world in general.

The apparent outcome of the act of inception perpetrated on Fischer is quite different from the unanticipated consequences of its prior success with Mal. Where Fischer starts out doubting himself, insecure because he had never felt accepted by his father, he walks away from the dream with renewed self-confidence and an increased capacity to trust in others. By contrast, to all appearances, Mal transformed from, as Arthur puts it with obvious affection, being "quite lovely," into what Ariadne describes in shock as "a real charmer," a jealous and untrusting and manipulative woman. Of course what we see of her in the film is only what Cobb remembered of her from the end before she took her life, a projection he also realizes in the end is no more than a pale imitation of the fascinatingly complex and lovely woman with whom he lived so long in life and in Limbo.

Mal isn't the only one whose doubts have made her dangerous to herself and others. As Ariadne emphasizes, Cobb is himself in danger of slipping from the real world and putting the rest of them in jeopardy, as a result of a combination of suspicion and self-doubt inspired by guilt. He's increasingly unable to trust or confide in others, is willing to risk their lives unknowing in the pursuit of his own objectives, and is losing sight of his own limitations and of his dependence on others to make up what he is lacking. His father-in-law Miles begs him, "Come back to reality, Dom, please," and the likely reason isn't, as some have speculated, because the entire film takes place in a dream, but because he has closed himself off to others, and refuses to allow himself to be vulnerable. One indication that he's losing his grip on reality is an obsessive reliance on his totem, the spinning top, that he tests every chance he gets as if it's delivering the fix he requires to cope.

How Do Totems Work?

The idea behind the totem, as Arthur explains to Ariadne, is that it's an object whose exact properties are known to its designer alone. "That way when you look at your totem, you know beyond a doubt that you're not in someone else's dream." The problem, as Descartes would insist, is that the totem does nothing to ensure that you're not in your own dream.

Cobb's totem, inherited from his deceased wife Mal, seems to be strangely unlike the others—Arthur's loaded die, Ariadne's chess piece—in that it's designed apparently to overcome this problem by behaving differently in dreams than it does in reality. In the real world, it behaves like a top, spinning for a time until it eventually topples over. In dreams, by contrast, it's endowed with perpetual motion, defying laws of friction and gravity in order to spin on indefinitely. Presumably, the weight and heft of the top is something Cobb would recognize, and that would help him tell whether he's in another's dream. His obsessive spinning of the top, however, seems aimed at ensuring he knows the difference between reality and anyone's dream including his own.

A bit of reflection, however, shows that his faith in the test is unfounded, since if he were the dreamer, there'd be nothing to stop him from deceiving himself and allowing the top to settle. That seems precisely to be what happened to Mal, who subconsciously allowed the top to stop, and then hid it away in a safe, thereby undermining any possible future doubts she might have that the dream was not real.

While the totem may manage to safeguard against dream deception by others, it doesn't safeguard against self-deception. The irony is that to overcome self-deception requires that one place trust in others, as Cobb comes to trust Ariadne, who helps him to see that he needs to work through his guilt over Mal. When Miles pleads with Cobb to return to reality, he means to return to the presence of other people, to allow once again the intimacy of trust that he attempts to protect himself from through his incessant use of the totem. While doubt may protect me against the deceptions perpetrated against me by my senses and by others, it also effectively excludes me from the presence of those others whose perspectives can offer essential correctives to my own. Only in the context of trust in others, a context that does not preclude caution and circumspection, can there be genuine intimacy, and it's only upon opening himself up to such intimacy that Cobb can truly go home.

Does the Top Fall? Does It Matter in the End?

The final moment of *Inception* is telling. Fans of the film inevitably ask whether the apparent wobble in Cobb's spinning top in the final moments means it will eventually fall, or whether the long awaited reunion with his children is itself only another dream.

In an interview with *Wired* magazine, Christopher Nolan insists that the most important thing about the spinning top at the end isn't whether it falls or not—that's meant to be ambiguous—but "the most important emotional thing is that Cobb's not looking at it. He doesn't care."

Cobb's own catharsis—a self-induced shift in perspective—amounts to a kind of reinterpretation of an idea expressed clearly by his projection of Mal. "Let's face it," she tells him, "you don't believe in one reality anymore. So choose, choose to be here, choose me." As much as he may want to, he can't choose her because he knows she's not real. Just as he could tell a fake from his genuine totem, his intimacy with the real Mal makes clear to him that she's not her. She asserts "I'm the only thing you believe in anymore," and he responds, "I wish. But I can't imagine you with all your perfection all your imperfection—look at you . . . you're just a shade of my real wife. You feel real but you're the best I could do."

What Cobb learns, though, is that he can choose, he can live in a world defined by self-doubt, paranoia and guilt, always rooted in the past, or he can live in a world defined by trust, always open to the possibility of intimacy and love. It's that choice that allows him to be welcomed back to reality by his mentor and father-in-law Miles, to rejoin the company of friends, to recapture the possibility of relations built on trust rather than contract and control. It's that choice that allows him to experience the reality of his children once again, and having made that choice he no longer needs to dwell on the possibility that he's being deceived. In the context of that choice, he can spin the top and look away and let it fall as it may.

4
Plugging in to the Experience Machine

MICHAEL RENNETT

"Who would wanna be stuck in a dream for ten years?" Ariadne makes a great point when asking this question.

Imagine that the last ten years of your life have actually been a dream and when you wake up tomorrow, you will revert back to your reality from ten years ago. Think about all of the experiences you may have had over this time frame—moments with loved ones, friends, family, pets, and so on—and then realize that it was all just one long dream that never actually happened. Suddenly, you're thrown back into making decisions that you believed you had already settled or perhaps realized that they weren't so important after all. How would you be able to reset your mind to begin living again in this old reality that now seems so far away?

Little does Ariadne know at the time she makes this inquisitive statement that she's speaking to somebody who has spent fifty years stuck in a dream: Dom Cobb. Cobb ended up in a dream state called Limbo with his wife Mal while the two were investigating the multiple levels of shared dreaming. Cobb explains they got "trapped so deep" in the dream within a dream that when they "wound up on the shore of our own subconscious"—in Limbo—"we lost sight of what was real."

Cobb is able to maintain his grip on reality while in Limbo, realizing that the world which surrounds him is all a dream, and eventually understanding that it's impossible for him to live a fake life; Mal, on the other hand, becomes so enamored with her life of growing old with her husband in the dream that she purposely leaves her totem—an object designed to distinguish a dream from reality—in a resting position that convinces her that she's living in the real world. Although Ariadne may not understand why a person would choose to live in a dream, Mal understands perfectly.

Inception also shows us a group of twelve nameless people who choose to live in a dream world instead of the real world. Yusuf, a chemist who creates sedatives that allow the user to have stable dreams for multiple dream levels, hosts a den where this group can come to take this concoction and enter into a shared dream state. As Yusuf's wizened old assistant tells Cobb, "the dream has become their reality." These people have chosen to live their lives in dreams instead of in the real world. Unlike Mal, their respective motives for living in the dream world are unspecified.

So while Ariadne and Cobb can't understand why a person would willingly live in a dream, Mal as well as Yusuf's dream-addicted clients believe otherwise. Mal's preference for the dream life even leads to her own suicide in reality as she attempts to return to that world (due in part to Cobb's first inception while the couple was in limbo—persuading her that the world surrounding her does not exist and that the only way to return to reality was through death). *Inception* seems to present both sides of this argument, allowing us to decide for ourselves whether a life in shared dreams would be better than living in reality. So, to rephrase Ariadne's question that begins this chapter, *Inception* is really asking us to consider why a person would choose to live in a dream instead of reality.

Choosing a Real Life over a Dream Life

In 1974, American philosopher Robert Nozick considers this question in his book *Anarchy, State, and Utopia*. He proposes the existence of an "experience machine" which would be able to "give you any experience you desired:"

> Superduper neuropsychologists could stimulate your brain so that you would think and feel you were writing a great novel, or making a friend, or reading an interesting book. All the time you would be floating in a tank, with electrodes attached to your brain. . . . Of course, while in the tank you won't know that you're there; you'll think it's all actually happening. Others can also plug in to have the experiences

they want, so there's no need to stay unplugged to serve them. (Ignore problems such as who will service the machines if everyone plugs in.) (pp. 42–43)

Inception offers a similar choice to its characters. By plugging into the dream machine, the subject's brain can take them to any experience that they visualize. Ariadne refers to the dream state as "pure creation" as she can create whole new worlds and defy conventional laws of physics while there. More specifically, a suave James Bond-type spy like Eames (Tom Hardy) can imagine a snowy, mountainside battle that seems straight out of the Bond film *On Her Majesty's Secret Service*; he's therefore able to experience this visceral thrill that was only available to him in the real world through a movie screen.

While it would be fun to live in a fantasy world where you could imagine any object and have it appear, play out your favorite movie moments, or perform any dangerous act with relative safety (since you wake up when you die in the dream), Nozick argues that we would choose to live a real life over the simulated dream life. He supports this claim with three reasons.

First, he believes that "we want to *do* certain things, and not just have the experience of doing them" (p. 43). As an example, let's pretend that Arthur has wanted to become a professional football player when he grows up, but for whatever reason (his skinny frame perhaps) he could never make a team. If he plugs into the experience machine, he could finally experience this fantasy life. However, when he eventually wakes from the dream, he will realize that he did not actually accomplish his lifelong goal. No matter how realistic the simulation, Arthur could not brag to his friends about his "accomplishment"—it was just a fantasy mapped out by his brain. In order for Arthur to truly complete his life's ambition, he would have to eventually make the squad in real life.

Second, Nozick argues that we should not plug in because "we want to *be* a certain way, to be a certain sort of person. Someone floating in a tank is an indeterminate blob. There is no answer to the question of what a person is like who has long been in the tank" (p. 43). We see this in *Inception* when we're introduced to the people in Yusuf's dream den. There are no distinguishing personality characteristics for any of these individuals. We only know that they come to Yusuf's to dream as a group each night. They might as well be indeterminate blobs floating in tanks.

Thirdly, Nozick thinks that "plugging into an experience machine limits us to a man-made reality, to a world no deeper or more important than that which people can construct" (p. 43). We can interpret this in one of two ways. Either Nozick is referring to a deeper connection that we can only make with reality or he's considering transcendent "higher plains" of religion like Heaven or Nirvana that could only be reached through reality. While the characters could imagine their own vision of heaven, they would still be limited by the constraints of the human mind. Additionally, the more the dreamer changes things, the quicker the subconscious projections attack the dreamer. This means that trying to dream of heaven would just result in the dreamer being torn apart by the subconscious.

It is this last point of maintaining a connection to reality that seems to influence Cobb to leave limbo with Mal. He describes his time in limbo to Ariadne:

> "We created. We built the world for ourselves. We did that for years. We built our own world. . . . It wasn't so bad at first, feeling like gods. The problem was *knowing that none of it was real.* Eventually, *it just became impossible for me to live like that.*"

Unlike Nozick's subjects who are unaware of their mental state, Cobb is fully aware of the fictitious world that surrounds him. He initially enjoys the power of pure creation in Limbo but realizes that this constructed fantasy does not compare to reality, mostly because he can't spend time with his children and watch them grow up. In fact, Cobb's motivation to see his children again drives his decision to leave Limbo. To coincide with Nozick's arguments, we can reframe Cobb's thoughts into three distinct points:

1. **I must leave Limbo to actually raise my children, and not merely experience raising them**

2. **I want to be a good father to my children; and**

3. **I must return to the real world in order to have a truly deep connection with my children.**

We could argue that since Cobb has the freedom to create anything he wishes while in Limbo, he could always imagine his children to exist in this world and then raise them. However, these projections would be inauthentic simulations instead of the genuine articles. Cobb would only be able to view them as toddlers since his consciousness would only know them as such. All of his advice would be sound and useful because his subconscious drive to be a good father would allow it to be so. Cobb's relationship with these projections would be empty and unfulfilling since all of the emotion would be one-sided; he could love these children, but they could never love him back.

Although Cobb could have the experience of raising his kids while stuck in Limbo, he wouldn't be able to truly replicate the deep interpersonal connection and journey of reality. Just as Nozick would argue, Cobb would only be able to accomplish this task in the real world and would rightly choose reality over the experience.

Making the Dream Real

While Cobb rejects the ersatz nature of Limbo, Mal is enticed by it and even begins to view it as her reality. Unlike Cobb, Mal chooses the false simulation over the real world. Given that she and Cobb have the same knowledge that they are in a dream world, why would she consciously choose to live in this artificial experience? By making this decision, she's effectively rejecting all of her ties to the real world—her friends, parents, and particularly her children—just to live in the dream. What could possibly be so important to Mal that would lead her to this conclusion?

Although her reasons are never explicitly stated, we can infer from the movie's dialogue that Mal is motivated by Cobb's promise to her that the two would grow old together. Mal constantly uses this moment to confront Cobb in his dreams, first in Cobb's individual dream and later in Limbo. The former is particularly important since this is a moment which Cobb regrets and is "reliving" in order to try to change its outcome.

Mal only asks about her children once, in the dream within a dream that opens the movie. Other lines of dialogue reinforce her unbreakable relationship to Cobb. The answer to his riddle about waiting for a train which he uses to convince her to leave

Limbo is "because you'll be together," neglecting any mention of their children. Mal's conflict with Ariadne in Cobb's dream also emphasizes Mal's connection to Cobb. As Ariadne sneaks off to the deepest part of Cobb's subconscious in order to understand him better, she comes face to face with Mal:

MAL: What are you doing here?

ARIADNE: I'm just trying to understand...

MAL: How could you understand? Do you know what it is to be a lover? To be half of a whole?

ARIADNE: No. . . .

Mal's comments once again disregard her children while stressing her relationship with Cobb. She isn't merely a half of a whole relationship, but a quarter of her entire family unit.

So why would this devotion manifest itself into her choice to stay in Limbo? Couldn't she continue to love Cobb and grow old with him in reality? And doesn't her decision to live in Limbo counteract her desire to grow old with Cobb since they aren't actually aging while in a dream?

The philosopher that can best help us delve into Mal's psyche and answer these questions is George Berkeley (1685–1753). Berkeley's philosophy, referred to as both "immaterialism" and "idealism," rejects traditional views of a material reality and instead regards the world as a system of ideas. According to Berkeley, there is no "real world out there," apart from what our senses tell us. There is nothing but the sensations we receive through our senses.

Our subjective senses are able to conceive a design of the world that surrounds us through signified ideas. For example, we can distinguish between an apple and an orange due to the differences in color, taste, feel, and so on. Our perceptions of one piece of fruit form an individual idea categorized under a single name while our perceptions of the other piece of fruit can be considered the other name. Berkeley summarizes his own views by stating that "it is impossible for me to conceive in my thoughts any sensible thing or object distinct from the sensation or perception of it." This is further condensed into Berkeley's famous dictum *"esse est percipi,"* or "to be is to be perceived." For Berkeley, the real can't exist independent of our minds since the real is only comprised of our ideas.

By applying Berkeley's philosophy, we can consider all of the events that occur during dreams in *Inception* to be real since the characters can perceive those ideas which surround them. Cobb tells Ariadne that "dreams feel real while we're in them," which can be rephrased in Berkeleyan terms to say that our brain perceives the dream world in the same manner in which it perceives the real world.[1] Although the dream is governed by different rules than reality, the characters still have to rely on their senses in order to understand the ideas of that world. Essentially, if the real can only exist in the mind and there is no mind-independent world which exists, then there is nothing preventing *Inception*'s characters from perceiving the world of their dreams as reality.

Since we have to use empirical evidence to perceive things, memory plays an important role in differentiating the two worlds. If the dreamer remembers the tangible elements of a real location while in a dream, it could become difficult to distinguish between the two since the dreamer could believe that he is in reality. For example, Saito is initially fooled by Nash's dream that is set in Saito's love-nest apartment since the physical details convincingly mirror his memory; it is only when Saito feels the polyester (instead of wool) carpet that he realizes that he's still dreaming. This slight tactile difference triggers his brain to comprehend the simulated nature of the dream. Cobb reinforces this point to distinguish the dream from reality when he teaches Ariadne the basic guidelines to creating a dream world. He urges her to "never re-create places from your memory" to build the dream and to instead "always imagine new places," warning that "building a dream from your memory is the easiest way to lose your grasp on what's real and what is a dream."

Mal's acceptance of Limbo as reality is a continuation of this Berkeleyan thought. She perceives the world around her, there-

---

[1] Since Berkeley would consider the ideas we perceive to be real, the differentiation between the real world and the dream world would be unnecessary. For simplicity's sake, I will use the term "real world" for the topmost layer in which a person is dreaming, and "dream world" for the imagined world which that subject is dreaming about.

fore it must be real. She has memories of the ideas contained in this world, therefore it seems real to her. Limbo is not only perceived in the same manner as reality, but it presents an idealized version of reality to Mal: she's able to live a long (possibly infinite) life with her husband where the two can grow old together. Any other world outside of this one could lead to any number of possibilities in which Cobb can't fulfill his promise. Perhaps the couple gets divorced. Perhaps he falls for another woman. Perhaps he gets trapped in Limbo and can't return to her since his mind has become scrambled egg. By accepting Limbo as reality, Mal doesn't have to worry about any of these potential outcomes.

But Is Berkeley Right?

Although Berkeley's philosophy helps us understand Mal's decision to accept Limbo as reality, it's by no means an infallible solution to our question of whether dreams can be perceived as real. Berkeley acknowledges that there are times when our senses can deceive us. Think about a pencil that you put into a cup that is halfway-filled with water. The light bounces off the water differently than it does air and this refraction makes it appear as if the pencil has broken. Since our perception of the part of the pencil that is dipped in water does not match our idea of a pencil, what we're seeing isn't true to reality.

Individual hallucinations or illusions are also not real. The ghosts which Cole Sear (Haley Joel Osment) "sees" during *The Sixth Sense* would also be considered not real by Berkeley. This isn't because the ghosts don't resemble anything in the world independent of our minds, since Berkeley argues that such things doesn't exist anyway, but because the ghosts don't resemble any ideas in other people's minds. Cole is the only person who can perceive these ghosts and interact with them; others would just see him speaking to an empty space. Since the ghosts only exist in Cole's mind, they must be an illusion. The same argument would apply to a drug-induced hallucination.

With this thread in mind, Berkeley would view our normal individual dreams or any brain-stimulated experiences in the experience machine as being unreal. A single individual can perceive these experiences but nobody else can perceive what we are individually dreaming. They are as illusory to others as ghosts or hallucinations.

But the dreams in *Inception* aren't normal dreams. Several people can perceive these experiences and effectively bring what transpires with them back into the non-dream world. For example, Cobb apologizes to Arthur after the two fail to successfully break into Saito's mind for Cobol Industries because Cobb's projection of Mal shot Arthur in the leg. Why does Cobb need to apologize for this incident if the event isn't real and therefore never took place?

To extend this point, we can consider the crush that Arthur seems to have on Ariadne since he asks her to kiss him during the hotel level of the dream within a dream. If she has a reaction to his advance, whether positive or negative, then it could have an effect on their future work together. Perhaps she's interested in him and they are able to form a strong relationship. Perhaps she's not interested and their future missions become awkward. Either way, there would be a non-dream world result from this action in the dream. However, if Arthur were to individually dream about kissing Ariadne or experience her kiss in the experience machine, then she would be completely unaware of his feelings and there would be no resulting effects (unless Arthur decides to tell her his feelings). These instances demonstrate that there is a major and distinct difference between normal dreams and the dreams in *Inception*.

So could these dreams be considered real? For the characters that perceive them, yes. And certainly the corporations that pay exorbitant amounts of money to hire extractors like Cobb and Arthur believe that the extractors are able to enter a subject's consciousness to gather secrets even if the heads of these corporations (except for Saito) don't actually see this world. So there is a general agreement that the world of the dream exists, even if not everybody can see the physical dream world.

Cobb, the skeptic who refused to believe that the experiences in Limbo were real, seems to admit the realness of his journey as he conveys it to Ariadne. Cobb describes himself and Mal as "old souls thrown back into youth," suggesting an emotional growth from their dream experiences. Similarly, when Cobb later finds Saito in Limbo, he implores the corporate businessman to return to the real world "so we can be young men together again," implying an actual passage of time within the dream state. By the end of the movie, Cobb confronts his own hesitations about accepting the dream as reality. When he confronts his subconscious projection of Mal, Cobb finally admits that what he had initially accepted as false was actually real:

MAL: You remember when you asked me to marry you?

COBB: Yes.

MAL: You said you dreamt that we'd grow old together.

COBB: But we did. We did. You don't remember?

By acknowledging the realness of Limbo, Cobb can finally find catharsis with his subconscious. He no longer has to feel guilty for breaking his promise to Mal since he fulfilled this act with her in Limbo. As Cobb tells himself, he doesn't "believe in one reality anymore" so it's up to him to decide in which reality he wants to live.

To briefly return to Nozick since he's the person who would argue most against this idea, the philosopher argues that we would reject the experience machine because the experiences we perceive wouldn't be real. But what if the base world in which the experience machine exists and the people in that world, including Nozick, are *also* not real? Would Nozick be as quick to say that this level should also be rejected and effectively obliterated? What if he were merely a dreamer's subconscious projection? Would he want to wipe himself from the annals of existence for the sake of finding the "true reality"? Probably not.

The films *Abre Los Ojos* (1997) and its American remake *Vanilla Sky* (2001) present this very scenario. The world shown in each of these films is a lucid dream imagined by its protagonist César/David Aames (Eduardo Noriega/Tom Cruise) with the other characters being projections of his subconscious. When the protagonist realizes that he's dreaming, his purely imagined psychiatrist (Chete Lera/Kurt Russell) pleads with him to not believe this since César/David's awakening would result in the psychiatrist's complete disappearance from existence.

Nozick's argument only seems to work if he knows that his world is indeed real. Since *Inception* presents multiple levels that could be perceived as real, and the characters can never truly know what is or isn't real, then the level of true reality becomes what each character believes to be real. The movie's final scene in which Cobb finally returns home to his children illustrates this point perfectly. Cobb spins his totem to see whether he's in a dream or not and the object continues to turn until the film cuts to black.

The viewer is ultimately left unaware of the true answer of whether Cobb has returned to reality or not since the top slightly wobbles but does not fall on-screen. But the most important part of this pivotal moment is that Cobb isn't even looking at his totem but at his children! In essence, Cobb is saying that it does not matter to him whether this world is real or not; he has accepted this world where he's reunited with his children as the one in which he wants to live.

The Power of Choice

Ariadne's skeptical question asking who would choose to live in a dream for ten years can now be reconsidered Ariadne questions living in the dream state for that long because she doesn't consider it real. Like Nozick, she chooses reality over the dream. However, as Berkeley argues, the concept of reality is only based on our perceptions. Ariadne believes that she's currently in reality because it's the only reality she knows. Perhaps she's just a projection in somebody else's dream. But she's *choosing* to believe that her reality exists, just as Cobb decides to believe in the reality of limbo.

Inception constantly reiterates the importance of making this choice. Ariadne chooses to believe in the world around her. Mal chooses to believe that there's a world outside of her life with Cobb. Cobb chooses his life where he's reunited with his children. Even classic philosophical arguments depend on this choice. The captive prisoners in Plato's Allegory of the Cave choose to reject the true statements of a different reality from one of their fellow prisoners. Despite the prisoners' being wrong in their beliefs, their experiences will feel no less real to them. It once again comes down to a question of choice. Reality becomes not only what we perceive, but what we believe.

Level 2

We're Not in *Your* Dream

5
You Have No Idea

JANET TESTERMAN

The seed that we planted in this man's mind may change everything.

—Cobb

Inception explores the possibility of changing another person's behavior by getting into his deepest dreams and implanting an idea in his subconscious mind. Cobb is hired by an über-wealthy magnate, Saito, to persuade another financially powerful young man, Fischer, to break up the colossal business conglomerate he has inherited from his father, thus leaving Saito's company in better shape.

To accomplish this feat, Cobb uses a co-dreaming machine, a device to which several people can, once sedated, hook up and share in one primary person's dream. Cobb and his cohorts enter several layers of Fischer's consciousness in the form of dreams within dreams so they can deposit the notion that Fischer will split up his father's empire. When Fischer utters the words "I will be my own man" at the end of the movie, the audience understands the inception, or inserted inspiration, is a success. The director, Christopher Nolan, would like us to conclude that Fischer feels it's his own conscious will which is deciding to fragment his father's empire, when actually Cobb and company planted the idea.

The viewer experiences a fabulous, magical suspension of reality while witnessing the elaborate manipulations Cobb and crew navigate as they get Fischer to unwittingly participate in their dreams, as well as the dreams of the dreamers. It's ironic however, that no one realizes that neither Cobb nor

Saito nor anyone else, for that matter, act from conscious will.

It would have perhaps been more productive for Saito, the initiator of the inception plan, to have done some introspection into the origins of his obsession with wealth and power, the proximate cause of his desire for a slice of Fischer's market share. Had he examined his own motivations he may have discovered he acted not from free agency, but from an inception of sorts which controls his own behavior, as such inceptions control all our behavior.

Some of the things we do seem consciously willed and others seem more automatic. Sometimes thoughts are obviously automatic. I don't think too much about accelerating, braking, and steering while I'm having a discussion with my son about the moral implications of wealth while we drive to the Grand Canyon. Fortunately, automatic thoughts run in parallel so we can do things like walk, talk, and notice the beautiful sunset simultaneously. But other thoughts seem to feel more intentional.

William James wrote that willful acts involve an "effort of attention" unlike other, easier thoughts whirling in the stream of consciousness which flows through our mental lives. He contrasted these more willful incidents with ones that seem more automatic, like feeling startled when the phone rings or swatting a mosquito as it bites.

> If, then, by the original question, how many ideas or things can we attend to at once, be meant how many entirely disconnected systems or processes of conception can go on simultaneously, the answer is, *not easily more than one, unless the processes are very habitual; but then two, or even three*, without very much oscillation of the attention. Where, however, the processes are less automatic, as in the story of Julius Caesar dictating four letters whilst he writes a fifth, there must be a rapid oscillation of the mind from one to the next, and no consequent gain of time. Within any one of the systems the parts may be numberless, but we attend to them collectively when we conceive the whole which they form. (*The Principles of Psychology*, p. 490)

After William James, John Dewey wrote extensively about the moral superiority of making a conscious effort to develop one's will power, and control one's urges. Dewey wrote that "The self isn't something ready-made, but something in continuous formation through choice of action" and "The good man is the man who, no matter how morally unworthy he has been, is moving to become better" and "There is no discipline in the world so severe as the discipline of experience subjected to the tests of intelligent development and direction" (*Experience and Education*). But Dewey never came up with a sufficient response to James's ponderings about why it was so difficult, even impossible, for us to control our own minds.

For example, it's difficult to keep a secret. Our subconscious is often disloyal to the very being who provides it with a home. There are tell-tale signs a person is lying, which emerge in the body language of a liar against his will (not to be caught in the lie). Researcher Paul Ekman has mastered the art and science of reading subtle facial muscle cues resulting when one's subconscious belies a lie "Once we had the idea that concealed feelings might be evident in these very brief *micro expressions*, we searched and found many more, typically covered in an instant by a smile" (*Telling Lies*, p. 17).

My own subconscious impulses betray me when I sometimes find myself eating the second bowl of ice cream which I told myself I wouldn't consume. And, sorry, Dewey, the harder I try to control my urges, the more powerful they become. So much for character-building through willpower, but, back to James, if I often can't control the contents and volume of my dessert, and if I don't wish to telegraph to observers the fact I am lying, who is performing these apparently willful, but unwilled behaviors?

There's a constant battle between the small, ever-present but only occasionally willful window of consciousness I consistently perceive and the roiling subconscious forces influencing my actions. Saito was on the right track in his attempts to change Fisher's behavior by planting ideas into his subconscious dream-world, but there are far less dangerous, less complicated means to manipulate a person.

In the following exchange in the movie, Cobb and Saito acknowledge our ability to manipulate another's mind in the short term simply by asking them to control their mind by suppressing a thought:

COBB: What do you want?

SAITO: Inception. Is it possible?

ARTHUR: Of course not.

SAITO: If you can steal an idea, why can't you plant one there instead?

ARTHUR: Okay, this is me, planting an idea in your mind. I say: don't think about elephants. What are you thinking about?

SAITO: Elephants?

ARTHUR: Right, but it's not your idea. The dreamer can always remember the genesis of the idea. True inspiration is impossible to fake.

COBB: No, it's not.

Asking another to not think about elephants is an even more powerful stimulus to think of elephants than the opposite request. Furthermore Arthur is, as Cobb points out, incorrect, at least in the conscious world. Initially, Saito will remember who told him not to think about elephants, but the message will swirl around in Saito's subconscious until long after the exchange with Arthur is forgotten. Later, the elephant exchange could become fodder which could contribute to Saito's subconscious will, to initiate action.

So Cobb is right, one can artificially cause another to feel their thoughts are a result of divine inspiration because no one ever knows the real origin of their own ideas. The only difference between being inspired and being influenced by previously planted ideas and inception-like concepts is the degree to which you recognize the origin of your own thoughts. The less you're able to attribute your own thoughts to other sources, the more inspired or unique your thoughts appear.

New York's Madison Avenue has mastered this process and exploits us by constantly presenting concepts in attractive or otherwise arresting packages which they hope will submerge into our individual and collective subconscious only to emerge in unexpected trips to McDonald's. Marketers' greatest hope is for people to find themselves mindlessly sporting Louis

Vuitton, Calvin Klein, and Chanel and, eating mounds of Pizza Hut and Ben and Jerry's ice cream, driving BMWs and never examining how they came to be the person they have become.

The unexamined life, contrary to Socrates, is perfectly suitable for living, since our metacognitive ruminations can expose only rudimentary, superficial foundations of behavior. Some force other than our own will conceals the most powerful stimuli of behavior in our subconscious minds. And as B.F. Skinner argued, even the ability to be able to contemplate the origins and implications of our choices isn't an act of self will, but the result of a stream of causes, most of them subconscious. The following arguments will show that Cobb and Saito's elaborate mind-heist is only a crude example of the evolution of an act of coercion that the actor experiences as free will.

The Feeling of Free Will vs. the Real Thing

Cobb believes he is free to will to become involved in the inception and Saito believes he's freely and willingly hiring Cobb to plant the inception in Fischer. But the experience of consciously willing an action and a person's conscious mind causing the action are two different things. Conscious will is a feeling, not a cause. According to Hume, causality isn't a property inhering in objects, but is something we infer. So in Cobb's and Saito's cases, there's a distinction between their phenomenal will, which they experience as their own agency, and an empirical cause of the apparent will and subsequent action.

Cobb thinks he freely agrees to participate in the inception plan and tells himself he does so in order to be reunited with his children. Saito devises a similar teleology: he's driven by his desire for wealth and power. Neither acknowledges the prior events and subconscious motivations that actually caused their actions. In other words, Cobb's and Saito's minds formulate experiences that lead them to believe they cause their own actions. They don't know the causes of their own decisions and actions. As Spinoza said, "Freedom is ignorance of the causes of actions."

There's a whole lot of research to support the fact that there's a gulf between the feeling we have that we're deciding what to do and the actual causes of what we do. There are people who experience acts which appear to observers to be totally willful yet, for which the actor lacks any feeling of will. Wilder

Penfield (*The Mystery of Mind*) applied direct electrical stimu-
lations on the brains of conscious patients. One electrical jolt to
a motor parietal area caused a patient's left hand to move in a
smooth fashion involving multiple muscles which appeared to
the observers as voluntary. The patient used her right hand to
stop the movement of her involuntarily moving left hand and
said "I didn't do that, you did." This instance of an apparently
willful act lacking the phenomenon of will allows for the potential for other, non-personal causes of action. (The devil made
me do it!)

In a similar experiment, a patient's brain was stimulated in
a way that caused his head to turn slowly, as if attempting to
look behind himself. When asked why he was making that
motion, the patient responded "I'm looking for my slippers."
Although he hadn't been the cause of his own action, he felt
inclined to attach the experience of conscious will to explain his
behavior to himself and others. Similarly, Cobb and Saito,
although acting at the behest of unconscious forces, feel
inclined to provide rational explanations for their decision to
become involved in the inception: Cobb wants to be reunited
with his children and Saito wants to be richer and even more
powerful. Their rationalizations could be unrelated to the
actual causes of their behaviors.

What then, of the feeling Cobb and Saito have of being the
masters of their own destinies? It's surely their experience of
the feeling of free will that goes along with the actions surrounding their inception scheme that gives them enough evidence to convince them that they are the cause of their actions.
Unfortunately, we know from brain science that their sense of
willing to do something arises in altogether different locations
in their brains than do their actual movements or deeds.
Functional magnetic resonance imaging (fMRI) research indicates the associated areas responsible for the experience of
willing, which are spread throughout the brain, are separate
from the motor cortex which is a localized area responsible for
physical movement.

This finding would be trivial were it not for the discovery
that brain activity initiating movement or action precedes activation of the associated areas which give rise to the experience
of conscious will. It's this consistent association of the feeling of
conscious will with actions which makes the illusion of con-

scious will so powerful and persistent. Cobb and Saito are smug in their confidence that Fischer has no idea that it was their manic scheming and dreaming which provided the origin of Fischer's new conviction to "be his own man" and dismantle his father's empire. Yet they have no lack of confidence at all while regarding themselves as the source of their own behaviors.

If actions are self-motivated, if Saito first decided to hire Cobb to perform the inception, then willed his mouth and lingual apparatus to make the requisite moves in order to articulate his wishes, then it would be necessary for Saito's will to have been the first brain activity evidenced on an fMRI. Astoundingly, we know from brain research that this just isn't the case. If researchers scanned Saito's brain under these circumstances, they would first observe brain activity initiating Saito's request before Saito had willed it!

In an experiment designed by Benjamin Libet, electrical potentials (voltages) of participants' brains were measured before, during and after a person was asked to voluntarily lift an index finger. An EMG (electromyography) was also performed in order to measure the muscle movement of the finger. Finally, participants were asked to watch a fast-moving, highly gradated clock to report the instant they became consciously aware of wanting to perform the finger movement. The participant was also asked to indicate when he became aware of actually moving his finger. Thousands of trials were performed. Oddly enough, the brain became active significantly before the person was aware of moving his finger but also before the actual finger movement. Somehow the brain has an awareness of the impending finger movement before the person who believes he is the cause of the action wills the movement to occur. The conscious willing of the action comes after the brain has begun preparing for the action.

Libet remarked that:

> free will . . . couldn't be the initiating agent, contrary to one widely held view. This is of course also contrary to each individual's own introspective feeling that he/she consciously initiates such voluntary acts; this provides an important empirical example of the possibility that the subjective experience of a mental causality need not necessarily reflect the actual causative relationship between mental and brain events. (*Neurophysiology*, p. 269)

What, then, was the cause of Saito's request of Cobb, if not Saito's will? Perhaps the brain activity prior to the experience of will precedes all acts, even those that don't feel voluntary. If this were the case, the extraneous brain activity could be explained as a precursor to any motor activity. But these electrical brain potentials which occur prior to conscious willing of action don't occur prior to involuntary movements such as tics. Perhaps the prior brain stimulation produces the desire to move. But what produces the prior brain stimulation? Subconscious forces.

All Experience Is Inception

Conscious will is even more sluggish when it responds to a faster, triggered action. Libet also found that when people are asked to push a button as soon as they feel a tap they become conscious of having responded four hundred milliseconds *after* they react. A response and a conscious response are more frequently than not, two different things. The source of the prior brain stimulation, since it isn't willfully produced by the person inhabiting the brain, remains inscrutable. Fischer, Saito and Cobb live in an epistemic illusion regarding the derivation of their own motivations and behaviors.

> COBB: I will split up my father's empire. Now this is obviously an idea that Robert Fischer will choose to reject— which is why we need to plant it deep in his subconscious. Subconscious is fueled by emotion, right? Not reason. We need to find a way to translate this into an emotional concept.
>
> ARTHUR: How do you translate a business strategy into an emotion?
>
> COBB: Well, that's what we're here to figure out, right? Now Fischer's relationship with his father is stressed, to say the least. . . .
>
> EAMES: Well, can we run with that? Suggest splitting up the empire as a "Screw you" to the old man?
>
> COBB: No, 'cause I think positive emotion trumps negative emotion every time. We all crave reconciliation—we love

catharsis. We need Robert Fischer to have a positive emotional reaction to all this.

EAMES: All right, well, try this. My father accepts that I want to create for myself, not follow in his footsteps.

Cobb's recognition that the inception's chances of success would multiply if it had an emotional theme is consistent with brain-based research as well. The brain has evolved in such a way that its core developed from the least evolved of our brain ancestors and its components became more complex as they developed radially outward toward the skull. The base of the brain has a composite of components that control autonomic functions such as breathing and heart beat. This interior base of the brain is often referred to as the reptilian brain. Another ancient layer deposited deep within the brain, is the limbic system which manages emotions. Anger and uncontrollable violent urges originate in the amygdala which is housed in the limbic system.

Millions of years ago it was adaptive for humans to have uncontrolled ferocious outbursts to protect themselves and their young from predators and competitors. Vestiges of the limbic system remain, but often the negative emotions they activate work counter to our best interests. Nonetheless, they are sources of neurotransmitters which, without our knowledge or approval, trigger reactions which often surprise and dismay the person who momentarily and regrettably loses control. The location of some anatomical brain components also correspond to their metaphorical significance.

In this case, Cobb wanted to deposit the inception deep into Fischer's subconscious. The most effective way to accomplish this goal was to enter the deepest part of Fischer's mind and brain by manipulating his emotions. Cobb recognized the power of subconscious suggestions with emotional content, so he planned to manipulate Fischer's anguished relationship with his father in order to exploit the deeply subconscious power of the limbic system.

Cobb's comment that "positive emotion trumps negative emotion every time" is accepted without question, but is not true. All it takes is a simple traffic jam or a long wait on hold to a credit card company to activate the amygdala and trigger a chemical cascade which results in anger and frustration. Happiness and other positive emotions are more elusive. People all over the world risk their mental, legal and physical health trying to obtain illegal substances which can, in the short run, make them feel joy or ecstasy. In either case, the conscious pursuit of the ends conceptualized is seldom achieved because of subconscious forces which often act at odds with the goals our apparently conscious selves prepare. Actions motivated by emotion, impulse, and habit seem less willful because the brain hasn't had time to fabricate the experience of will.

If the inception team wanted to get the idea into Fischer's subconscious they should have chosen a less expensive, dangerous, and elaborate method. Many simpler, more elegant and effective methods abound. The foot-in-the-door phenomenon is one such useful technique. A person is asked to agree to make one small concession to perform an otherwise unappealing act, which eventually opens the door to influencing that person to make more major violations.

For example in one study ("The Counterfeit Self"), people were given designer sunglasses to wear, but half of the participants were told they were knock-offs, imitations of the real, more expensive shades. Subsequent tests on the same participants showed the ones who had been told they were wearing fake sunglasses indicated they were significantly more likely to lie during simple computer games and low-stakes betting situations than the people who believed they were wearing the genuine, expensive glasses. Apparently the foot-in-the-door phenomenon correctly predicted that once people comply enough to participate in even a mildly unethical behavior, they are more likely to become subconsciously predisposed to continue to push the ethical envelope. Cobb and his colleagues could have gotten Fisher to agree to sell off a minor part of his father's empire, and then later encouraged him to sell still more, in a gradual decomposition of Fisher's financial empire.

Exposing Fisher to some video clips containing subliminal messages of his father indicating his desire to dismantle his empire would have also done the trick. Cobb and Saito could have utilized John Anderson and Lynn Reder's elaboration (*Elaborative Processing Explanation of Depth Processing*) of our tendency to think about an item's relationship to other things and ourselves to surreptitiously influence Fischer's subconscious. They could expose Fischer to situations involving people similar to him, as they become more powerful or respected as a result of selling some of their businesses. Fischer would internalize and personalize this idea and perhaps act on it in his own world.

Unlike co-operative dream manipulations, these methods are doable, but effective to varying degrees. On the other hand, research by William Swann would support the inception, since this investigation determined that people seek circumstances that substantiate the verification of their prior view of who they are. The inception employed this finding to change Fischer's prior concept of himself as a failure in his father's eyes, to a success, but only if he were to drastically change the course of his father's business plan. Unfortunately, although Swann's research supports the basic idea of altering Fischer's prior view of himself in order to affect his future actions, the method by which the inception is planted in the movie is impossible.

Group Will

The *Inception* team dreamed together and co-operated with one another during their communal dream. Although each member of Cobb's team experienced their own illusory sense of free will, there was also an interesting group will that is common among people who work toward a common goal, like football team members who all want to win the championship. Actions the group performs may be perceived as independent of what the individuals do. Cobb's faction had a mutual wish to implant the inception, but there were differences as to its execution:

ARTHUR: What about his security? It's gonna get worse as we go deeper.

COBB: I think we run with Mr. Charles.

ARTHUR: No.

EAMES: Who's Mr. Charles?

ARTHUR: Bad idea.

COBB: The second we get in that hotel with Fischer, his security is gonna be all over us. We run with Mr. Charles like we did on the Stein job.

EAMES: So you've done it before?

ARTHUR: Yeah, and it didn't work. The subject realized he was dreaming and his subconscious tore us to pieces.

Nonetheless, despite these willful disputes over details of the mission, the common goal remained intact. From where did the group will originate? The party who thinks of the group's objective before the group embarks on its exploits is perceived as the more willful agent. Although Saito was the initiator of the plan, Cobb often called the shots so the others followed—to an extent, their wills became identical to his.

The individuals in Cobb's group automatically analyzed the internal and external cues available to them to decide which actions were personally willed and which were coercive and thus developed a theory of their own agency and identity. This automatic process is carried out by everyone as they proceed throughout their daily lives in order to maintain the fiction of personal identity and agency. So when group goals become very far removed from individual motivations, people have to be reminded about their original reasons to have become involved in the group's activity.

Cobb, for example, is involved in the inception because he hopes if he does this favor for Saito, the latter will use his influence to reunite Cobb with his children. We're frequently reminded through Cobb's dreams and thoughts about his family, of his personal motivation, but not of the other members' reasons for participating in the heist. Their devotion to the plan remains steady, however, despite the danger involved, so their personal motivations are assumed to be quite strong. Saito's desire becomes the desire of the group, ultimately, and no one questions Saito's motivations presumably because they have reasons of their own to be involved. Heck, Saito doesn't even ponder his own rationale for his desire for crushing power, even though it's the root of the entire scheme.

The origin of his behavior, and thus the behaviors of the members of his group, are unfathomable. It's as if a Hegelian historical movement provokes Saito's behavior through causing associated areas of his brain to conspire to give him an illusion of freely willing the inception, then a symphony of collaborating pseudo-wills of the group coagulate in a similar way to pull off the culminating scheme. It's as if the entropy-defying progress toward ever more complex systems of thought and action are willing themselves to become. Even so, Cobb and his colleagues still find satisfaction in a job well done.

It's certainly possible then, that at the end of *Inception* as Christopher Nolan would like us to believe, though he seemed to be experiencing free will, Fischer may have been responding to a subconscious inception created by Cobb and company. We can never be sure of the cause of our behavior, though, because as Pierre Laplace wrote, actions are "so complex that the project of understanding the causation of even a single human action is a vast challenge to scientists, perhaps an impossible one."

B.F. Skinner also acknowledged his own lack of agency after a lifetime of examining operant and conditioned behavioral responses. When asked about the course of his life, Skinner said "I did not direct my life. I didn't design it. I never made decisions. Things always came up and made them for me. That's what life is."

Nonetheless, Saito hedged his bets by implanting a subconscious idea in Fisher, thus bolstering his own sense of clandestine agency by creating an idea in another man's mind without that man knowing it. *Inception* appears to be an illustration of the ultimate mind-manipulation, an invasion of one man's free conscious will. But since our brains act before we ever desire to act, it's all manipulation. The brain's ability to give us the sensation of freely willing our own behavior, but only *after* the behavior has been performed, lends an air of irony to Saito's and Cobb's inception.

6
The Business of *Inception*

DANIEL P. MALLOY

The major players in *Inception* aren't the characters—they aren't even people. They are corporations. Cobol Engineering sends Cobb after Saito. Saito, acting as head of Proclus Global, sends Cobb after Robert Fischer. Fischer becomes a target, not because of anything he's done or even knows, but because of his impending ascension to the chairmanship of Fischer-Morrow.

In all of this, the people are just pieces, moved about at the will of the company. This is most obvious in Cobb's case. His life is threatened because of his failure to deal with Saito. His salvation comes in appeasing Proclus Global by sabotaging Fischer-Morrow. But Saito and Fischer are pieces as well—they're just more important pieces than Cobb. They are the kings to his pawn. And just like kings in chess, they are more valuable pieces, but they are still subject to the whims of the players—the corporations.

This power to move people about like pieces on a chessboard raises serious questions about the ethics of doing business, both in the world of *Inception* and in our own world. Does Cobol Engineering have the right to punish Cobb for his failure? For that matter, does either Cobol or Proclus have the right to hire Cobb in the first place? His services are of questionable legality at best, and there's little question about their immorality.

Further, should the CEO of Proclus Global have the power to get a suspected murderer off the hook with a phone call? Is either corporation responsible or answerable for what Cobb does in their service? And what of Fischer-Morrow? When Saito hires Cobb, he gives two reasons for wanting the job done.

First, because Proclus Global can no longer compete with Fischer-Morrow—a clear, practical, economic reason. Second, he says that Fischer-Morrow is on the verge of having a monopoly on half the world's energy supply, making the corporation effectively a new super-power. Thus, his second reason is an ethical one—a global monopoly on energy wouldn't be good for the world. But how genuine is this second reason? We can easily guess—if Proclus Global were on the verge of creating such a monopoly, Saito wouldn't break up the company.

These questions, in turn, are based on a deeper question about the nature of corporations. If a corporation can have a right, or a responsibility, or even be said to do anything, then it follows that the corporation is a person or at least an agent. But, common sense tells us, corporations plainly aren't persons. If common sense is right, then Cobol has no rights against Cobb and Proclus has no responsibility for the kidnapping (more or less) of Fischer.

In the US, it has been legal precedent for the past century and a half or so that corporations are persons, endowed with the same rights and responsibilities as any flesh-and-blood person. As such, a corporation has, for instance, the freedom of speech, although it has no mouth with which to speak. Likewise, a corporation can be prosecuted for crimes, though in a very real sense it is incapable of committing crimes—or any other action, for that matter. But there's an important distinction between legality and morality. Just because Cobol and Proclus are legal persons that doesn't necessarily imply that they are moral persons.

This Isn't the Usual Corporate Espionage

Inception opens, appropriately, in a dream. First, Saito's dream. Then we flashback to how the whole affair between Saito and Cobb started: another dream. In this second dream, Cobb is offering his services to Saito, but the offer is a ruse. He simply wants Saito to reveal a key piece of information, or, more specifically, where he has hidden a key piece of information. Cobb wants to know because he wants to steal that information. In truth, Cobb has no interest in the information itself—it is of absolutely no value to him. But it is of value to his employer, Cobol Engineering. This information is, in Hitchcock's term, a

MacGuffin—an object, meaningless in itself, that sets the action going. Tellingly, we never discover what information it is that Cobb wants. But then, neither does Cobb.

Now, I don't think there can be much debate about the morality of Cobb's actions. Extraction is a violation of another person's mind, pure and simple. The fact that, in this case, that other person happens to be the CEO of Proclus Global in no way mitigates the violation. Think about it: if another person hacked into your e-mail account, or stole your credit card numbers, or broke into your house, that person has undoubtedly done something wrong. Cobb broke into Saito's mind, and more or less kidnapped him to do it.

Or, to draw another parallel, Cobb is a corporate spy. Extraction is a form of espionage. Aside from breaking and entering, we could draw a parallel between Cobb's activities and stalking. Arguably, this mitigates some of the violation involved in extraction. Rather than stealing, Cobb is simply gathering information concerning a person who doesn't want him to have it. No big deal, right? Wrong. Of course it's a big deal. It's an invasion of privacy, and a worse one that any other conceivable. This is not going through someone's garbage—it's rummaging around inside someone's mind.

But, some might say, the fact that Saito was the CEO of Proclus Global is a mitigating factor. While it is no doubt wrong for one person to invade another's privacy, or to break in to someone else's house, these aren't people we're dealing with here: they're corporations. Corporate espionage is an accepted business practice; it's the price of doing business. The reasoning here is somewhat similar to the common (and fallacious) reasoning offered by the paparazzi when they invade the lives of celebrities: this is the price they pay for wanting to be famous. In Saito's case, in becoming a CEO, he has created such a strong connection between himself and Proclus Global that what one corporation is allowed to do to another, it is allowed to do to him. He, to put it simply, is Proclus Global, and vice versa.

One of the major differences between corporations and flesh-and-blood people is that corporations are almost by their nature in direct competition with one another. Because of that competition, they, like states engaged in war, are justified in gathering intelligence about their competitors. This activity has to go beyond the limits established between individuals. If I hide a piece of information from you, it may not concern you at all. If I tell you a piece of information, it may concern you or it may not. In the case of competing corporations, however, whatever one lets out in public is sure to be of no use to the other: that's the whole point. The surest way of losing whatever edge one has in the marketplace is to be loose with information. So, in order to gain useful information, corporations must engage in corporate espionage.

That explains the necessity of corporate espionage, but not its morality. Too often, we confuse the expediency of a particular action with its morality. Just because corporate espionage, in our case extraction, is a useful means for achieving our ends doesn't mean that it's a justified one—or, for that matter, that the ends are justified themselves. In our case, we don't know why Cobol Engineering wants or needs the information they sent Cobb after. Presumably, it had something to do with the competition between Proclus and Cobol, and would have given Cobol some sort of edge in that competition. This inference would be dangerous to make if humans were the primary actors here, but as they are corporations, we are on fairly safe ground. The primary purpose of a corporation, after all, is to make profits. Therefore, we're safe in inferring that any activity engaged in on behalf of the corporation will serve that end in some fashion or other.

What we should take away from this is the fact that Cobb kidnapped a fellow human being and invaded his mind, but it wasn't personal. He had no connection to Saito, no grudge against him. On his own, Cobb would never have bothered Saito. It was only the influence of Cobol that caused Cobb to act at all. Is that enough for us to consider Cobol Engineering, and by extension, other corporations, moral persons? No, not yet. But we have seen a couple of factors that could lead us in that direction. First is the fact that while Cobol can't act, it can cause others to act on its behalf. This distinguishes Cobol from other possible causes of action—being hit by a car will cause a person to act as well, but not in the same way. Cobol Engineering, unlike the car, has interests. These interests can influence the motives of others. Further, these interests aren't directly identifiable with the interests of any particular flesh-and-blood individuals.

The individuals may have interests that coincide with Cobol's—for instance, stockholders have interests in Cobol making a profit—but they aren't identical to Cobol's. If, for instance, Cobol is bought out, that would bring an end to Cobol's interests, because it would end Cobol, but the stockholders' interests remain, now having shifted from Cobol's profits to those of the new parent company.

You Know the Corporation Who Hired Us Won't Accept Failure

When Cobol Engineering hired Cobb and his team to go after Saito, they formed a contract of sorts. I say "of sorts" because a contract that obliges one of the parties to do something illegal or immoral is generally considered invalid. However, let's grant that this is a contract for the sake of argument. If that's the case, then it implies that Cobol Engineering is capable of forming contracts. To make a contract means two things. First, both parties are persons—only persons can form contracts. You can't make a contract with your dog or your computer, because they aren't people. But we make contracts with corporations all the time—for our cellphones and Internet service, for cable TV and employment. Secondly, it means that Cobol Engineering has rights. At the least, in the context of the contract, Cobol has rights. The corporation hired Cobb to do a job. It has the right to expect that Cobb will do that job, or, failing that, compensate Cobol for not accomplishing his mission.

This capacity to have rights is one indicator of personhood. Typically, moral personhood is linked to legal personhood by this commonality: both possess rights. A legal person is the bearer of legal rights, while the moral person is the bearer of moral rights. This distinction is not immediately obvious, particularly in the US, where many of our moral rights are also legal rights. One way to make this distinction is to think about the protections afforded to citizens and non-citizens. Citizens, for instance, have the right to vote, where non-citizens don't. Voting, then, is a legal right. Free speech, on the other hand, is a right protected for citizens and non-citizens alike; it is a moral right. So, given that corporations have legal rights, in order to discern whether or not they are moral persons, our next step in to decide whether they have moral rights.

In some cases, the answer is obviously no. There are some moral rights that it would make no sense to assign to corporations, because they simply couldn't exercise them. I, being male, don't have the right to give birth. Similarly, corporations, being organizations, don't have a right to have children.

But there are many moral rights that it makes perfect sense to assign to corporations. For instance, property rights. In essence, a corporation is itself a collective exercise of property rights—stockholders pool their property in order to do things that their properties individually are incapable of doing. In *Inception*, we can see this in Saito's response to the problem of how to get access to Robert Fischer. As his co-conspirators are debating the complexities of assuring that they'll have enough time and privacy to carry out their plans, Saito interrupts: "I bought the airline. . . . It seemed . . . neater." Now, it is doubtful that Saito himself bought the airline—very few people have those kinds of resources. In the shooting script, he says, perhaps more accurately, that *"We* bought the airline." *We* being Proclus Global. Saito, acting as CEO, used the resources of the corporation to purchase another corporation in order to further his criminal scheme. Now, put yourself in the place of Proclus Global—someone else has just used your money to buy something. You'd be a bit put out, to say the least, and rightly so.

The case, however, is not exactly parallel, because Saito is the CEO of Proclus. Contrary to what we were saying earlier, this does not make him identical to Proclus. Rather, Saito is Proclus's representative. In acting as he does, he is carrying out his role. He bought the airline to further the interests of Proclus Global—the same reason he hired Cobb in the first place. So long as he's using Proclus's resources to this end, he's respecting the rights of Proclus Global. Were he to take Proclus's resources and use them to further his own interests, as distinct from the corporation's, then he would be embezzling. The case is quite similar to elected representatives. In theory, an elected representative has the duty to pursue the interests of his or her constituents. When elected representatives fail to do this, it may be a sign of simple incompetence, or a sign of conflicting ideas about what those interests are. On the other hand, when an elected official takes a bribe, he or she is plainly pursuing his or her own interests above the interests of the constituents.

The flipside of rights is responsibilities. A moral person must be responsible for his or her actions. In *Inception*, this gets complex. When Saito hires Cobb, he's acting as Proclus Global's representative. Cobb then becomes an employee of Proclus. So, who's responsible for the kidnapping and inception of Robert Fischer? Well, in any contract to perform a specific task, both parties must take some responsibility. If I go out and hire Bob to kill Joe, then Bob is responsible for what he does to fulfill that contract—murder or attempted murder, depending on his competence—but I'm also responsible for hiring him. We'll both be tried for the crime. In the same way, Saito and Cobb share responsibility for what they do to Robert Fischer.

And the corporation? The same logic holds. Saito is Proclus's legal representative, and so Proclus is responsible for anything Saito does in the name of the corporation. Note that there are limits to this—Proclus only bears responsibility for actions Saito undertakes in his role as CEO. Had he hired Cobb to perform inception on his mistress, Proclus would in no way responsible for that.

So, even though corporations can't act for themselves, and can't claim or exercise certain moral rights, there are some rights that they are entitled to. Likewise, there are certain actions, undertaken in their names that the corporation bears responsibility for. Note once again that, like the interests of the corporation, this responsibility is not reducible to the responsibility of the stockholders or any other individual. As for the stockholders, part of the point of the corporate structure is to minimize the responsibility of individual stockholders for the actions of the enterprise. If I'm a stockholder in Proclus, and Proclus loses a billion dollars, I haven't lost a billion dollars. I may have lost some money, but it won't be anywhere near a billion dollars. Similarly, the responsibility borne by Proclus is not identical to that of Saito or Cobb.

This is harder to see in Saito's case than in Cobb's, because the responsibility of the corporation is more directly tied to the decisions and actions of its CEO than to those of its employees or third-party contractors. Nevertheless, there's a distinction between the responsibility of a corporation and the responsibility of its CEO. The easiest way to see this is to reflect on the fact that the CEO can be held responsible by the corporation itself. For instance, suppose Saito, as CEO of Proclus Global, made decisions which lost the corporation a billion dollars. First, Saito is not responsible for that billion dollar loss, any more than any of the shareholders are. Second, Proclus Global would be perfectly within its rights to fire Saito, to hold him responsible, but that firing wouldn't mitigate Proclus Global's responsibility for the billion dollar loss.

We Want the Heir to a Major Corporation to Break Up His Father's Empire

If we take what's been said so far for granted, it seems to make a good case for the moral personhood of corporations. A corporation like Cobol Engineering or Proclus Global may be incapable of acting, but it has interests, rights, responsibilities, and the ability to cause others to act in its place. Corporations even, in a certain sense, have the ability to make decisions. Every corporation has some decision procedure that distinguishes the decisions of the corporation from the decisions of the individuals who make it up. But, some claim, all of this is insufficient for moral personhood—it is sufficient only to prove that corporations are moral agents. A moral agent, as distinct from a moral person, is capable of acting and being responsible for those actions, but may not have interests or rights.

There are two reasons offered for this distinction between personhood and agency, both having to do with emotion. First, the argument states, a corporation is not a moral person because it is not capable of moral emotions. Corporations aren't capable of emotions, period, as far as that goes. The distinction is fairly simple: moral emotions are the ones that allow us to relate to other people. Sympathy, compassion, and the like. They are related to other emotions, no doubt. Anger, for instance, is not a moral emotion, but indignation is. Moral emotions, so this argument claims, are necessary for moral personhood because without them one can't really understand moral standard.

To borrow an example from Gilbert Harman, imagine a person discovered a gang pouring gas on a cat, preparing to set it on fire. This person should respond with repugnance. It's not just that the action is morally wrong—it goes beyond that. Harman says that we can imagine an entity who would know that setting the cat on fire is wrong, and yet not feel repugnance about it—a being, that is, with morality but without moral emotions. This being would condemn the action, but, we would say, she wouldn't fully understand why it is wrong. Likewise, while a corporation may perform morally praiseworthy or blameworthy action, it's incapable of fully understanding the morality of its own actions because it is incapable of emotion, and therefore of moral emotions.

A similar argument runs that we must deny moral personhood to corporations because they can't have virtues or vices. Virtues and vices are moral habits, patterns of behavior that persons display when given the chance. Again, this is a valid point. There are many ways to describe corporations—profitable or unprofitable, efficient or inefficient, national or international, and so on. But if someone were to call Cobol Engineering brave, or Proclus Global generous, or Fischer-Morrow patient, they would be abusing the language. Cobol Engineering's management may make bold moves, Saito may use Proclus Global's resources for charitable ends, and Maurice Fischer may lay out strategies far in advance, but these are policies, not habits or traits of the corporation. If the corporation can't have habits, then it can't have virtues or vices either. Therefore, the argument goes, the corporation is not a moral person.

I'm looking at these objections together because they suffer from a single confusion: they both fail to distinguish between moral personhood and personality. Moral emotions aren't necessary for moral personhood—if they are, then psychopaths, who, by definition, are incapable of them, aren't moral persons. That is simply not the case. Psychopaths are moral persons—they're just not good persons. Their personalities lack certain key facets which would make them good people. Similarly, virtues and vices are important for defining the kinds of persons we are, but not for making us persons. I think these objections both put the cart before the horse. One must first be a moral person, and only then can one acquire moral emotions and virtues and vices. Think about it like this: in Harman's example, what makes setting the cat on fire repugnant? I would argue that it is the understanding of the wrongness of the action.

A further argument claims that a corporation is not a moral person because we don't feel moral emotions toward it. For example, in *Inception*, we may feel bad for Robert Fischer—the end is good for him, and may make him a better man with a happier life, but nonetheless he has had his personality changed in a fundamental way against his will. However, all of our sympathy for Mr. Fischer will never transfer over to Fischer-Morrow. We understand that he's going to break up the company, effectively ending its existence. There will be no memorial service for Fischer-Morrow, as there's one for Maurice Fischer.

When we hear that a corporation is being broken up, or swallowed up in a merger, or going bankrupt, we don't feel bad about it. Or, we may feel bad about it, but we don't feel bad for the corporation. We may feel bad for its employees, or because a tradition is coming to an end, or for a variety of other reasons, but we don't feel bad for the corporation. Whereas if we hear that some friends of ours get divorced, or a relative has died, or that a person was dismembered, we feel bad for them. Since we don't sympathize in this way with corporations, the argument goes, corporations aren't moral persons.

This argument fails. Primarily this is because the moral personhood of an entity can't depend on the recognition of others. If it does, then we must conclude that people of color and women were not moral persons until the twentieth century. That conclusion is morally repugnant. So, our recognition of personhood is not a necessary condition for personhood. Further, it is not a sufficient condition. In Harman's example, we are meant to feel sympathy for the cat, in a way that we never would for a corporation, but this does not mean that the cat is a moral person. We can call it J. Wentworth Tiddlesmire III, Esq., dress it up, and teach it to use the toilet, but the cat still won't be a person.

Each of these arguments is an attempt, I think, to defend our intuition that in order to be a moral person an entity must be made of flesh-and-blood, even though a corporation may be a legal person. Each fails because it tries to include too much in the concept of moral personhood; a concept which is, almost necessarily, somewhat thin and formal. There's a greater connection between the concepts of moral and legal personhood than these arguments will allow.

The World Needs Robert Fischer to Change His Mind

A final consideration: if the corporation's a moral person, it seems to follow that it has moral obligations. Saito hints at this in one of his reasons for wanting Fischer-Morrow broken up. The move, he claims, aside from profiting Proclus Global, will be good for everyone. Fischer-Morrow is on the verge of becoming a new superpower. Given that this is the case, and that such an extensive monopoly, particularly on energy supplies, would be detrimental to the greater good, does Fischer-Morrow have a responsibility to break itself up?

There are two perspectives we could take on this question. The first, advocated by economist Milton Friedman, is that the corporation's only responsibility is to its stockholders. By Friedman's logic, Fischer-Morrow's responsibility is to generate profit for its owners. Say what you will about monopolies (and economists since Adam Smith himself have said that they're bad for business), they are excellent ways to generate profit. Therefore, if Friedman is correct, then Fischer-Morrow's responsibility is to consolidate its monopoly, not to break up.

On the other hand, one could argue that if the corporation is indeed a moral person, then it is part of a moral community. As such, it has responsibilities to the community. Since monopolies are bad for the community, Fischer-Morrow must break itself up.

There's a logic behind both positions. On Friedman's side is the fact that the very purpose of corporations, for the most part, is to generate profit. A corporation that doesn't do that is a bit like a hammer made of pudding: pointless. On the other side, the corporation needs the community if it is to fulfill its purpose. Hurting the community ultimately hurts the corporation.

Put this another way: imagine the corporation as a dog. Now, if I have a dog, I expect it to treat me in ways that it does not treat other people. That is, I expect my dog to get excited when I come home; I expect it to wait patiently for me, to obey me above others, and so forth. At the same time, my dog must treat others in a certain way if I am to keep it. It can bark at people, no problem. But if it mauls someone, I've to get rid of it. The good of the community outweighs the good of dog ownership. Similarly, corporate stockholders can expect the corporation to generate profits insofar as whatever it does to generate those profits does not interfere with the greater good of the community. Fischer-Morrow and Proclus Global and Cobol Engineering may be exempt from contributing to that greater good, but they may not hinder it, as Fischer-Morrow would if it became a monopoly.

Cobol's Backyard

So, corporations are moral persons for at least three interconnected reasons. They make decisions, have rights, and can be
held responsible. I find it difficult to say that any one of these
reasons is more or less important than the others, but I would
argue that each is necessary for any defensible definition of
moral personhood. A being that had rights and responsibilities,
but no ability to make decisions, wouldn't, I think, be a moral
person. Likewise a being without rights or responsibility. The
first scenario is the easiest to imagine, though, because we see
it happen. Coma patients have rights and can be held responsible—after a fashion—but lack decision making ability. Thus,
a human being in a coma is not, so long as she remains in the
coma, a moral person. Before the coma, she was a moral person;
after the coma, she will be again. During the coma, however,
she is a person only in a metaphorical sense. If this is correct,
what does it mean for us? If corporations are moral persons,
what follows?

Quite a bit, actually, but not as much as some may think.
There are still limitations on the moral personhood of corporations—limitations brought out in the previous section. Being a
moral person does not entitle the corporation to all of the rights
that flesh-and-blood individuals have, because its personhood
is of a different sort. Just as corporations aren't entitled to the
right to vote by their legal personhood, they aren't entitled to
all moral considerations by virtue of their moral personhood. A
corporation has no right to life, for instance. Not being alive in
any but a metaphorical sense, its "life" can't be defended.

However, there are certain rights that corporations can
claim, and given their status as moral persons, these rights
should be respected. In *Inception* they often aren't. There are
several examples, but most of them are questionable—each
time a corporation engages a worker to do a job, it has a right
to expect that that job will be done. But, its right is doubtful
when the job in question is illegal. So, when Cobb fails to perform the job Cobol hired him for, it is doubtful that Cobol's
rights were violated. However, in attempting to perform that
job, there's no doubt that Proclus Global's rights were violated.
Similarly, the rights of Fischer-Morrow are violated by the
attack on Robert Fischer.

This is all old hat by now. What about in real life? Well, in real life many people have no problem violating the rights of corporations, on the grounds that they are corporations. "No one gets hurt," the justification goes. And it's true, when one steals from a corporation, no flesh-and-blood human being is directly harmed by one's action. But a moral person is still harmed. Stealing things from the local Mega-Mart, sneaking in to movies, and stealing cable are all examples violating the moral rights of corporations. Just because no individual human being is directly harmed does not mean that the action in question is morally right, or even permissible.

A further implication concerns responsibility. Corporations are held legally responsible in all sorts of ways—regulations, fines, and so forth. There are even more ways to hold them morally responsible. To get some idea of what I mean by holding a corporation morally responsible, think about someone who has wronged you without breaking the law. Maybe they violated your trust in some way, or talked about you behind your back. As a result of this action, you probably took some action of your own. Perhaps you went the eye-for-an-eye route, and just did the same thing to that person. Or perhaps you simply cut her out of your life. Whatever you did, it was your way of holding her morally responsible.

And, in just the same way, we can hold corporations morally responsible. When a corporation engages in immoral behavior, we have various means of bringing social (but not legal) pressure to bear on them. Boycotts are probably the most obvious example, but there are others. Letter-writing campaigns, petitions, Facebook groups, and advertisements are all ways of holding corporations morally responsible, and thus, of treating them as moral persons.

7
Mental Burglary

MARCUS SCHULZKE

Dreams have long been considered a source of insight into the unconscious mind—a way of finding hidden memories, desires, and fears. The content of dreams can reveal things that dreamers wish to conceal from the world and even things they attempt to hide from themselves.

Dreams are also personal. The experience of the dream is something that can't be reproduced or shown to others. It's difficult to describe dreams because descriptions lack the feeling of immediacy and dissociation from the waking world that make dreams seem real at the time. The exploration of dreams, as it is depicted in *Inception*, destroys the privacy of the dream world; it grants outsiders access to both the content of the mind and the feeling of being inside of it.

Inception shows how the characters react to the threat of invasion by increasing their psychological defenses. Cobb hides his memories and Fischer militarizes his mind to fight intruders. However, these efforts are futile, as neither skilled extractors nor billionaires with unlimited security resources manage to protect their own minds. The world of *Inception* is one in which private mental life is impossible.

The Defenseless Mind

In the world of *Inception*, extraction—learning people's secrets by going into their dreams—is known to be possible and has become routine, though it is expensive. Inception—going into someone's dreams to plant a really new idea in their mind, that will then seriously influence their beliefs and behavior—is not generally accepted as practically feasible, and whether it is possible at all is open to debate.

Arthur, Cobb, and Saito discuss the possibility of inception early in the movie. Arthur, who doubts that inception is possible, uses a classic problem to demonstrate the way that direct thought manipulation works. He tells Saito not to think about elephants and, consequently, Saito can't help but think of elephants as he tries to keep them out of his mind. Arthur gives Saito an idea, just as communication of any sort can cause others to think about something, but points out that the source of the idea is clear. Since Saito knows the idea came from Arthur he can resist it and prevent the idea from taking hold of his mind.

Arthur's example is somewhat misleading. Psychological defense isn't as simple as tracing the origin of an idea back to an external influence. To some extent, something rather like inception is already possible in our world, even without the ability to enter dreams. Thought control through brainwashing, hypnosis, propaganda, peer pressure, and advertisements are among the most familiar forms of thought manipulation. Although the effectiveness of these kinds of techniques is still controversial, they can at least have some definite effect under the right circumstances.

Kathleen Taylor argues that "even if we wished to avoid all attempts to influence us, we simply don't have the cognitive resources to detect and counteract each and every one" (*Brainwashing: The Science of Thought Control*, p. 247). Outside attempts to influence thought are so common that even a well-defended mind can't track new ideas and question their source, as Arthur implies that we should be able to. Thus, it should come as no surprise that Arthur's skepticism about inception turns out to be misguided.

Given the similarities between inception and other kinds of influence, inception should not be viewed as some completely foreign idea that exists only in this movie. However, two important differences set it apart from other forms of thought control. First, there are fewer opportunities for resisting inception than other types of influence. Although advertising is everywhere, it's possible to limit and control our exposure to advertising messages—by installing adblocker software on an internet browser, avoiding television, and reading newspapers and magazines selectively.

We can avoid exposure to propaganda or peer pressure in much the same way, by limiting exposure to it. Brainwashing is more direct and may be more difficult to defend against, but it can likewise be resisted and risk situations can be avoided. Inception is far more powerful. Those who, like Fischer, have trained their minds to detect and attack intruders may be capable of resisting inception. However, the movie assumes that even the best security can be overcome by a skilled extractor.

Inception could be a far more powerful influence than advertisements or propaganda. They tend to have a subtle influence on people, pushing them towards behavior that is consistent with their beliefs and personality. An advertisement may induce a beer drinker to try a new brand, but it will probably lack the power to convince a teetotaler to start drinking.

Even the most sophisticated brainwashing techniques tend to fall far short of their objectives. Inception, by contrast, allows dream burglars to enter the subject's mind and implant an idea that is radically different from anything that's already there. As Eames explains, inception requires a carefully formulated idea. "It's not just about depth. You need the simplest version of the idea, the one that will grow naturally in the subject's mind." The idea must be capable of spreading and altering other thoughts. The idea must appear natural, as though it were the subject's own and this can only be accomplished by allowing the implanted idea to reshape the subject's mind. This makes inception more versatile and powerful than other forms of influence; it can completely change a person, rather than just push them in a certain direction.

The simplicity of the implanted ideas makes them extremely dangerous. Eames and Cobb repeatedly insist that inception can work only for the simplest ideas because they must be allowed to grow within the subject's mind. This simplicity introduces serious risks of unintended consequences. The idea may take root in the subject's mind, only to influence that person in a way that no one expected. One of the movie's central themes is how psychologically damaging inception was for Mal. Cobb gave Mal the idea that her reality is an illusion. This was, as Mal said, "a simple little thought that changes *everything*." She became obsessed with the idea that the world was an illusion, so much so that she lost attachment to any world and to anyone except Cobb. Cobb's life was also destroyed; his use of inception ultimately made him a criminal, forced him to work as an extractor for dangerous employers, and separated him from his children.

Cobb explains the extent of inception's power to Saito and warns him that the implanted idea may do more than Saito expects. "This isn't the usual corporate espionage, Mr. Saito. This is inception. The seed of the idea we plant will grow in this man's mind. It'll change him. It might even come to define him." Worse still, the implanted idea can't be eradicated once it begins to spread. Earlier in the film Cobb explains how strong and resistant to change ideas can be: "Resilient, highly contagious. Once an idea's taken hold in the brain it's almost impossible to eradicate. A person can cover it up, ignore it—but it stays there."

This is a frightening claim, as an unwanted idea that comes to define a person's character must lead to an inauthentic existence. It would be difficult to determine the extent to which a person's actions are voluntary or coerced when they are driven by motives that may contradict or at least be alien from the values they held before inception.

Losing Autonomy

Inception introduces many ethical problems, but the most fundamental is that it represents a violation of personal autonomy. Autonomy is a person's ability to think and act without outside control. It is the capacity for self-governance.

Many philosophers have discussed the concept of autonomy and developed its moral implications, but Kant's ethical theory of autonomy is one of the strongest. Kant argues that every person is morally obligated to respect the autonomy of other people. Kant's rule for moral action is that we must treat all persons as ends in themselves and never merely as means to our ends. Kant calls this rule a categorical imperative because it is a rule that all persons must follow at all times. It applies universally, regardless of circumstance.

While extraction may sometimes be ethical, inception is clearly immoral because it violates the subject's autonomy and, in doing so, disrespects their humanity. Fischer's inception provides a clear example of this, as it is done for mainly self-interested reasons, and certainly not for Fischer's own benefit. Each member of the team treats Fischer solely as a means to an end, not as an end in himself. Saito cares about Fischer only insofar as he can make Fischer break up his father's empire. Cobb only cares about completing the mission so he can return home to his children. The other members' motives are less clear, but none seem to be entering Fischer's dreams for any reason aside from personal advantage. The way they execute the mission adds another dimension to the disrespect. They not only plant an idea in Fischer's mind, but they also trick him into becoming a willing participant in his own deception. Fischer sacrifices his own autonomy, but does so because he has been so deeply misled as to believe that the people inside his mind are parts of himself.

But must inception be as bad as all that? A therapist might enter a patient's mind and implant an idea that could lead to healthier behaviors. Inception could even serve as a quick way of curing behavioral problems without requiring patients to undergo lengthy treatment. However, even if inception were only used in this way, Kant would still consider it morally off-limits because it would deprive subjects of part of their autonomy.

Mal's inception is more difficult to assess than Fischer's because Cobb performs inception on her with good intentions. He clearly loves Mal, cares about her safety, and has a desire to bring her back into the real world. He thinks that giving her the idea that the world is an illusion will convince her to commit suicide, thereby leaving the dream world. Given Cobb's good intentions, Cobb may not be disrespecting Mal. He does not treat her as a means to an ends in the sense that he's using her for his own benefit.

However, for Kant, even an action that benefits a person or that does not disrespect them as an individual may be immoral if the action disrespects humanity. Cobb violates Mal's autonomy by implanting an idea in her mind and, by attacking that which makes Mal human, Cobb disrespects humanity. He does what he thinks will benefit Mal, but he does so by refusing to treat her as a real person capable of self-determination. It is only fitting that the Mal he's left with after Mal's suicide is one whom his own imagination constructs and who has no freedom.

Fischer's inception shows a purely instrumental violation of autonomy, in which people used another person for their own gain, and the more general disrespect of humanity. Mal's inception provides a more difficult case because Cobb only commits the second form of disrespect. According to Kant, both are immoral on these grounds alone, but the violation of autonomy is even more serious than the categorical imperative reveals. Autonomy isn't important only because it's a mark of being human, but also because you must be autonomous in order to be responsible for your actions, and only when you are responsible for your actions can you truly act morally. For a person or a person's actions to be described in terms of good and evil, that person must actually be responsible for those actions. Actions performed under coercion or under thought control aren't usually considered blameworthy.

Kant's categorical imperative states that each person must act as though they were the legislator of universal laws of action. In simpler terms, this means that everyone ought to act as though they were setting an example that all people would follow. Each person's ability to create laws of moral action that are true for all people is the reason that each person deserves respect and that humanity as a whole deserves respect.

After inception is performed on Mal and Fischer, it becomes impossible to determine which of their decisions result from their own desire to legislate universal laws of action and which of their actions are performed because their minds were altered. Given this ambiguity, Mal and Fischer can no longer act according to the categorical imperative. It's impossible to determine when they are acting as they wish and when they are acting as someone has programmed them to act. Because the simple idea that is planted in their minds grows and reshapes other thoughts, even actions that seem unrelated to the implanted idea could be indirect results of it.

Kant says that every person must act as though every action implied a universal law that could govern every person's action. If this universal law would result in a contradiction when followed by every person, then it's wrong for any single person to follow it. For example, murder is immoral because a world in which anyone can kill without punishment would be unsustainable; each person would face a constant threat of attack that would lead to the breakdown of social institutions and of mental health.

The problem with inception is that the person who lacks autonomy can't be held responsible for obeying or failing to obey coherent universal laws. When Mal appears in Cobb's dreams, she's a malicious figure who knowingly attacks people and attempts to keep Cobb trapped in the dream world. However, in Cobb's memories she's a more sympathetic figure—deeply confused and eager for Cobb's support. Her conception of reality has been undermined and she's unable to cope with the constant suspicion that her entire world is illusory.

The real Mal's actions are akin to those of a person with a severe mental disorder. She neglects her children and shows little concern for her own life, but she isn't motivated by a desire to hurt her family or herself. Although the movie leaves open the possibility that she may be right to doubt her reality, Cobb thinks she is delusional. Her lack of awareness of reality, combined with the fact that she's not responsible for her condition, makes it difficult to blame her for her actions. Mal does not seem to be responsible for her actions and has therefore lost her capacity to be a moral actor.

Inception disrespects the subject whose thoughts are controlled and it disrespects humanity by treating the mind as something to be manipulated for personal gain. It also deprives the subject of both the ability to make rules of moral conduct or to follow them. We can conclude that Kant would oppose inception, even when it is carried out with the best of intentions.

Stealing Thoughts

Although the movie tells us little about extraction, it does make clear that this process is commonplace, at least for those with plenty of money. It seems to be a standard means of espionage, used by large corporations to gain an advantage over their competitors. We're not told much about Cobb's customary uses of extraction, but it's clear from his legal troubles and his employer's willingness to use violence that extraction is often used immorally, to violate people's autonomy. Although extraction is performed by clandestine operatives, many of whom must hide from law enforcement and from retribution, these operatives seem to work for regular employers and have business contacts that are prepared to transport them safely between jobs.

The movie therefore makes extraction appear to be a relatively minor crime that is routine to the point of being often overlooked. Even Cobb, who's portrayed as one of the greatest extractors in the world, is only wanted for Mal's murder and not for his many mental burglaries. Extraction is much simpler than inception because it only requires finding secrets and exposing them. It does not require the extractor to change the subject's personality or to rob them of their capacity to be moral actors. In other words, it does not attack personal autonomy.

Extraction is possible because people lower their defenses when they're dreaming. While awake, people carry many secrets, perhaps even some which are unconscious. Alcohol and drugs can lower a person's inhibitions, bringing out some of these secrets. In more extreme circumstances interrogation and torture may be used. No matter how rigorously they are applied, any of these traditional means of extracting information may be insufficient to make a person reveal some of their most guarded secrets. However, secrets are routinely manifested in dreams, which is why so many psychoanalysts have considered dream analysis to be an essential part of treatment for mental disorders.

Hidden fears and secret thoughts, even those not acknowledged by the dreamer, arise outside the dreamer's control. In fact, the concentration required to protect secrets during waking hours may make them weigh more heavily on a person's mind and make them more likely to appear in dreams. Anyone with the capacity to not only watch someone else's dreams, but to manipulate them and to bring certain secrets to the surface, could have the power to see every secret, every hidden wish, and every repressed memory. For a skilled extractor like Cobb, no secrets are off-limits.

Extraction, like inception, has some counterparts in our world. Some of the closest may be computer hacking or corporate espionage that involve infiltrating a rival company and breaking privacy laws to find information. Yet even in their extreme forms, these are far less intrusive than extraction. Conventional espionage violates privacy, but extraction makes privacy nearly impossible. The widespread use of extraction would mean the end of private dreaming, which in turn would virtually bring an end to private mental life. Real privacy would only exist for short periods of time. New thoughts might arise during time spent awake and not be discoverable until the next time a person sleeps, but this would only yield a very limited measure of security. More enduring information that is part of a person's conscious or unconscious memory over time would always be subject to theft.

If extraction were possible, every person would have to think about deception in a new way. There would be no safe secret, no matter how well hidden. Worse, as Cobb explains the practice of extraction, the most carefully guarded secrets may also be the easiest to discover. When explaining his craft to Ariadne, he says that building a secure place like a jail or bank vault will lead dreamers to fill that space with the secret that they're trying to protect. This allows the extractor to quickly sort through the immense amount of information stored in a person's mind and makes extraction even more threatening to privacy.

Although extraction might be used infrequently, people would live under the constant threat that a suspicious partner, a rival, or a potential employer might sneak into dreams and steal guarded information. The risk of extraction, however small, would probably be enough to lead people to reconsider personal privacy, just as terrorism, which directly harms only a relatively small number of people has caused widespread security concerns. The end of secrecy introduces serious risks. For example, government thought police, in order to locate and punish dissidents and spies, could gain access to secret security information.

Invisibility or Honesty

Extraction provides an answer for one of the oldest thought experiments in Western philosophy. In Plato's *Republic*, Glaucon tells the story of the Ring of Gyges. The ring gives its bearer the power of invisibility, allowing that person to act without any fear of retribution. The story is told to force Socrates to defend his belief that people should act justly even if they have no fear of punishment. Socrates provides several answers to the problem. He argues that using the ring for immoral purposes would distort the wearer's character and that it would lead to punishment in the afterlife. The first of these claims receives the most attention. If the ring's wearer was unrestrained and satisfied every desire, no matter how base, that person would become a slave to their desires. In other words, that person would lose autonomy without even being a victim of inception.

Extraction adds a third reason to this list. Even if a person could be invisible while committing unjust acts, the marks of those acts would be permanently engrained in that person's mind and vulnerable to an extractor. If something as powerful at hiding actions as an invisibility ring existed, extractors could still hold its user accountable by entering that person's dreams and finding evidence of all the actions performed while invisible. A person with the ring would be faced with the difficult choice of whether to act justly or to remain invisible even while sleeping. In other words, the only choices would be honesty or to retreat from the world and hide.

Those without a Ring of Gyges would face a similar decision. For past actions, beliefs, and wishes, people would have to decide whether to retain their secrets in the hope that no one would bother looking for them or to volunteer the information to others, so as to minimize the damage. For future actions, the choice would be even simpler: to deceive others and hope that the deception isn't discovered or to be honest and have no fear of mental espionage. In some cases, exposing secrets could help to protect those who the subject may intentionally or unintentionally harm.

Inception shows us an excellent example of a situation in which extraction saves lives. While preparing for the mission, Ariadne notices that Cobb is taken into the dream state every night and she decides to enter his dreams to see what he's doing. She discovers Cobb's hidden memories, even the one that he tries hardest to hide. As she discovers these secrets, she realizes that Cobb is a threat to the mission. He could allow Mal into his dreams to destroy everything the team was working for or even endanger the lives of the other team members. Ariadne decides not to tell the other members of the team how dangerous Mal's influence on Cobb really is, but she does warn Cobb and helps him cope with his problems. She even accompanies Cobb into Limbo to counteract Mal's speech to persuade him to stay.

In the end, Cobb refuses to remain with a person who is only a fragment of Mal. He decides to let her go and continue living for their children, because of Ariadne's help. And so, Ariadne's use of extraction on Cobb not only helps to protect the team from Cobb's deception, it also helps Cobb himself. This use of extraction to expose dangerous lies indicates that there's a positive dimension to extraction. This is best understood by returning to Kant's ethics and looking at his controversial critique of lying.

Kant objects to dishonesty because it often leads to contradictions. Failing to keep a promise creates a contradiction between the promise and the action. Telling a lie creates a contradiction between the description of an event and what actually occurred. These contradictions may be relatively harmless. Failing to keep a promise about meeting a friend for coffee or lying about a late report may not actually harm anyone. These lies are often excused because they cause little damage and because they are so common. White lies may produce good consequences. Lying about a person's appearance or their weight can give that person reassurance and greater happiness. Moreover, telling white lies is obligatory for anyone who wants to maintain their friendships. For moral consequentialists— people who judge actions by their consequences alone—these instances of lying are excusable, provided they have more good consequences than bad ones.

Kant, by contrast, thinks that telling any lie—even the nicest white lie—is wrong in all circumstances. In addition to the contradiction between promise and action or between story and event, there's a far more serious contradiction of the first formulation of the categorical imperative. The act of lying implies the rule that "lying is acceptable for me." If this rule is universalized, as Kant's first categorical imperative says that it must be in order to judge its morality, then it leads to the rule that "lying is acceptable for everyone."

This law would lead to a world in which all rational actors could lie whenever it suited their purposes. It is an untenable rule; the social consequences would be terrible. Trust would breakdown and society as it is now would cease to exist. All of the collective agreements that make social life possible— promises, contracts, money, and any kind of organization – would be impossible without trust. Money would have no value without the confidence that other people would accept it, and exchange would be extremely difficult with nothing to prevent people from cheating to get a better deal.

Many people are willing to accept that lying is wrong and that it should not be done, but it seems to be low in the hierarchy of immoral actions. Lying is rarely punished with anything more serious than a stern warning. Only a few kinds of lies—such as those about infidelity, stated while in a position of responsibility, or stated while under oath—are treated as serious transgressions. Moreover there are times when lying can save lives and prevent serious wrongdoing. For example, lying to members of the Gestapo about the location of a Jewish person during the Holocaust would be a life-saving lie that many people would judge to be morally defensible.

Kant would say that even lying to save a life is wrong. His reason for remaining firm on this point is that he thinks it is dangerous and contrary to the purpose of moral values to grant exceptions. For him, morality must be universally binding to be meaningful. The rules must apply to all people, at all times or they will unfairly favor certain people and be susceptible to manipulation. Moreover, as this chapter has already discussed, the first and third categorical imperatives are applied by universalizing an action to determine whether it could be acceptable for everyone. If exceptions were granted for some actions that can't be universalized, then these rules of moral conduct would be far less certain and less fair.

Kant's opposition to all lies might lead him to see some merit in the practice of extraction. The prevalence of extraction would encourage honesty. If people living with the threat of dream espionage responded by becoming more honest and less inclined to do things worth hiding, then they would be more inclined to tell the truth. Given the advantages of occasional lying and its low costs, it seems that only a threat to privacy as significant as extraction could induce most people to follow Kant's admonition to always be honest.

Although it's unlikely that inception or extraction will be real concerns in the near future, they are worth serious consideration as the technologies of influencing thought and monitoring actions become increasingly sophisticated. *Inception* provides a compelling thought experiment that helps us to think about what it would be like if the barriers that now protect our minds were to be breached. *Inception* forces us to reflect on the morality of technologies that don't yet exist, but which are foreshadowed by modern surveillance techniques, brainwashing programs, and data monitoring.

8
Right and Wrong in Dreams

JOSEPH GARVIN

What sort of things have you done in a dream? Have you ever woken up from a dream and worried about what it says about you, or is that just me? On the other hand, have you ever felt proud of dreaming something, not so much because it was interesting, but because it seemed right? Our behavior in dreams does sometimes seem to be ethical or unethical, though few people would consider someone a good or bad person purely on the basis of their dreams.

All of this leads to one simple question: Does it make sense for us to say that what we do in a dream is either good or bad? The question is obviously important when you aren't simply going to sleep and dreaming, but planning and arranging a dream in advance, and then being in control of your own actions in the dream. However, it's still relevant, if less immediate, in our ordinary dreaming. While the shared and lucid dreaming of *Inception* makes the issue crystal clear, the basic issue is one that still might nag at us, if we wake up having dreamt of violence, or of an intimate encounter with someone other than our partner.

The questions specific to *Inception* itself are pretty much new to philosophy. Shared dreams, as they don't occur in reality, have rarely been a subject for discussion by philosophers, though obviously this is changed, at least in a small way, by this very book. However, dreams and the ethical content of dreams have been a subject for philosophers in the past.

The Catholic philosopher and theologian, St. Augustine, discussed how dreams can be immoral, especially sexually immoral.

However, his work, as well as not mentioning *Inception*-style shared dreams, focused on the idea of sins of thought—lust, primarily. But we do other things in dreams that might be considered wrong: we tell lies or commit acts of violence.

The Shared Dream

Are the characters of *Inception* doing something that could be either right or wrong? Their actions are the sort of things we would usually consider wrong—they lie, kill, and steal. Or, at least, they pretend to be something they are not in a place where everything is not what it appears to be, fire dream-guns at dream-opponents, and find out things that the target would prefer to remain hidden. This last one is both the simplest and the most difficult, in a way. Stealing information from a dream is in a way no more or less ethical than stealing information from a computer or a filing cabinet. Unfortunately, the question of whether it's right or wrong to steal such information deserves a lot more space than I have here—as the extensive arguments over Wikileaks have shown.

The first and second ones, however, are easier to approach. In the first case, Cobb and his team lie extensively. Cobb twice pretends to be a subconscious security expert, rather than a thief. Eames's primary role in the team is to pretend to be other people, taking on their appearance in the dream. The entire team deceives Fischer when they pretend to be his security team. This sort of deception would normally be considered unethical. However, in the dream, it isn't so immediately obvious. It's the very nature of dreaming to be deceptive. We've all dreamt of something that seemed so real that when we wake up, it takes a few minutes to remember it didn't happen.

> Our dreams feel real while we're in them. It's only when we wake up we realize things were strange. (*Inception*)

So, Cobb and his team are pretending to be something that they aren't in a "place" where nothing is what it seems—a place that isn't even really a place at all. The argument could be made that there's nothing out of the ordinary in their dreaming. It isn't necessarily unethical to lie to someone who is constantly lying to himself, as we do when we dream. Indeed, the lies they use on their trip into Fischer's dreams can be seen as beneficial ones, helping the person being lied to.

ARIADNE: So you destroy his one positive relationship?

COBB: No. We repair his relationship with his father and expose his godfather's true nature.

EAMES: Hell, we should be charging Fischer as much as Saito.

The fact that they're in a dream changes the way that we can judge Cobb and his team's deception. This applies even more because it's implied that Fischer most likely won't remember that he's been invaded in this way, and will instead simply believe that he has realized something about his relationship with his father. The lies told in the shared dreaming are not as simple as lies told in reality.

Cobb and his team also regularly use force within the context of the dream, from Cobb's break-in to gain access to Saito's secrets to Eames's use of a grenade launcher to clear a path for their van in the first level of Fischer's dream. There isn't much of a question here about the ethics of the use of force in reality. In Christopher Nolan's previous movie, it's only the Joker, as the primary villain, who makes extensive use of weapons and violence, implying that Nolan doesn't see violence as a particularly justifiable action, especially lethal violence. However, in *Inception*, none of the characters have any hesitation about opening fire on the projections, with the only question being not about the ethics of killing them, but rather its effect on the real person—Fischer.

ARIADNE: These projections, they're part of his subconscious?

COBB: Yeah.

ARIADNE: Are you destroying those parts of his mind?

COBB: No, of course not. They're just projections.

Do Projections Matter?

The question of whether it could be wrong to kill projections the way it's wrong to kill a person simply never even arises for the characters of *Inception*. Yet, at the same time, they are using a wide variety of weapons, all the way from pistols to a car, in what would normally be a lethal manner. The obvious justification for their behavior is, as Cobb puts it, that those they are killing are "just projections." All they are is figments of Fischer's imagination and so, if they're killed, they aren't really dying. Instead, they simply cease to be dreamed of.

So, can we say that the actions of Cobb and his team are good or bad? It's pretty clear that the fact that they are in a dream affects how we can think about their behavior. However, the rules of ethics do still apply. In the case of lying, the answer is relatively easy. As the dream is shared, any lies they tell are to the dreamer. If lies are wrong (and most of us agree that they are, most of the time), then the deception practiced by Cobb's team are wrong, as they are lying to Fischer. The fact that dreams are themselves a form of deception is mostly irrelevant. Fischer is subconsciously complicit in his deception, but that does not mean that Cobb is not deceiving him. This wouldn't normally apply in a dream, as normally, we are alone in our dreams. However, the entire point of *Inception* and the "dream-share" is that dreams are experienced together. Communication in a shared dream isn't drastically different from communication in the real world, and so the rules we apply to communication (it's wrong to lie, wrong to be hateful, and so on) apply to shared dreams.

The case of violence is more difficult, though I think that here, too, the ideas of good and bad behavior are still applicable. It's true that most of the team's violence is not directed towards Fischer himself. However, it's still violence. Does being a figment of a dreamer's imagination mean that there can't be any right or wrong about what's done to you?

At a very basic level, we wouldn't feel a drastically different level of moral outrage at seeing an immoral act committed on a dream-projection than on a person, were we to be bystanders. Seeing someone, to take a rather overblown example, firing a machine gun into a crowd while laughing maniacally would lead to a feeling that that is morally wrong, whether the crowd were in the real world or in a dream. However, if we were to see someone doing the same to a crowd of clothes shop mannequins, we wouldn't feel it to be wrong—though we would probably think there might be something wrong with the person doing it. The distinction between shooting a projection and shooting a shop mannequin seems pretty clearly to be in how convincing or unconvincing the two different illusions are.

The dream projections are—like the dream itself—utterly convincing. In *Inception*, even those who know they're in a dream can be fooled by the presence of projections, as when Saito believes Fischer's projection of Browning to be Eames's illusion of Browning. They are near-perfect simulations of people. They are not exactly like the real person they are a projection of, such as Maurice Fischer's transformation from an uncaring to a caring father, or Mal's lack of "perfection".

> COBB: I wish you were. But I couldn't make you real. I'm not capable of imagining you in all your complexity and . . . perfection. As you really were. You're the best I can do. And you're not real.

However, though the projection of Mal is not enough like Mal to convince her husband, a projection of someone you don't know would be more than sufficient to convince. So, are the projections "just" projections, as Cobb says?

If a projection is able to act independently, able to communicate intelligently, visually identical to a human, and in general is indistinguishable from a person, then how can we distinguish between them and a person? This is almost the same as the famous Turing Test for intelligent machines, except in that case, one can find out if the other person is a human or a machine by looking behind the curtain, as it were. In a shared dream, only waking up will let you know if the person you spoke to was a fellow dreamer or a projection—and that may not even be enough. So, either you can't tell if the individual you're about to shoot is a projection or a human, or it makes no difference, as a projection is as deserving of rights as a human, because it is, within the dream, indistinguishable from the human.

The Un-Shared Dream

So, the dreamers in *Inception* are bound by the same ethical rules within the dream as outside of it. However, its' not clear if the same rules apply to our ordinary, unshared dreams. When we dream, our dream actions occur in total isolation. They affect no one else at the time, and have no direct after-effects. It would seem, therefore, that ordinary dreams don't have any sense in which they can be ethically right or ethically wrong.

But it that really true? We can still feel a sense of moral wrongness from a dream, especially from violent dreams. Either we're mistaken to feel that sense of wrongness, or we can still behave rightly or wrongly in dreams.

Does lying in an ordinary dream have the same moral impact as lying in the waking world? To answer this, we have to think about what is meant by lying in a dream. It's different from the lies in the shared dream of *Inception*, as all the participants (the only participant, the dreamer) are deceived about the nature of the experience. When we dream, we believe things and take things as normal that were never the case in the waking world nor could ever have been—such as talking animals, rooms that are larger on the inside, speaking to historical figures, and so on.

However, it doesn't seem that this is what we mean when we say someone is lying. This is closer to being mistaken. Our sleeping minds can't make the distinction between what exists in reality and what we create in our imagination. If we were lying, we would know what the truth was, and would be pretending it was something else. The ordinary strangeness of dreams isn't itself a form of lying, unless someone were to be creating that dream to fool us. In that case, the conditions that apply to Cobb's team in *Inception* would apply here.

St. Augustine's position resembles this. For him, it's a sin to lust after another. If one lusts in a dream, as is common enough, is that a sin? St. Augustine worried that it might be, as lust is a sin of the mind. His response was to say that the difference between him awake and him asleep was sufficient to make him awake not responsible for what he did when asleep. However, I would argue differently. Lust seems to be analogous to lying—it's something mental, and so something which is indistinguishable between a dream and reality. We may feel lust for someone we meet in a bar in reality, or we may feel it for a dream-version of them. Either way, if lust is an immoral thing, then dream-lust, just like dream lying, is not immediately immune to ethical judgment.

However, there still can be lying in an ordinary dream. Even if we were inside our childhood bedroom that is now the size of a ballroom, talking to a badger and George Washington, if we knowingly deceive, then that would be a lie. But it's still not clear that there would be anything wrong with that lie. Though there are some who would argue that any lie whatsoever would be wrong, it could be argued that this lie is of no consequence. As there's no other person sharing the dream, only the projections, it's as if someone was to speak a lie to an empty room. Though it's a lie, there's no one being deceived.

Does violence in a dream have the same impact as violence in the waking world? The most immediate response is that there is no victim and that violence in a dream is the equivalent of striking at a cardboard cut-out. In the dream, everything that exists is a projection of the sleeping mind. Therefore, there is only the dreamer in the dream. Any violence is nothing more than shadow-boxing or target shooting.

However, in each case there is still the problem of the basic deceptiveness of the dream. Much as in the case of the shared dream, it's the fact that it is convincing that makes what happens within it ethical or unethical. If the dream is convincing enough that we don't know it is a dream, then what we do in the dream, must be subject to the same ethical and moral rules we follow in the waking world. Though the idea of talking to a badger and George Washington is absurd, in the dream we're convinced of its reality. Even the strangest things can seem entirely normal. When we lie in a dream, we believe we're lying to a real person. Similarly, when we are violent in a dream, we believe that the target of our violence is a real person. If we are so completely deceived, then we are subject to the same ethical rules that we are subject to in the waking world.

Does This Matter?

There's one final issue that affects the ordinary dream, though not the shared dream. How does our control or lack of control over dreams affect the ethics of the dream? In the shared dream, the dreamers are in complete control of their actions. Even the deceived dreamer, the subject of extraction or inception, is in control of their actions, though they are only in relation to what they believe the world around them is, not in relation to what it actually is. However, in our own dreams, we don't always seem to be in control. It's one of the most distinctive aspects of dreaming that our actions are in some part out of our control. We continue walking down the dark corridor even though everything about it makes us want to turn back. We want to stay talking to the badger and George Washington, but the dream seems to drag us away—or we go, even though it isn't what we want or chose to do, but we do it anyway.

Does this mean that all of the moral rules that I've just argued apply to dreams are irrelevant? The usual view among ethicists—and I think it's correct—is that if you're not in control of something, then it can't be your fault. If someone else commits a crime, and you had no influence over them, then absolutely no guilt can apply to you. If someone else cuts your brake cables, and you run into a pedestrian, it's not your fault, and no guilt applies to you.

So, if we're in a dream, and we're not in conscious control of our actions, then we can't be morally responsible for those actions. However, our actions in dreams are not totally outside of our control. Some of our actions are outside of our control—just as, in the waking world, some actions are also out of our control. We do still have a sense of decision making in dreams, from a very minimal level right up to lucid dreaming. Admitting that some or many of our actions in dreams are out of our control does not mean admitting that moral rules are irrelevant to what we choose to do in our dreams.

The actions of the characters in *Inception* show us how the things we do in dreams are open to the same kind of moral and ethical judgment as actions in the waking world. This applies to both the science-fiction concept of the shared dream and to our normal, everyday dreams. Accepting this, what are the consequences? Are we all to spend all our time feeling deeply guilty about what we have dreamed? I don't believe that most of us dream terrible things all the time. Indeed, most of us probably dream very 'normal', in terms of dreaming, dreams. Whether we're dreaming pleasantly of a nice walk with long-lost friends, or unpleasantly of a fall from a tall building, most of our dreams don't contain the sort of things that would make us worry ethically. As for those that do, the best way to view them is not as something that we should find a way to make up for, but as something we might, if they worry us enough, look to avoid in the future.

Level 3

The Infinite Staircase

9

Ariadne's Clue to Life, the Universe, and Everything

THOMAS KAPPER

> I woke up in between
> a memory and a dream.
>
> —Tom Petty

Cool. The film *Inception* is cool, certainly. How could it not be when referred to as an "existential heist film." But its coolness is exceeded by its hipness. In the fifteenth century, an African king who brought peace to his realm was awarded the name *Ewaure*, "it is cool." Thereafter, cool meant stability in a society and has come to refer to composure in an individual. While cool is cool, it is still surface behavior, waves covering the enormity of the sea, a kind of mask.

Hip, on the other hand, goes deeper. It encompasses the intelligence behind the cool mask. Hipness engages you fully, spurs you to think and spin out your own ideas. The hippest movies are those that cause you to chat about them to your friends, maybe even argue (even argue frivolously about the difference between cool and hip). Films like *Inception* frequently raise more questions than they answer.

Am I Dreaming Now?

It's a seemingly simple question, but not at all easy to answer with certainty. At the heart of *Inception* there lies a subtle distinction. The question is not so much what's real but rather how we know what's real. This is how the film differs from another recent, philosophically rich film, *The Matrix*. In *The*

Matrix, the nature of reality is at issue (metaphysics) rather than how we know what is real (epistemology).

"Am I dreaming now?" is an ancient query. In Western culture, Plato was the first great philosopher to ask how we could recognize if we were indeed dreaming. (He did this in a Socratic dialogue with a man called Theatetus, whose name is so close to the word, theater, I find it amusing given the current topic). Dreaming has bedeviled philosophers ever since.

As Cobb says in the film, "Our dreams are real while we're in them. It's only when we wake up we realize things were strange." But do we wake up or do we just think we do? René Descartes wrote in his *Meditations* (1641), "There are never any sure signs by means of which being awake can be distinguished from being asleep." He goes on, "What if there is a deceiver of supreme power and cunning, who is deliberately and constantly deceiving me?" Dreams can be sitting in a darkened theater, or reading a chapter in a book.

Let's leave aside for a moment that you may be dreaming that you're reading these words and conduct a thought experiment. What happens at night in our beds when we close our eyes? If your dreams are anything like my own, they are usually unintelligible, mostly incoherent, and mainly gibberish. My dreams are in fact quite similar to music videos from the days when MTV still played music videos. These nocturnal excursions are far more confusing than those dramatized in *Inception*. They're just images and emotion (sometimes with guitars and a drum kit). Coherence is probably added by me when I relate the events the next morning to my tolerant spouse or reconstruct it later for my therapist.

With mention of my therapist, we've arrived. Sooner or later in any discussion of dreams the bearded, cigar-smoking elephant in the room must be addressed. That elephant is Sigmund Freud, founder of psychoanalysis and author of *The Interpretation of Dreams* (1899). He told us there is an unconscious aspect to the mind (called the subconscious in contemporary usage) and he saw dreams as the royal road to getting into that unconscious world. The way Freud sees it, in dreams the unconscious is attempting to resolve some sort of conflict, but the conflict is disguised and symbolized because it's too much for the conscious mind to bear. The question goes unasked as to whether the dream world is in any sense real. The dream is just the activity of the unconscious, and the unconscious is part of what Freud conceived of as the mind as a whole.

In Freudian dream work, there has long been discussion that perhaps the symbolic aspect is overemphasized. As one of Freud's close friends once said to him, "Sometimes a cigar is just a cigar." Throughout Freud's career he was keen on mythology, from Eros to Thanatos, from Oedipus to Electra. The mythological thread brings us back to *Inception* and the introduction of Ariadne.

Who Is Ariadne?

In *Inception*, the character of the architect is called Ariadne. It's quite an unusual name. It's not listed in the top one thousand most popular baby names over the last decade. (That will probably change after *Inception*.) We can make a fairly safe assumption that such a name appearing in a story must have some import. With a little digging we find that Ariadne made her debut in Greek mythology.

According to myth, on the island of Crete, a labyrinth was constructed to confine the Minotaur, a half man, half bull. This labyrinth was a maze so complex no gates or bars were necessary to make it an effective prison. The hero Theseus journeyed from Athens to do battle with the Minotaur. Ariadne gave to Theseus a ball of thread to unravel in his venture into the labyrinth so that he could find his way out after dispatching the monster. This thread is known as 'Ariadne's clew', from which our modern word 'clue' derives.

In *Inception*, the labyrinth we wander is the dream world. As in the myth, Ariadne provides the clue. The clue, in this case, is architecture.

Is Architecture Necessary?

That depends on what you mean by architecture. For most people architecture is buildings: homes and skyscrapers. But naval architecture is the building of ships, and landscape architecture can be seen as the space between buildings. Our concern is with the architecture of dreams. What might that be?

The architect of dreams must create a place. Space is already there in the cacophony of the subconscious. What Ariadne provides as the architect is a place for humans to interact in a narrative context. She constructs interiors and cityscapes. In other words, she builds the stage where the show can go on.

(Excuse a short digression on God—and all digressions on God should be short. If, as Shakespeare wrote, all the world's a stage and we are but merely players, what does that imply for the builder of that massive stage? It spells Architect with a capital "A." But Ariadne in *Inception* is certainly not the omnipotent God of monotheism. Perhaps she could be reasoned to mythic goddess status; she does have a mythological pedigree after all. Still that's a rather tenuous argument to pull out of *Inception*.)

Ariadne builds the world of the dream, thus is designated as the dreamer. Then the subject, Fischer, fills it with his subconscious, populates it. Cobb and his team enter as self-contained entities, but their own subconscious natures leak through. Cobb's mind unleashes a train in the middle of the street; Yusuf causes it to rain due to a full bladder.

Dream architecture must support an intelligible human narrative. It has to make room for men and women as social beings. A subconscious as messy and incoherent as my own from last night would be very difficult to raid for ideas. In *Inception*, the concept of dream infiltration is glossed over, taken as a given. But I believe we would be terrified if others could enter into our dreams and our minds. Having our hearts, fantasies, and fears naked before intruders is worse (maybe) than having them exposed before our loved ones. It's fear of intimacy carried to the ultimate level.

The ancient Greek philosopher Heraclitus said, "Only the waking share a common cosmos; each sleeps alone." I am confident that others haven't entered my dreams. If there is no getting around the notion that the world is entirely my dream, then there is a clear implication that there are no "others" to break in. A book is a dream that can be shared, as is a film. But the interaction is only in one direction.

So is dream architecture necessary? Yes, if we wish for a story to unfold. Is it sufficient? For the movie, yes, it's a story-telling medium. But if by sufficient we mean is it sufficient to let us know if we are dreaming, the answer is less certain. Ariadne's clue, her gift, is place. She takes chaotic dream space and creates a structure for meaning in the form of architecture. But it is only a clue, which is a hint not a solution. Ariadne's clue is to help us to experience the dream world, the labyrinth, and make enough sense of it for rational narrative to take place. That may be exactly the worst thing to do if the goal is to wake up.

Can I Wake Up?

Cobb advises the architect to never recreate places from your memory. Always imagine new places. "Because building dreams out of your own memories is the surest way to lose your grip on what's real and what's a dream." The characters have totems, supposed keys to how they know if they are still dreaming. In his notebooks, Ludwig Wittgenstein commented that "The argument 'I may be dreaming' is senseless for this reason: if I am dreaming, this remark is being dreamed as well." You and I could easily be dreaming of totems. "Pinch me, I'm dreaming," won't work either.

I am dreaming (maybe). Can I wake up? I can awaken with a kick, say my chair tips over backwards. Or if in a dream, I awaken by dying. For the film says you can't die in dreams; it merely wakes you up. There is a tense point in the plot when it's revealed that when you get in too deep, dying means really dying. But what torments Cobb is not that death may occur if he's in too deep with his team, but rather that he hasn't tried to awaken enough times, that maybe Mal was right, and he just has to die one more time.

How deep are we now? How many times must we wake up? Which will be the last—the real one?

Do We Have to Talk about Death?

The playwright Tom Stoppard wrote that every exit is an entrance somewhere else. When I awaken, the dream ends. But am I just entering another dream in another place? If life is but a dream (as the "Row, Row, Row Your Boat" song says it is), maybe death is waking up elsewhere. Which is more real, the here or the elsewhere? Maybe then we wake up from the elsewhere too.

How Many Times Do We Have to Die?

Forty-two. You have to die forty-two times. Those of you who just chuckled receive bonus points (forty-two of them) for your appreciation of the writer Douglas Adams. You also no doubt well understand the thinly veiled homage to him in the title to this chapter. But of course my answer is a jest. As an aid to our inquiry into the numerology of death, let's look to the East and their cultures.

Cobb also journeys eastward. When he seeks the chemist he flies to Mombasa. The basement of Yusuf's pharmacy is filled with dreamers, the scene looking for all the world like a nine-teenth-century opium den. It's ironic that the most beautiful opium-fueled discourse on dreams comes from Western culture and the English poet Coleridge:

> What if you slept? And what if, in your sleep, you dreamed? And what if, in your dream, you went to heaven and there plucked a strange and beautiful flower? And what if, when you awoke, you had the flower in your hand? Ah, what then?

Mombasa is not quite far enough to the east for our purpose. It is on the coast of Kenya, and our destination is across the Arabian Sea to India then north into China. We will dip into three great wisdom traditions in an appallingly shallow way, Daoism, Hinduism, Buddhism. I mean we only have the one question, How many times do we have to die? How hard can it be?

In a similar vein to the Coleridge poem (minus the opium), there is an often repeated story of the Daoist sage Zhuangzi. As Hiu Chan explains in her chapter in this book, it's reported that Zhuangzi once slept and dreamed he was a butterfly. When he awoke, he didn't know whether he was a man who had dreamt he was a butterfly or a butterfly now dreaming he was a man. The story has been retold as a King having the dream and then asking Zhuangzi whether he was the King or the butterfly. Zhuangzi is to have replied, "Oh King, only you the dreamer are real. But who are you?" This was echoed many centuries later in the West by Descartes who felt he had defeated the cunning deceiver with his iconic, "I think therefore I am." (He hadn't really. He may have begun modern philoso-phy, but he had to bring in God to defeat his deceiver which I have always thought was sort of cheating).

So, More Than Forty-Two?

The labyrinth is not a dream. It's a vast array of dreams. In Hinduism, there is the myth of Indra's net, a net the size of the universe. At every knot there is a perfectly polished jewel. Every single thing that exists now or has ever existed is one of the jewels, as is every dream in the cosmos. And each and every jewel is reflected in every other.

In another Hindu myth, the world rests upon the back of the great elephant Maha Pudma, who is supported by the great turtle Chukwa. When a native was asked what Chukwa rested upon, the response was another turtle. And what supports that turtle? "Ah, Sahib, then it is turtles all the way down." The German philosopher Arthur Schopenhauer touched the same theme, "The universe is a dream dreamed by a single dreamer where all the dream characters dream too." This is somewhat dizzying and kind of makes me want to lie down.

Surfacing. When I awaken it's like breaking onto the surface of the water. I didn't know I'd been holding my breath. Then I awaken again. Again I did not know I had been holding my breath. Perhaps we dream and wake up infinitely. Is it a problem? That depends on your point of view. If life is a dream and death is waking up into another life, in a way that is living forever. Everlasting life is the goal of the world's monotheistic religions (Christianity, Judaism, Islam), and just the opposite for religious traditions of the East. An old story goes that Christians are afraid that they may not live forever and Buddhists are afraid that they very well might. A Buddhist tries to escape the cycling of birth and death.

But death is distinguished from waking up when one world is more real than the others. The early twentieth-century philosopher William James coined the phrase, "stream of consciousness." As he wrote in *The Varieties of Religious Experience* (1902), we have many consciousnesses separated from each other by "the flimsiest of screens." But which ones can we know? Is only one truly me? We tend to believe the real us is the consistent one, the face we see in the mirror every morning. This is the case even though Emerson warned that a foolish consistency is the hobgoblin of little minds.

Can We Figure It Out?

We must experience it all from the outside, perhaps sit in a darkened theater and watch images flicker at twenty-four frames per second.

The universe as a totality (think Indra's net) can't be understood by anything inside the universe. A thorough understanding requires a step back. And we cannot, by definition, step back out of the universe. It's all there is. Thus, rationality is brought to its knees.

If you want to wake up, architecture won't help you. As Ariadne and Cobb emerge from the surf, you see the buildings crumbling along the beach. The tapestry Ariadne wove with her thread exists to let you realize there is no solution. The dreamer's world crumbles. Life is a labyrinth so complex, there is no way out alive. Waking up is not a story, although it may be both the beginning of one and the ending of another.

Buddha means awakened one. The sayings of the Buddha are collected in writings called sutras. The root of "sutra" is the basis of our word suture (think surgery), it is a thread that binds things together.

At the risk of oversimplification, Hinduism claims everything we see is an illusion; Buddhism claims that everything we think about what we see is an illusion. We are dreamers. Does that help you sleep more soundly at night?

If you never awaken there is no certainty that you're not dreaming now. Death is a drastic test. Is there an alternative?

Do You Have Your Ticket to Mombasa?

In a Buddhist view, realization is like peeling an onion, waking up one layer at a time. When the onion's gone, ah what then? Nirvana. Nothing is there and nothing is not there. The Hindu's call it Satchidananda. This is truth, consciousness, and bliss—the completeness of reality as experienced by a fully enlightened being. I read somewhere that the joy of the drop is to die in the river.

Is it worth the bother? I mean do we *really* want to know?

Here's an illuminating exchange from Aldous Huxley's novel, *After Many a Summer Dies the Swan*:

I like the words I use to bear some relation to facts. That's why I'm interested in eternity—psychological eternity. Because it's a fact.'

'For you perhaps,' said Jeremy.

'For anyone who chooses to fulfill the conditions under which it can be experienced.'

'And why should anyone wish to fulfill them?'

'Why should anyone choose to go to Athens to see the Parthenon? Because it's worth the bother. And the same is true of eternity. The experience of timeless good is worth all the trouble it involved.'

'Timeless good,' Jeremy repeated with distaste. 'I don't know what the words mean.'

'Why should you?' said Mr. Propter. 'You've never bought your ticket for Athens.'

Buddhism and Hinduism claim you can wake up in this life by fully realizing that it's a dream. How? Sit quietly in perfect stillness. When I try to do it—and I've been practicing Zen for fourteen years—I often fall most certainly asleep. What do I dream? Of sitting quietly in perfect stillness.

Cobb is obsessed with his totem, the spinning top. The Buddhist concept of Nirvana pertains when the idea of real or dream stop pertaining. That is how the movie closes. Cobb turns away from the spinning top on the table to attend to his life. The top is left to do what it will.

Do We Give Shakespeare the Last Word?

William James noted that philosophy bakes no bread. This is a sentiment that resonates with the Henry David Thoreau line that the best philosophy is all untrue.

To sleep.
Perchance to dream.
Ay, there's the rub.
For in that sleep of death what dreams may come. (*Hamlet*)

We are such stuff as dreams are made on. (*The Tempest*)

10
Once Upon a Time

RANDALL E. AUXIER

Just Because We're Paranoid . . .

I admit I'm worried. Worried and suspicious. I think Christopher Nolan has been messing with my mind and maybe I have been inceived, or incepted, or whatever it is he does when he plants a doubt in my brain that won't stop nagging me.

Maybe you know what that's like, huh? But first, before we deal with our deeper misgivings, here's an easier one, just a little riddle: Remember when Cobb tells Ariadne to make him a maze in one minute that takes two minutes to solve? Why is that a test of whether she can be a dream architect? I think maybe it's because the dream architect always needs to be a couple of (dream)-minutes ahead of the dreamers, anticipating where they're going and providing them with specific passages, twists, and turns. And no matter how clever the dreamers are, they should never be able to catch her turning a space back on itself.

I bring this up because, well, I don't know about you, but sometimes I feel like Nolan is the Architect and I'm the hapless dreamer lost in his dreamscape. And sometimes I think I can just catch a glimpse of his shadow as he leads me on. That's surely one way to approach directing a movie—especially if you're also writing the script. If you control both the story and the images someone takes in, that's a lot of power, and that is one attraction of film as an artistic medium.

I'm convinced that the greatest artistic geniuses of the last hundred years have been increasingly drawn to film—the best writers are writing scripts, and the best actors establish themselves in film so as to command the attention (and salaries) they want when "returning" to the stage. Meanwhile really accomplished sculptors, painters, and even some architects are designing sets and costumes, while the best photographers are now cinematographers, and the most creative technical people are developing special effects of all kinds. Needless to say, the coolest orchestral composers are doing movie music, and so on. All artists want an audience and they want to make a living. It's no wonder they're drawn into working together in the amazing, all-encompassing, all-consuming medium of film. There is an audience, and hence, there is a living for those who can get in on the action.

. . . Doesn't Mean They're Not After Us

Among all these artists, the "writer-director" is the arch-creator, the puppet-master of the medium. In a recent interview one of the members of Clint Eastwood's "team" (speaking of his film *Hereafter*) made the remark that a lot of directors would love to have Eastwood's team, but the team draws its liveliness and purpose from the way Eastwood works (collaboratively and loosely).

Who would've believed, watching Eastwood's early Sergio Leone films that the grim, silent, smoking, spitting, executor of cowboy justice was really a latter day Picasso of filmmaking? But there Eastwood is, writing scripts, composing scores, directing, still acting, and being a renaissance man in everyone's admiring estimation. And who could resist that kind of artistic power? We love Eastwood, now, with something like the affection Florence must surely have felt for Michelangelo. In the last ten or twelve years you would think Eastwood could do no wrong (people have evidently forgotten how awful *Blood Work* was).

We're not quite ready to gush like that over Christopher Nolan, though. We don't really trust him, yet, but I notice that he rates highly with his peers. They speak of him with considerable reverence because, unlike most of us, they know how he gets us to experience whatever he wants, and they all know that it isn't so easy to cover one's own tracks as a director (especially from others who belong to the guild). Since no director, no matter how brilliant, can completely conceal his art, there has to be a thread. It's like that in life too, you know. There's always a thread (one can usually follow a money trail . . . almost no matter what one is tracing).

That traceable trail is the reason it pays to be on your guard when you feel yourself being propelled toward a conclusion you didn't produce spontaneously in your own cogitations—and after all, that's what "inception" means in Nolan's world: to obscure the process by which an idea that propels us toward a course of action has been implanted. We mistake for our own, apparently, whatever viral ideas we can't trace to anyone else.

Claim Your Own Baggage

So I want to ask you a question. You may have thought of it already, but I think it is pretty revealing. There is a moment, near the end of *Inception*, when the dream-invaders are claiming baggage at the airport. In that scene, Cobb comes face to face with Robert Fischer, the "target" of the inception plot. Remember, they all just spent the last ten hours dreaming together, and lucidly dreaming at that. I would interpret the look that Fischer gives Cobb in that moment to be ambiguous. Maybe it has to be ambiguous because this is a place where the story doesn't quite hang together. Why doesn't Fischer seem to recognize Cobb? Or maybe he does, but if so, what is Fischer thinking? Is his expression one of private recognition, perhaps even gratitude? That would make sense, but probably that's not it.

More likely: Cobb looks familiar and Fischer is trying to remember who he is, having the common difficulty we all have in recalling our dreams. But now remember, Fischer is trained to resist dream-invasion. Wouldn't this include not only the discipline of lucid dreaming but also training in remembering dreams? It seems odd that Fischer is formidable enough to require a "Mr. Charles" gambit to neutralize his defenses, but he can't remember his dreams. That isn't believable, is it? Surely he ought to recognize Cobb at baggage claim.

But the situation is actually even less believable than that. Maybe it occurred to you too, but obviously Robert Fischer must recognize all these people from waking life who were with him in First Class. We have all been on flights and we do recognize in baggage claim the people we sat near on a flight, especially if it's a long one. These are also the people with whom Fischer just traveled through three dreams (or four if you count the dream in which Mal kidnapped him), and the climax of the third dream was profoundly emotional for him. Even if he can't remember them all, surely he remembers Cobb. And in waking life, what were these people doing on his flight, and in his head? Does he think their presence in his dream on the plane was "day residue"?

In any case, Fischer didn't call the police on them, didn't say a word. Perhaps he even believes they are all his own security people. But if so, wouldn't he recognize his own people? In a nutshell, what's the deal when they land? What does that look really mean? When the flight is over, what does Robert Fischer know and what does he not know?

In our present flight of fancy, feel free to think of this question as a baggage claim check. You can redeem it at the end of the chapter for an answer. But in the meantime you have to keep me out of your head because I'm dead set on rearranging your ideas before we land. You can trust me. I promise I'm on your side. Really.

Training Day?

The reason that over a hundred generations of the human race have preserved and returned to and built upon the story of Ariadne and Theseus is because there's something in that tale that plucks the taut strings of our collective being. Myths don't just inform our cultures, they well upwards anew in every generation to tell us who and what we are.

We can't really even prevent this renewal, and we wouldn't want it to stop even if we could. But that doesn't keep us from wondering whether we ever really say anything new or do anything genuinely novel. Are we not also confined by the pre-conscious "archetypes" of the human race, telling us what we must do? We fall in love, or strive to free ourselves from our parents, or try not to wound our children, but in spite of our efforts we end up being the same old warriors and kings and tricksters and eternal children that our human race always begets from the womb of our unconscious, collective past.

I don't know about you, but I can't keep myself from re-enacting the human drama any more than I can quit puzzling over Nolan's damnable labyrinth of a movie. I don't even feel free to slow myself down as I barrel toward whatever diabolical end he may have prepared for me and my little ponderings and putterings. So I'm wondering whether I might be able to militarize my unconscious, become trained to resist Nolan and his army of archetypal images and mythic plots. Robert Fischer has somehow gotten such training, much to the surprise of our team of the dream-invaders. In the opening scene, Cobb and Arthur are offering that sort of training to Saito. So there must be some sort of possible training in how to dream, in the Nolan universe.

What sort of training is that? Does Fischer have a Zen master who teaches him to empty his mind? That seems more like something Saito might have pursued. Fischer's defenses are of a military character, closer to Rambo's with guns blazing than to Zen masters and silent Ninjas. This militarization of Fischer's unconscious mind is not driven by ideals of honorable combat, and even if it is about mind-control, in some sense, this militarization isn't brain-washing. The discipline Fischer has learned seems to be a kind of control over the way the subconscious energies enter the conscious mind, and the aim of the training appears to be the identification and total, violent elimination of foreign presences in one's dreams. But how can "foreign" presences in a dream be identified? All kinds of stuff ends up in our dreams, after all.

We can work this out, and maybe even get ourselves some training, but the path is a bit circuitous. I need to talk a little bit about brain chemistry (in Nolanland) and a bit about dream architecture. I wouldn't want my offerings to be mistaken for actual brain chemistry (about which I know very little), or actual architecture, (no one would want to use so much as a staircase of my design—I'm no Ariadne). But I'm guessing that you and I know as much about this kind of brain chemistry and dream architecture as Nolan does, and besides, the "facts" here are driven by the demands of the story, as we also know, and within the framework of what we can plausibly believe for the sake of the plot.

It isn't rocket science and it definitely isn't brain surgery. But explaining group lucid dreaming in *Inception* is a little bit like trying to explain how the transporter works on *Star Trek*. There is a certain sense to it, but thinking through it, using what is known about our physiology and our dream states, and filling in the rest with plausible suppositions, we can have an account of how dream architecture is possible, how it could "actually" work in a way that is consistent with the clues provided by Nolan. I'm not saying that what follows is the only way it could work, but the "right" story would surely be akin to the one I'll now tell.

Sharing the Dream

Yusuf is our crack chemist-for-hire in *Inception*, and from him we learn the basic facts about what happens, physically, that makes group dreaming possible. Group dreaming has to be possible before dream architecture can be done, so let's look just at group dreaming, first off.

There is the vague suggestion in the movie that the knowledge of how to dream in groups is ancient (and African), at least as it concerns the drugs to be used. We have old African men gathering in the dank cellars under the apothecaries of Mombasa (or Nairobi, or wherever) to "share the dream." Yusuf tells us that they do this because it's the only way they can still dream—together, as assisted by these chemicals.

This connects the idea of group dreaming to mythic consciousness, and perhaps we're meant to think that modern life has made group dreaming impossible, and that in these unwise times, the wise yearn for the kind of attachment to each other and their dreams that existed before civilization became so much controlled by greed and technology. We're led to imagine a world in which elders would gather around a fire in a sacred circle, take the drugs and share the dream. Here the ancestors would instruct them together in the ways of war, peace, and spirit.

The reason the old men can't dream together (anymore) without Yusuf's chemical help is that the puny dreams they have alone are not real dreams at all. When one has shared the dream with others and has explored the possibilities of that world, it's difficult to take seriously the impoverished dreams of a lonely dreamer. One could even see such a dreamer as "lost," and modern dreamers don't even know they are lost—

and that's as lost as you can be. Something similar might be said for our modern form of waking consciousness. We wrongly believe it is individual in form, when in truth we are all fragments, using very little of our brain power because we don't know how to reconnect with what is real. Waking consciousness was once collective as well. We re-experience that in ecstatic praise and worship gathering, or rock concerts.

Mythic consciousness, on the other hand, is a shared consciousness, and it is the measure of genuine reality. Individual consciousness is an aberration, a pathology of consciousness in which the individual foolishly mistakes his tiny perspective for reality. But in every isolated individual lies the common memory of the race and the power to find the way out of the labyrinth of modern consciousness and into genuine, shared, collective consciousness. Our group dreaming is the training for finding the path toward shared waking consciousness. Some kind of story like this lies behind Nolan's depiction of the old men in the basement, and Yusuf is more than an apothecary, he is more like the Medicine Man.

But anything can be commodified in the modern world, packaged, sold and enhanced with the latest technologies. In a world so misguided, people might break into one another's dreams and steal things, or worse yet, leave things behind. There is no human thing, no matter how pure, that can't be misused, and the discipline of group dreaming is no exception.

Better Living through Electro-Chemistry

So how does the science work? The suggestion I would make about the chemicals is that perhaps they have an effect on our brainwaves similar to the way that a laser beam works with light waves. A laser device takes variable light waves that would normally cancel each other out and aligns them so that they are mutually reinforcing. What if some psychotropic concoction could bring about a similar effect on our brainwaves? And what if, to such a mixture, we add a sedative, nay, a "powerful" sedative, carefully adjusted to the aim of going down extra levels?

We can imagine something along these lines being accomplished with drugs, and in the same way that a laser beam can be intensified by concentrating more and more energy into the same mutually reinforcing wave-pattern, what about an organizing of brainwaves that employs increasingly more of the brain's total "neural capacity"? Such an idea is suggested by Cobb when he reminds us of how little of our brain capacity we use in waking life. Perhaps the chemically controlled alignment of brainwaves can unlock something like our greater "neural capacity." So we could think of this enhancement of "neural capacity" as a measurable electro-chemical ratio, where the effect of the drugs is to produce an iterated electromagnetic field within a field within a field, and with each incremental increase of neural energy, we can skip down more deeply into the dynamics of that nested field. The field is also open to electrical manipulation.

Perhaps the electromagnetic field can jump incrementally in intensity: as energy is added, at a certain point, the "next level down" becomes sufficiently organized to "visit." And if that's right, then the temporality of each deeper level might be like the Richter scale for earthquakes, so that when the intensity of brainwave alignment is cranked up, the effect is a leap to a frighteningly greater and greater expansion of actual time. So, to supercharge the serum, as Yusuf does, creates the conditions for a three or four-level expansion of the same five actual minutes, pulling those minutes apart to the point of approaching a quantum minimum of time, a smallest "time-particle" or something which would make a second seem like an eternity, if you could experience it (this is my best shot at saying what "limbo" is in this movie, by the way!). And so maybe there is a minimum "time burst," a set amount of required expansion when one goes to the next "level," or maybe there isn't, but to keep using chemicals to align brainwaves only really gets us access to smaller and smaller drops of experience. Each deeper level is built from more rarified or subtle waves.

This is all pretty weird to contemplate, but here is an analogy that may help: If you run audio or video tape faster across a magnet, less information goes on each physical segment of the tape as it passes, and the effect is higher fidelity. Less information spread across more space, due to the faster passage of time, preserves that information more faithfully. When you run the tape slower, more information is packed into less space, and the result is a lower fidelity. So maybe our experience of dream-time is sort of like that. The more it's expanded into nested levels of space, the slower it goes, but in this case, we get less "lucidity" (that is, "fidelity"), because the brainwaves are so rarified. In other words, maybe it becomes harder and harder to maintain the dream architecture and to interpret one's own dream experience as we pack more and more of it into the same five (waking) minutes—or ten hours of the plane ride, or whatever.

The margin of error for variation in the individual wave vibrations would become increasingly thin, and the manipulation of the electromagnetic field produced by those waves becomes more and more delicate, while the experiences had by the dreamers become harder to interpret as the waves are more rarified. One result of wandering around in a dream that is three or four levels removed from waking life is the increasing loss, then, of lucidity and the onset of a kind of "psychosis of forgetting" that replaces the lucidity. One could go so far as to suppose that the wanderer in limbo is physically lost in a quantum foam.

The Ghost in the Machine

Then we have to consider that for our team of inceivers, there is the dream machine they carry around in various metal suitcases. There is such a machine in Yusuf's basement as well. Precisely what the machine is, and how people might have dreamt en mass without it, in ancient days, is something we don't know. But I think we're supposed to infer that the drugs do something of a chemical nature to our brains and bodies, while the machine, which seems to have electrical leads that can transmit impulses of some sort from one dreamer to others allows for the manipulation of the electromagnetic field created by the sympathetic alignment of our brainwaves.

It's not important that we know exactly how this process works, but I do think that it needs to seem plausible to those who watch—not because all stories need to stay within the bounds of plausibility, but because this particular story would quickly lose the kind of profoundly human interest it has unless we can persuade ourselves of the premise about group dreaming. Not content with the idea that this is an ancient art, Nolan adds on modern technology.

I think it's probably safe to infer, from what we're shown, that perhaps "group dreaming" is the only ancient part. The elders remember when the great grandfathers told them about sharing the dream and meeting the ancestors there, but some of the old magic is now lost, so they depend on the machine (and that is sad, as Yusuf seems to imply). But maybe even crude electrical leads from dreamer to dreamer would suffice for conducting the impulses of a shared experience, at one level down, and maybe it is the leads that enables one dreamer to produce images in a dream that belongs to another dreamer. Perhaps the ancients never got that far. They weren't interested in manipulating the shared dream to their personal advantage. The fancy high-tech machine is needed for the kind of highly organized invasion and theft that are practiced by our hired team, and for going two, three or even four levels into shared dreaming.

It's notable that Nolan chose to represent this technology as electrical rather than electronic. To introduce computers into the narrative would change the story greatly. It seems to have been important to him to stay away from the idea that the ways we can control dream architecture involve computer manipulation. He wanted this to be a skill one learns by controlling one's thoughts (like a shaman), not by manipulating a computer (like a geek). Part of the reason I'm certain that Nolan wants to invoke our sense of mythic consciousness (apart from the obvious clues, like laying the story out over the lattice work of the myth of Theseus) is that he so obviously avoided introducing electronic elements into the story.

Once upon a Time

So what is mythic consciousness anyway? There are a number of theories out there, and not much agreement among anthropologists, psychologists, and other theorists (including philosophers). I will give you the brief version of one theory that meshes well with what Nolan does in this movie. I am not sure I buy this theory, overall, but I do admit that I'm convinced by the part I am going to tell you about.

The theory belongs to a philosopher named Susanne Langer (1895–1985). She wrote a famous book called *Philosophy in a New Key* (1942) in which she provided a theory of mythic consciousness that used narrative principles to explain what mythic consciousness is and how it works.

The basic idea is this: the difference between a dream and a myth is that dreams slip around, all over the place and myths do not. In a dream, one thing can turn into something else without warning, and that's what we expect from dreams. It surprises us sometimes, and sometimes it doesn't, when (for example), a seashell is suddenly a bird that talks to us, or our parents are suddenly our children, or our companions become trees, or some other such transmogrification. But since it's a dream, we always know this is a possibility. In Langer's theory, the reason dreams can behave this way is because we don't have to communicate them to others. If you really must communicate something to someone else, you will have to put it in a time sequence and make it conform to the boundaries of narrative communication—there will be a beginning, middle, and end, and a sort of plot thread. But dreams don't have to behave that way. We do put them in that order when we tell others about our dreams, but we always know it's a bit artificial to impose narrative order on the experience.

Langer doesn't talk about lucid dreams, but they would exist in between ordinary individual dreaming and storytelling. Lucid dreams do have narrative structure, but they are still dreams. It's just that the dreamer is aware that he or she is dreaming and presumably has some control over the narrative. I suppose seashells can still become birds spontaneously, but in a lucid dream we could get some control over that process: make things become other things—or prevent it—by using our minds and wills. And here we begin to get close to the idea of "training" the dreamer. Perhaps it is possible to train people to generate images in a lucid dream that become elements of the narrative, regardless of who is in control of the narration.

Castles in the Air

It is believable that a person could be better or worse at this interposition of images, as a matter of natural aptitude (like being good at math or music). Practicing could improve the capacity to generate these images in one's own dreams. Ariadne has a gift for this sort of thing, for generating images of spaces, and she learns to do it regardless of who is narrating the dream. For his story, Nolan needs it to be possible for more than one dreamer to be lucid at the same time, in group dreaming, but I think that idea is consistent with the story of group dreaming I already gave you.

There's a sort of structural regression to group mythic consciousness made possible by the drugs and the machine, where the form of collective consciousness is mythic, but individuals still carry their modern abilities of narration with them when they "travel" this way. It's like Mark Twain's *Connecticut Yankee* having a dream of an even more primitive time.

The same idea may explain how Robert Fischer is "trained" to generate images of a well-armed Delta Force or SWAT team that comes to rescue him if he is trapped in a dream narrative that poses a threat to his secrets. I'll say more about that training, but the point is to recognize that whatever Ariadne is doing to get better at dream architecture is probably closely related to what Fischer is doing to "militarize" his unconscious mind. But the unconscious is a little more unruly and a little less responsive to simple habituation than is the conscious mind. So no amount of conscious practicing will perfect the militarization of the unconscious.

No matter how much we habituate ourselves to certain patterns of conscious thinking, and no matter how hard we try to tame them, our unconscious minds still have a spontaneous tendency to supply images to our waking minds and to our dreams that we don't create with our wills. Freud's way of distinguishing the conscious from the unconscious mind is to say that there is a sort of sentinel, the "ego," who guards the threshold between consciousness and the unconscious, but sometimes (especially in dreams) unconscious desires slip past our defenses and become images. This idea explains Cobb's limitations and failures controlling the images that show up wherever he goes in the dream world. All of this tug of war between the conscious and the unconscious seems to happen in the liminal domain of lucid dreaming, somewhere between the world of conscious story-telling and the world of dreams.

Langer goes on to say that as we attempt to communicate the crazy swirl of our inner conscious lives, we increasingly restrict what "counts" in our stream of thought, that is, what we actively pay attention to, and we select just those aspects of conscious life that we can place into narrative order. I don't know about you, but if I tried to actually communicate to you what goes on in my inner life, well, you wouldn't want to know. It's a perfect chaos, when I try to survey it as a whole.

The demands of communicating our inner lives to others, with all the organizing and censorship we impose, are severe and we eliminate most of what we think and even more of what we feel. In time we acquire the habit of ignoring things we can't easily communicate, pretending those thoughts and feelings don't really exist. These habits explain not only how we move from the rich imaginative life of childhood into a less lively adult world, but also how the human race loses its mythic childhood as it takes on the strictures of "civilization," in which science takes the place of magic, and written novels replace oral traditions, and solemn worship replaces ecstatic rites. What counts as an acceptable story for "civilized" people must be "rational," which is to say, highly regimented.

As you can see, these ideas about mythic consciousness and the narrowing of consciousness into "civilized life" have some implications for the story of inceiving the mind of Robert Fischer. As our team knows, to inceive successfully requires the use of symbols and those symbols have to spread through the target's unconscious mind and eventually break past the sentinel, the ego, and manifest themselves as hunches, or as notions, or even as ideas, but not as images. It would do no good for Robert Fischer to suddenly have an image in his mind of the pinwheel his father gave him. He would go "humph" and dismiss it. Rather, to inceive, the symbol's meaning has to be taken up as a disposition to behave one way rather than another. I would suppose that the way a symbol spreads through the unconscious is by a series of transformations that preserve the essence or the basic energy or tendency of the original symbol. By the time the symbol has pervaded the unconscious, it is no longer traceable to its source.

What this hypothesis of mine implies, putting it all together, is that inception would actually be easy for "primitive" people but difficult for sophisticated, modern "civilized" people, whose defenses are always up, and whose over-active egos are so thoroughly "protected" against any genuine contact with the inner life of another, as well as from their own unconscious desires. "Primitive" people would be open, would have no secrets to protect, and would be taught to believe that the distance between waking and dreaming is not great. That's why the interpretation of dreams is received as a useful art among them. Such people would not fear inception. They might even welcome it and practice it as a kind of gift-giving or hospitality. Upon encountering modern people who can't be inceived easily, perhaps they would be sad for such people. The modern person is so alone, so confused, and is forced to endure such a narrow, uninteresting world, a world in which everything must be just what it is and nothing else, a world of impoverished signs and with no living symbols, that the situation is pitiable.

To the "primitive" mind, language teems with living symbols, while to the supposedly "civilized" mind, language is a dead conveyer of abstract signs. With this small bit of Langer's philosophy of myth, we are now in a position to return to the film itself with a better understanding of what happens and how dream architecture works, along with getting a grip on the process of inception itself.

Whose Dream Is This, Anyway?

One thing you might not have worked through is the question of who is the principal narrator of each dream. That turns out to be an important point because apparently one principle of Nolan's dream architecture is that the architect is most effective when she/he is not the dreamer. So Ariadne is in all the dreams, but she is never the dreamer. It also appears that being the dreamer may eliminate you from descending deeper. You can appear in your own dream, but if someone else is dreaming within your dream, you can't appear in the deeper dream (apparently). The first dream on the airplane is Yusuf's, which is why he stays in the van "awake" (in his own dream, narrating it lucidly) while everyone else dreams of a hotel. The second dream is Arthur's, which is why he stays in the hotel while everyone else dreams of a snow fortress.

But whose dream is the snow fortress? There are a few clues. First, when Ariadne has prepared her physical models for each dreamer to study, Eames walks to the model of the snow fortress. Second, remember that Fischer believes that Eames is Peter Browning, and in the hotel (Arthur's dream), Fischer believes he is going into Browning's dream, to break into Browning's dreamsafe, and that is in the snow fort. Of course, Eames is Browning. Third, all the other characters except Eames appear at the deeper levels, below the snow fort —Fischer, Ariadne, Cobb and Saito. So the snow fort is really Eames's dream, and he is maintaining that dream level as its narrator, but he is dreaming as Peter Browning in order to deceive Fischer. That's why they keep referring to "Browning's defenses" and "where would Browning put it?" and so on, when they're in the dream of the snow fort.

All the architecture in the first three dream levels is Ariadne's (with some invasions by Cobb's projections), until they unexpectedly find themselves having to go into Cobb's dream, where Mal has taken Fischer hostage. So when Ariadne and Cobb go to sleep in the snow fortress, they go into Cobb's dream. He is the architect, but it was built a long time ago and is now falling apart.

The key to understanding the planned inception of Fischer is to look at the snow fort that Eames is dreaming about. Ariadne has built the safe there for Maurice Fischer's Last Will and Testament, but she left the safe empty, as is the rule for heavily defended secret places (we learn that early in the movie, when Cobb and Arthur are in Saito's dream). So, if I've worked through this rightly, Eames is the one who puts the pinwheel in the safe—that is the inception—and he figures out what to do when the picture of Maurice and Robert with the pinwheel is in Robert's wallet, which Eames has lifted when he is disguised as a bodacious blonde bar patron in the bar in Arthur's hotel.

A Pinwheel and a Picture

I think that maybe, just maybe, that picture is Robert Fischer's totem. Eames recognizes its importance. Granted, Fischer doesn't know he's going to be spending time in other people's dreams when he gets on the airplane, but he is trained in "dream defense" and a totem is something these dreamy people always keep with them. There must be some way that a person's totem crosses from waking reality into all these dreams, right? It makes sense to believe that these people are all trained to generate the image of that totem in any dream (along with the absence of some secret characteristic it possesses only in waking life). We already know that handling another person's totem gives one great power over that person.

So the picture of Robert with his father and the pinwheel shows up in Arthur's dream, and Eames is the character who keeps it and says it will be useful.

Eames, then, placed the pinwheel (from the picture) in the safe (as a generated image), following the clue he picked up in the stolen picture, but the inception only works because Robert Fischer believes he has placed the pinwheel in there himself, unconsciously. The Will is what Browning has supposedly put there. Remember Robert is trained, his mind is "militarized," so he knows that Browning will fill the safe with something secret from his own unconscious. But in fact, Robert is the one who puts the Will in the safe. It is actually his own projection because it is what he expected to find. Yet, he discounts the Will because he wrongly believes Browning has put it there, unconsciously. The switcheroo is that the pinwheel is such a powerful symbol that Robert believes he has put it there himself, and the meaning it carries is that deep down he knows his father always loved him and isn't disappointed. Robert drops his defenses for just that moment and connects with a feeling about his father—one that will spread.

Do You Doubt Me?

Fischer doubts whether Peter Browning has really been kidnapped (the doubt suggested to him by Cobb), and Fischer also suspects that Browning is the one behind the attempt to invade his dreams. So Fischer is convinced by the Mr. Charles gambit to turn the tables on Browning by going where Browning didn't expect him to go, which is into Browning's own dream, to discover what Browning was trying to hide (the true contents of the Last Will and Testament of Maurice Fischer).

Part of the standard "Mr. Charles" gambit is to convince the target to reveal his secret while believing he is revealing someone else's secret. But in this case, no one is interested in Robert's secrets; the mission is inception, which adds a twist to the standard Mr. Charles routine. What seemed like a revelation of a secret was actually an implant.

A doubt is easier to inceive than a positive idea, but as Cobb briefly says, it's better to use positive symbols, things that evoke good feelings. Doubt tends to tear down meanings, not build them. Doubt arrests action rather than motivating it. If you want your target to do something he wouldn't otherwise do, you have to relieve doubt, counteract it. Both doubt and its opposite, the relief of doubt, will spread in the unconscious. Doubt is what overtook Mal's unconscious (see my other essay), and Cobb has learned from that what not to do in attempting inception.

Proceed to Carousel One

I promised you an answer to what Fischer does and does not know when everyone (except Saito) is at baggage claim. I think the key to it is to understand that a doubt has been lifted from Fischer, although he doesn't think the dreams he had are the reason it disappeared. He probably feels like his own man for the first time in his life. And here we learn something like the moral or the "theme" of the whole tale. Modernity is an age of doubt and doubt spreads across the unconscious, manifesting in millions of ways. We are all so very afraid, so guilty, so lacking in confidence in our own judgments, in the work of our own hands, and so isolated from one another that we substitute emotional bravado for genuine healing.

The same deep structures of consciousness that make it possible for us to dream together are the ones that lead us to doubt each other. Doubt is easy to create in modern people and difficult to relieve. But for traditional people, the ones who live in closer proximity to the world of dreams, and to one another, it is the other way around: belief is easy to create and doubt is hard to implant. They know who and what they are and they have no deep-seated doubt in their unconscious minds. The unconscious is the place where the ancestors speak, and so long as it is approached with reverence and awe, the ancestors will be benevolent. Robert Fischer has touched that place—his father, now the departed and revered ancestor, speaks and is in fact benevolent. Robert has recovered himself by getting below the doubt to what our collective and primitive selves have always known, which is that our ancestors desire our happiness.

So when everybody wakes up, Fischer doesn't say anything to the people he has just spent the last ten hours dreaming with. Maybe he recognizes them, from the dream, but either he believes they are his own security people, in waking life, that they helped him defeat the attempt to steal his secret and instead, perhaps they got Browning's knowledge of the Will, but it really doesn't matter. Maybe all of that was "just a dream." Robert is confident and not suspicious and fearful now, and it doesn't matter who these people are. Otherwise I guess he would have had everyone arrested when they landed.

Saito has disappeared when they land, by the way, so Robert probably believes Saito was Browning's co-conspirator. That would make sense. Robert surely knows who Saito is, what he looks like in waking life, and would have been naturally suspicious of him, as his father's main competitor. The fact that Saito is not at baggage claim would tend to confirm that if someone was trying to steal Robert's secrets, it was probably Saito, and the people on the plane were sent by Browning, or someone else, to protect Robert on the flight. Something like this story would supply the unstated narrative moves that finish out the "whodunit" aspect of the tale.

Day Residue

I'm not absolutely certain how "dream architecture" works, but I believe it requires the waking co-operation of the dreamer, in order for the architecture to "take." The dreamer has to be lucid enough to choose the architecture created by the architect, and I think they have to study it together. The dreamer dreams the superstructure and the architect supplies the particulars about the space. The architect can build in some features the dreamer doesn't know about, but the comprehensive whole has to be chosen by the dreamer, I'm pretty sure. So the superstructure is what dream theorists call "day residue," stuff that carries over from your daily activities and experiences and shows up in your dreams without being transformed by the dream state. So if you are studying for a math test, you dream about actual math, and so on.

Robert Fischer believes the first dream is his own dream, at the very least (it is really Yusuf's). But at the baggage claim, he has the option of believing all the dreams were his own, and that the people in them were day residue, just as I suggested at the outset. But I also said I would try to inceive something in you. Since you are a modern, civilized reader, it is far easier to get you to doubt something, and for that doubt to spread, than to get you to do something I want you to do. But I'm better than your average inceiver. If you are still reading this, I managed what I set out to do, which was to keep you reading to find out what I was trying to inceive in you. You mainly doubted that I could really do it, I'm sure, and maybe now you're disappointed, but if I managed to get your suspicion of me to work as a lever to get you to the end of the chapter, I succeeded in the waking inception.

I also promised some training. You now know that doubt spreads more easily than does its opposite, for the people you care about. Your training is, then, an object lesson in resisting the urge to plant doubts in the unconscious depths of the people around you. If you make a habit of doing that, you may not be able to keep them from spreading. You don't want to leave anyone in the position Robert Fischer was in.

On the other hand, if you want to protect yourself from being inceived by Christopher Nolan's movies, stay away from the movies altogether. To place yourself in the theater is to place yourself at his mercy, to invite him into your dreams. He knows that you go to the movies to be able to dream, with others. And after all, Nolan is Cobb.

11
The Story of Reality

EMILIE DIONNE

"What is the most resilient parasite?" Cobb asks Saito as they meet in the fancy hotel of the dream sequence. Is it a bacterium, he suggests, or a virus? No. It's an idea, he claims.

When you think of a parasite, it usually involves some kind of illness, and the presence of a host onto which the parasite latches itself. It implies that the equilibrium of an organism is shattered by the introduction of an invader and that the life of the host is threatened by such a parasite. So how can an *idea* be a parasite? Or, more importantly, how can an idea be capable of such virulent power and, as Cobb points out, be so "resilient"?

Of course, what we realize in *Inception* is that the 'ideas' proposed by Cobb aren't just isolated words out of context, like the scattered contents of an overturned garbage bin. The 'idea' needs to be solid, stable, and coherent; it should be articulated *through* a well-thought-out story-line. It requires a logical narrative on which it can flow and eventually take on a life of its own in a person's mind. This is usually what parasites *do;* they evolve, grow and feed themselves.

It's an idea *as* a story that Cobb hopes to implant in a person's mind; the idea, in the form of a narrative, becomes a parasite that could reshape how a person sees the world, engage with others, and even understand herself. And this is what happens in *Inception:* when Cobb invades Fisher's subconscious. It's with a story (*"My father doesn't want me to follow in his footsteps"*) extrapolated from the idea to incept (*that Fischer dismantle his father's empire*) that Cobb and his team will theatrically invade the subject's deepest refuge.

But what becomes evident as the audience follows Cobb in his quest—and not merely the Trojan-horse tactic of invading Fisher's subconscious—is that Cobb's mind itself is fueled by an idea that animates each and every one of his thoughts and actions. Much like the goal Fischer develops as he shares tears with his dying father and Cobb's desire to return to his children which leads him to accept Saito's proposition, these stories, as dreams, are necessary features of life that we *incept* in the deepest refuges of ourselves. Recall that, according to Cobb, an idea can change a person's mind and even come to *define* who she is. If an idea is a parasite, can't we claim that an individual is not the host, but a collection of ideas, of those well-planted stories that fuel every one of our decisions?

We need ideas that define who we are. Every day we cultivate stories in which we should truly believe if we are to engage with the world and with others to acquire knowledge and to act. These stories are not just *any* ideas; they need to be logical and to make sense. We strive for coherence, and when facing the meaninglessness of a cluster of things that exhibit little to no coherence with each other, we instantaneously feel the urge to create a narrative from this inchoate mass. In the words of Cobb, "humans strive for positive logic."

A story is a tool we use to make sense out of apparent meaninglessness because the threat of meaninglessness leaves us petrified. But stories are not just innocuous *words*; therein lies their inherently virulent and dangerous nature.

Dreams as Realities

In their first shared dream experience, Cobb explains to Ariadne that in dreams we're unaware that we create what we see *as* we perceive it. Cobb argues that our imagination works at an increased rhythm when dreaming, which makes the creative part almost indiscernible from our perception of it. The processes of creation and of perception happen almost simultaneously, and while we're dreaming, we're *unaware* that it's a dream. As Cobb suggests, this process is *accelerated* in the dream, but we will see that there's only a difference of *degree* between dreams and reality, not a fundamental difference of nature. But let's first look at the realm of the dream.

In our dreams worlds are created as we walk through them, and we fill in the gaps with our projections—individuals—and scattered memories—architecture such as streets or buildings. As Ariadne discovers the realm of dreams, she senses that the *texture* of things feels *real:* the physics, the fabric, the smell. What she recognizes is the inseparability of *all* senses and the fact that, although vision seems omnipresent to us, a dream is not a collection of visual experiences, but of an assemblage of bodily sensations. We don't merely *witness* what's in front of us; we *live* it.

Much like in a dream, we're never mere spectators to our experiences. As *beings-in-the-world*—that is, as individuals situated both in time and space and that have a body we can't escape—it's impossible to extirpate our "mind" from our perspective of where we are and who we are. The very fact that we're *embodied* means that we're always already engaged with the things and the environment in which we live and breathe, and that we're never *just* spectators, be it in reality or in the dream.

Our actions and decisions are informed by our perception of things, but we also *create* these perceptions. For the nineteenth-century philosopher Henri Bergson, our embodied condition affects how and what we perceive because we never cease to be part of this dynamic world. The world and what it contains attracts or repulses us, it invites or frightens us, and we actively participate in its materiality. This means that each act, even perceiving itself, is partial, biased, and contaminated with vested interests; it is mediated, negotiated through our memories, our expectations, our desires and our past experiences. Bergson says that we're always invested in how things present themselves to us and always prepared to *react* to them.

This is also what quantum physics is all about, as pointed out by Karen Barad: "to "see," one must actively intervene" (*Meeting the Universe Halfway*, p. 51) and this participation introduces a motion through the very act of *seeing*; it changes how things appear to us. Later Barad says that "part of seeing is also being convinced about what one sees," insofar as it *demands* that we act in relation to what we see. We can never fully know, or know *for sure,* that things are one way and not another. Yet, because we're part of *this world,* we can't afford *not* to act. Inaction could be fatal. And this is precisely what's at stake in *Inception:* the contingency of the dream and, by extension, of reality, requires some sort of *belief.* This strangely echoes the leap of faith Saito and Mal ask Cobb to take.

Memories and Desires as the Fabric of Reality

Think of a street you walk by daily to go to work; the act of walking is informed by a specific goal, and many things may remain unnoticed to you, except were they to interfere directly with you. Walking the same street with no specific goal will translate into a completely different experience where objects or individuals can appear in a new light. You might notice a house you've never seen before or even find romance along the way. Remember how, in *Inception,* Cobb's fear of the memory of the bridge Ariadne has built is what *triggers* the projection of Mal, not the bridge itself.

For Cobb, a word or the sensation of the wind brings to surface a memory or a regret that he can tame only with much difficulty. This happens when a smell or a touch brings back to memory a person or a feeling that submerges you. Of all things, it's almost impossible to *remember* a perfume, but smelling a similar fragrance will change our perception of an event because our perception is necessarily mediated through memories, past experiences, and desires.

The contamination of past memories is quite vivid in Cobb's case; he has no control over those apparitions. This is not to say that the other characters in *Inception* are immune to such experiences, but rather that it's *through* Cobb's perspective that we jump into the story. A story is always a view *from* somewhere.

Because we're *embodied,* we're limited to our perspective on things. As *beings-in-the-world,* in actively participating and not being just witnesses, to make sense of the new things that constantly hit us, we're forced to interpret what's happening *through* the lens of past experiences, even though the process is already in progress at a subconscious level. Even if we achieve multiple perspectives on an event, these always bring their own load of *interested* views. Hoping to reach the god-like, detached, and disengaged viewpoint is a mere fantasy and never achievable.

Perception, assaulted by the weight of memories, works through analogies. In other words, things that are fundamentally *different* may appear as similar *enough* and, as they do, we transfer what we know about one thing to the other. Those analogies that we perceive are actually productive *errors*, that is: illusions that become the ground of further knowledge. This is what we usually call *intuition,* a faculty Cobb excels at. According to Friedrich Nietzsche, life as such is only possible with error and illusion, and to assume that truth is *better* is to fallaciously deny how errors can also be productive and *good*:

> It is no more than a moral prejudice that truth is worth more than appearance; it is even the worst-proved assumption that exists. Let us concede at least this much: there would be no life at all if not on the basis of perspectival evaluation and appearances. (*Beyond Good and Evil,* II, §34)

Illusion, tricks, resemblance are inherent to nature and to life, for some to survive, or others to escape. Most scientific research is *developed* from a hypothesis, a simplified model, that is applied to reality subsequently in order to understand reality further. A narrative creates a sense of stability, of unity, which is needed to engage with the materiality of the world.

The Story-Making of Reality

Story-telling is a process through which perception and creativity are intermeshed together in such a dynamic and progressive way that it becomes almost *impossible* to perceive the movement from *perception* to *creation*. Yet to create analogies is also to *partly* misconstrue what we see. This is due to the fact that, because of our embodied condition and the need to make decisions, we have only a certain amount of *time* to reflect on the course of action to follow. In *Inception,* the characters are limited by the projections of the subject's subconscious; they need to decide quickly on what to do next before the projections catch up with them. This is also brought to our attention as Saito is shot by Fisher's projections. Even if, in the state of dream, time expands, external events require of Cobb's team that they act with no time wasted.

In dreams as in reality, we constantly face the contingency of a dynamic world. Therefore, the passage from ignorance to knowledge is carried out through translation, which is also quite unstable. To know means to understand what is unknown through what we *already* know. And, in this process, what we already know and what we just learnt mutually contaminate each other. To perceive what is unknown means to translate and interpret it *through* past experiences and through what is already know. Simultaneously, what we already know is *transformed* by the new analogy we perceive *and* create between the two things.

Art is a good example: a new art movement, such as cubism or expressionism, will expand our understanding of art, and retrospectively we will reassess other work of art in relation to this new development. We don't look at art the same way before *and* after Picasso. To perceive is to interpret; it's not a perfect translation of what things are in and of themselves.

Given this constant state of contingency, our lives depend on our capacity to stabilize, momentarily, what surrounds us. As embodied beings, there's another illusion that we need to acknowledge: the fiction of a stable and autonomous self. We're vulnerable due to our bodily limitations; we depend on others to understand our words and our gestures to communicate. Yet at all times, our body can experience trauma or illness. But as pointed out by Cobb, even *ideas* can change us. Thus to think of ourselves as stable entities is, at best, a temporary fact.

Striving for Positive Logic

Stability, however, is not something we necessarily *consciously* strive for. As Cobb explains, it's a profound desire, an irrational drive, that, as humans, we all experience. Cobb says that, deep down, we strive for positive logic, even if this comes to the cost of *denying*, willfully rejecting a *truth*:

> Positive emotion trumps negative emotion every time. We yearn for people to be reconciled, for catharsis. We need *positive* emotional logic.

Likewise, Nietzsche maintains that: "something might be true although at the same time harmful and dangerous in the highest degree; indeed, it could pertain to the fundamental nature of existence that a complete knowledge of it would destroy one" (*Beyond Good and Evil*, II, §39). Therefore, we don't *naturally* strive for truth but rather for harmony. Due to this, Nietzsche also claims that "we remain necessarily strangers to ourselves . . . we *must* mistake ourselves" (*The Genealogy of Morals*, Preface, §1) because of the visceral, irrational desire that animates us and makes us who we are at a subconscious level. If an idea is a parasite, individuals are not the host but a *collection* of ideas that make us *become* who we are. The more resilient the idea, the closer it is to who we *truly* come to be.

That we *yearn for* coherence is no proof that there *is* coherence. A desire isn't a fact but an interpretation of a fact. This desire also constantly mediates our perception. As I said before, we have to recognize the impossibility of a *disinterested* point of view because even the most *disinterested* perspective at the very least conceals a *desire* of being as disinterested as possible. This yearning for logic usually takes the form of a coherent story, but often it speaks to this visceral, invisible and often subconscious *desire,* which is made visible in dreams. This role, as Cobb explains, is filled by the presence of projections.

The projections, which emerge from an individual's subconscious, are wary of all elements that introduce chaos in the harmony effective in the dream. "What happens when you start messing up with the physics?" asks Ariadne. To this Cobb replies that the projections, sensing (or assuming) the foreign nature of those elements, will eventually look for those who are invading and interrupting the flow of the dream.

Passers-by stare aggressively at Ariadne and push her around as she makes her way through the streets she changes at will. Visibly annoyed, she bluntly suggests to Cobb that he *control* his projections, to which he replies that he can't exercise any authority over them: "this is why it's called the *subconscious.*" According to Cobb, the subconscious *desires* harmony without the interference of external parasites that would redefine the nature of the narrative. The projections in *Inception* strive to eradicate all foreign elements that threaten this coherence; an invader of the dream needs to walk the fine line situated in between perception and creation, hence becoming invisible to the subject's subconscious.

The architect must make its presence as subtle as the distortion of an echo, like the waves formed by a pebble in the water. In penetrating another individual's dream, the architect can give the illusion to the subject that *she's* the instigator of the dream. Otherwise, as the projections "feel the foreign nature of the dreamer" explains Cobb, they will "attack, like white blood cells, fighting an infection." Yet, if the architect succeeds in incepting the idea, the idea itself, *as an infection,* will grow exponentially, "like a cancer."

An idea, says Cobb, is the most resilient parasite. And the consequences of *incepting* an idea are not to be taken lightly. The most simple and apparently innocent idea can evolve to the point of redefining the mind, behavior and emotions of a person. "The seed of the idea we plant," explains Cobb, "will grow in this man's mind. It'll change him. It might even come to define him." In this sense, ideas are not just words uttered in the air that vanish as their echo fades. They have real, material consequences; they can change the *nature* of an action or an event and redefine their significance.

Cobb maintains that the subconscious strives for the genesis of the idea and will reject what *appears* foreign to itself. But is it the genesis of the idea that the subconscious will reject, or the elements that fail to fit the picture? The language of "health" is predominant in how Cobb describes the process of inception and the impact of ideas. If he agrees to perform inception on someone else, it should be obvious to the audience that he couldn't care less about how the idea will evolve in Fischer's mind after the inception. In fact, he maintains that no one can fully control what will happen to the idea once absorbed by the subject. He knows this for a fact, and only submits to Saito's request to settle his own faith: to see his children again.

Films as Dreams

When discussing the idea behind *Inception*, Christopher Nolan said that the story he wanted to tell *worked its way through* the figure of cinematic worlds. *Inception* explores a way to make a story work: it is a meta-narrative on a narrative, Fischer being the spectator who needs to be convinced by the story Cobb, the director, has to offer.

With the help of the architect, Ariadne, Cobb creates a world, texturizes it, gives it a sense of *realness* to the subject of the dream who can *forget* that she dreams, which is, ideally, where a director *hopes* a movie will take you. Fischer, as the audience, experiences through fictionality a whole array of authentic emotions. These emotions—the tears he sheds for his father—are the truest expression of his experience. It might be all *inspired* by a lie, but what Fisher *feels* and the experiences his subconscious absorbs become real. What he sees becomes meaningful as he *believes* in the story Cobb *incepted,* and gives it a sense for himself. The ideas materialize; they have real, concrete impacts, and they change who Fisher is.

Yet if some are to *believe* in the story, Cobb maintains that others need some sense of security to avoid being lost in between the different levels of the dreams.

Leap of Faith

The dreamer and the architect work in and through a dream, and they constantly risk being targeted as invaders by the subconscious of the subject. As Cobb informs Ariadne, a dream is never "*just* a dream. While we're in it, it's real." Thus Cobb and Arthur suggest that she forge herself a *totem*. This *totem* is an object whose weight and feel only she knows. Were she to doubt *her* reality and suspect herself to be in someone else's dream, she could settle this suspicion with the help of her totem, for its specific characteristics, known only to her, could not be replicated accurately by another's subconscious.

The totem is a curious object in *Inception,* especially because while Cobb *does* have a totem—Mal's—the audience actually doesn't know *how* the totem operates *for Cobb.* Even more stunning, he spins it whenever he doubts reality. Yet Arthur clearly specifies that the totem should be used to verify if one is in *someone else's dream*, someone who wouldn't know the details of the totem itself. Therefore, a person can still be locked in his own dream and fooled by his subconscious into taking the dream for reality.

The danger of mistaking dreams for reality is always present, and it's complicated by the fact that there's only one way to know *for certain* if you're asleep: ending your life. If the dreamer finds herself questioning the reality *of* the dream, she

must take a leap of faith: her actions are thus constantly negotiated through the highly contingent nature of the dream and,
by extension, the nature of reality.

This danger, as Cobb explains, cuts both ways: you can convince yourself that you have returned to reality all the while
remaining in a dream. This is why *architects* should be wary of
creating from memories because in doing so they blur the line
between reality and dreams for themselves. "Is this what happened to Mal?" asks Ariadne. "Yes. She'd decided to forget that
our world wasn't real," answers Cobb.

Here, I'd like the reader to take a similar leap of faith: Cobb,
once again, is talking about *dreams* and he wishes to maintain
a clear distinction between reality and dreams. Yet it isn't clear
that his *dreams* aren't his reality. In fact, as Arthur tells
Ariadne: "You must have noticed by now how much time Cobb
spends doing things he says never to do," Cobb's dreams *have
already* become his reality. In his dreams, Mal is still *alive*.

Furthermore, the story he tells himself takes on a life of its
own and evolves in ways that he doesn't fully control. His *subconscious* succeeds in contaminating the narrative, as is exem-
plified when a train almost annihilates Cobb and Ariadne in
the first level of Fischer's inception. Dreams are like stories;
but the danger in every story is to *believe* in something that
could threaten your existence.

Stories are tools that allow us to acquire knowledge about
the world, but this knowledge is built on unstable ground that
can, at any moment, tremble beneath our feet. To *know* is also
to believe, and you have to assume the consequences of your
choices. Cobb chooses to go to his children and we're left alone
watching the spinning, wobbling top.

At this point the top is no longer Cobb's totem. It's now *our*
totem for the reality of the narrative. But how can we assume
that the top is what's real? The only thing the spinning top
reveals is an *interpretation* of a fact, not a fact itself, something
that's made unsettlingly clear when the movie ends. There is
no fact of the matter as to the fate of the top (or of Cobb), there
is only our interpretation, at once exhilarating, frustrating, terrifying, and profound.

12
Butterfly and Spinning Top

Hiu M. Chan

At the end of the nineteenth century, Freud tried to understand the unconscious mind by interpreting the meaning of dreams and thus showing the way dreams relate to reality. Daoist philosophy, on the other hand, suggests that there's no such division between dreams and reality. According to Zhuangzi, someone who dreams doesn't know he's dreaming. The indistinct border between what's real and what's not is the key to the Daoist concept of dreams.

Christopher Nolan once revealed in an interview: "My interest in dreams comes from this notion of realizing that when you dream you create the world that you are perceiving" (*Inception: The Shooting Script*, p. 8). Nolan's idea of "creating" a world in dreams is crucial to the plot of *Inception*: it's a movie about being able to create a world in the subconscious. The word "create" determines a degree of consciousness—the intention to separate dream from reality and to have control over the dream world. However, in Daoism, dream and reality are difficult to distinguish and, as a consequence, there is no such impulse to separate these two phenomena.

Inception fits the mold of the post-classical Hollywood narrative film which uses dreams as parts of its story line. According to Thomas Elsaesser and Warren Buckland, post-classical cinema maintains the traditional patterns of narrative and style of classical cinema, but also contains a playful knowingness. While *Inception* follows a classical narrative structure, Nolan also introduces an element of playfulness through multi-layered dreams and through an ambiguous ending. While this playfulness challenges our perception of the film, the Daoist philosophy of dreaming gives us an alternative way of understanding *Inception*'s narrative structure.

Dream in Daoism

Zhuangzi (369 B.C.–286 B.C.) was an ancient Chinese philosopher famous for his contribution to the development of Daoist philosophy. In his works, Zhuangzi writes extensively about dreams, the best known of which is 'the butterfly dream'. Here's my translation of 'the butterfly dream':

> Zhuang Zhou (Zhuangzi's real name) once dreamt of a butterfly, a butterfly fluttering and flying around happily. For a while, he forgot that he was Zhuang Zhou. Suddenly, he awoke and there he was, unmistakably Zhuang Zhou. He did not remember whether he was Zhuang Zhou dreaming of a butterfly or if he was a butterfly dreaming to be Zhuang Zhou. However, there must be a distinction between Zhuang Zhou and the butterfly. [How can this be explained?] This must be the transformation and unity of things in nature. [He was himself and at the same time the butterfly.]

Zhuangzi's 'butterfly dream' revolves around three main ideas: 1. the forgettable self-being; it is through dreaming that your own existence in reality can be forgotten by being transformed into another existence; 2. dream as life and life as dream; 3. the idea of transformation and unity.

These three ideas come from the profound attitude that Zhuangzi held towards reality. To Zhuangzi, reality is false. Instead of fighting against the false in order to obtain individual freedom within reality, Zhuangzi chooses to escape from reality through spiritual imagination. The free world is beyond reality and beyond dreams, in a realm where 'I' no longer exist as an individual but as a part of the *whole* (nature). It does not matter if Zhuangzi's being defines reality or if the butterfly's being defines dreams; what matters is that Zhuangzi and the butterfly are united at the end.

Through the experience of unity, we learn to let go, to forget and to go with the flow. We learn to accept that both reality and dreams are outside of our control. To think of dreams in Daoism is a way of practicing the Dao; it's a mediation enabling us to experience the transformable nature of things. It is a "Way" that enables spiritual imagination. This understanding of dreams differs from traditional Western ideas. The Indian philosopher Radhakrishnan once wrote that "we have in the West the realism of the men of action; in the East we have the sensitivity of the artist and imagination of the creative dreamer" ("Dreams in Buddhism and Western Aesthetics," p. 65). According to Thorsten Botz-Bornstein, the Western concept of dreams makes a stable link between dream and reality.

Western theorists have often objectified dreams in order to interpret their meanings from the point of view of a non-dreaming status (p. 67). In traditional western psychoanalysis, for example, dreams are interpreted through signs. Semiotics and structuralist film theory also adapt the code of dreams in order to establish a meaningful reading of movies. Dudley Andrew has explained that "movies are now thought to be a specific melange or system of codes of meaning whose elements and interrelations could be detailed" (*Concepts in Film Theory*, p. 57). Through analyzing the various signs, we are able to uncover the underlying unconscious meaning of movies.

If we read *Inception* from a semiotic perspective, the spinning top that Cobb uses to remind himself whether he's in reality or dreaming is objectified. If it keeps spinning, this *means* that he's in a dream. In other words, the spinning top defines the status of dreaming, it is an object, a symbol. However, if we think of dreams from a Daoist perspective, the spinning top has no specific meaning. If it ever had one, this would have been exactly the same meaning that it has in reality: a spinning top.

The butterfly in Zhuangzi's dream had never been defined as anything else; it was merely the existence of a butterfly, just like any other butterfly in real life. In *Inception*, on the other hand, the spinning top is supposed to mean something—it signifies the status of dreaming and this meaning is crucial to its narrative logic.

Zhuangzi's Dream versus the Story of *Inception*

If Zhuangzi's 'butterfly dream' invokes three meanings (the forgettable self-being; dream as life—life as dream; transformation and unity), then the "dreams" in *Inception* are exactly the opposite. In *Inception*, the self-being hasn't been forgotten but is constantly highlighted; there's a clear division between dream and reality, or at least an intention to separate them. There is no transformation and certainly no unity.

The Non-forgettable Self

Cobb has never forgotten his self-being. Cobb's existence is central to the story. He and his partner Arthur illegally enter their targets' subconscious in order to extract valuable information by using a "dream within a dream" strategy. Being able to "enter" someone's dream is a proof of self-existence. The person who enters the dream needs to remember who she is and what she wants. Cobb plans his actions before entering a dream, and he even plans the dreams themselves in order to achieve his goals.

On the other hand, when Zhuangzi was dreaming of a butterfly flying around, he didn't expect that he would be turned into a butterfly in his dream. What happened did so by accident; it was unpredictable. This is precisely how he managed to forget his Self. Cobb's self-being, on the other hand, cannot be forgotten because he has to function within his missions. In a word, Cobb breaks into *minds* instead of *dreams*.

Moreover, his self-being is also highlighted across the narrative through his personal trauma. Cobb's wife Mal was involved in his inception experiments. She struggles to tell apart her dreams and reality and eventually commits suicide. Mal's death became Cobb's trauma. His guilt and sorrow towards his wife's death comes to determine his actions, behaviors, and consciousness. This becomes evident through flashbacks such as Cobb's memories of Mal which appear in the film.

Although Cobb's trauma isn't fully revealed until the second half of the film, the entire inception project had been sparked off by his trauma. It is central to the story. Being charged with Mal's death, Cobb is exiled from his home and children. Meanwhile, a rich business man, Saito, promises to help Cobb to return home on the condition that Cobb accepts the inception assignment. This project is unlike any of the others, for it requires Cobb and his team to enter a three-layered, shared dream with Robert Fischer as the target. It's a risky assignment. According to Cobb, the deeper you enter into a dream, the more likely you are to lose your grip on reality.

How can you know whether you're dreaming or not? Zhuangzi said that you don't know that you're dreaming until you awake from a dream. However, dream and reality are not opposed to each other in the form of black and white. Once you wake up from a dream, there's a bigger dream: life. You believe yourself to be awake, but the biggest dream is actually reality. It is in reality where people get lost, confused, and trapped.

In Zhuangzi's understanding, dreams don't trap people; on the contrary, dreams allow people to escape from their fragile reality, to forget their self-being as well as their problems. In contrast, Cobb believes that people get trapped in dreams, somewhere deep down in their subconscious. Therefore, the self must not be forgotten.

How can we not forget ourselves when dreaming? Unlike the world that Zhuangzi used to live in, the world of *Inception* is full of advanced technology. Via these technologies, Cobb and his teammates are able to control dreams and to remember their self-existence by separating dreams from reality.

Dreams as Narrative

What defines a dream? Was Zhuangzi dreaming while being a butterfly or was the butterfly dreaming while being Zhuangzi? The division between reality and dream is unclear. Marc Chagall, in his 1924 painting "The Dream, or the Rabbit" presents a similar problem. Is the rabbit dreaming of carrying a person, or is the person dreaming of being carried by a big rabbit? There is no clear answer to either question.

The Dream, or the Rabbit, 1924, Marc Chagall

According to Zhuangzi and Chagall's painting, dreams are as real as reality; there's no division between the two. In contrast, in *Inception*, dreams and reality are fundamentally separated. In order to maintain their self-being, Cobb and his teammates need to control dreams from the outside. How can a dream be programmed? This can be done through science and technology as is shown by Cobb and his team in the film (though, in fact, Nolan doesn't show us very much of it: all we learn is that we need a drop of liquid and to press a certain button). In the end, the dream becomes a computer program. Every single element within the dream is translated into symbol, number, and code.

How can a dream be programmed within a film? Nolan achieves this through narrative: the programmed dreams are revealed through a linear narrative structure. In the film, reality and dreams can be told apart. Audiences are also reminded via codes of the particular dream-layer that they are watching. Christian Metz developed an understanding of the psychoanalytic narrative as a body of codes through which the symptomatic meaning of the film can be clarified. In dreams and fantasies, the code or the language are manifestations of the unconscious mind which can be signified by films. The dreams in *Inception* are also coded, but the difference is that these codes define the dreams themselves. The plot of *Inception* is structured by four layers of dreams. As the dream goes deeper, the narrative simultaneously progresses. The following figure presents the progression of the story line.

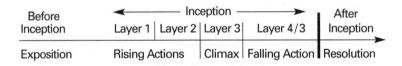

Figure 12.1. Structure of Narrative and "Dreams"

The idea of multi-layered dreams might confuse our perception of the plot. However, at the same time, the narrative structure follows a classical model. If we break down the narrative of *Inception*, its logic turns out to be quite simple. The figure above represents an understanding of its structure. The numbers of dream layers are not really important, what matters is that all the characters have problems to solve. This means:

Exposition (reality): Cobb needs the inception project in order to return home.

Rising action (dream layers 1–2): In the first layer of the dream, problems appear: Saito is injured and the team is attacked by Fischer's militarized subconscious projections. These problems continue within the second layer. The only way to solve them is to keep going forward (that is, downward).

Climax (dream layer 3): In the third layer Fischer gets shot before he manages to identify his father's secret. Fischer is unconscious. What he needs to find out, and also what the team needs to implant in his mind, is the idea of his father's wish of Fischer setting up his own business. Meanwhile, Saito is also unconscious. Another layer is needed to bring Fischer and Saito back to the third layer.

Falling action (dream layers 3–4): The falling action of the narrative crosses somewhere between layers 3 and 4. Fischer is brought back from the fourth to the third layer by Ariadne. He opens the safe and finds the secret. Back in layer 4, Cobb "wakes" up Saito, and they both return to reality.

Resolution (reality): The mission is completed. Cobb reunites with his children in America.

The Codes

In *Inception*, the dream within a dream model is not complicated. The story is almost linear and it contains the three basic narrative elements: the beginning (exposition), the middle (rising action, climax, falling action) and the end (resolution).

Because the movie depends on such a structure, the dreams cannot be random. They need to be controlled and constructed. The more control the characters have, the more obvious becomes the division between dream and reality; and the clearer becomes the progression of the narrative. Therefore, codes such as motifs and cues in the movie are used to mark out the different layers of dreams as well as the process of the narrative progression.

Motif 1: The Dream Machine. The dream machine appears before the team enters each dream layer. In the movie, the machine enables the team to enter a shared dream by connecting the members with wires. The wires tie the protagonists together within the same narrative (they are all working on the same mission).

The dream machine is also used as a reminder to mark the beginning of each new dream layer. The machine becomes crucial. Without the machine, the team cannot enter a dream, and the narrative cannot be continued. Because of the dream machine's repetitive appearance in the movie, this is how the audience knows exactly when he's watching a new layer of dream (a new section of the narrative).

Motif 2: The Spinning Top. Cobb's personal trauma causes him to confuse dreams and reality. As the hero of the molvie, it's his responsibility to narrate a coherent story. Separating dreams from reality is therefore important for making sense of the story development. The narrative only moves forward when the dream goes downwards.

The progression of the narrative follows the order of dream layers as explained in Figure 12.1. Layer 1 marks the beginning of the inception project and layer 4/3 marks the end of it. A spinning top is used for Cobb himself and also for the audience to distinguish dreams from reality. While the top keeps spinning, Cobb is in a dream; when it stops, he's in reality.

In the fourth layer, Cobb needs to bring Saito back to consciousness. Both Cobb and Saito are so deep down in the dream structure that they almost forget that they are dreaming. Saito spins the top, and it continuously spins. Only then do they realize that they need to return to reality, to approve the agreement which allows Cobb to return home. The top appears in the film several times before the actual inception project. We remember what the top means to Cobb (and to us).

Motif 3: Cobb's Children. Images of Cobb's children also appear to be a narrative motif to remind the audience that Cobb is dreaming. Cobb's children appear in his dreams because of his wish to reunite with them. However, in Cobb's dreams, we never see the children's faces. The image of the faceless children becomes a sign of Cobb's dreaming status. The only time we see the children's faces, is in reality when Cobb returns home after the inception mission.

Apart from the use of certain motifs there are also other codes. Certain cues are used to separate dreams from reality, as well as to distinguish different dream-layers in the narrative.

Cue 1: Location and Weather. Different locations keep reality and the multi-layered dreams separated. The following table explains how different locations work as cues:

Reality before inception	airplane
Layer 1	van
Layer 2	hotel
Layer 3	the complex tower (Browning's secret base)
Layer 4	beach, Saito's castle
Reality after inception	airplane, airport

The different locations allow the multi-layered dreams to be linked together as a narrative. At the same time, within the inception project, Cobb reveals that the fact of building different places within each layer can help the team to remember their mission process. The dreams need to be imbedded in a structure, just like the narrative.

Also, the weather is used as a cue in the film. Almost every layer has its own unique weather so that it becomes a cue:

Reality just before the inception takes place	indoors (airplane)
Layer 1	outdoors, raining
Layer 2	indoors (hotel)
Layer 3	outdoors, snow
Layer 4	mostly indoors
Reality after inception	indoors (airplane)

Cue 2: Special Effects. If this isn't obvious enough, there are computer-generated special effects helping to make sense of the structure. In dreams you can create almost everything, even things that don't exist in reality, Cobb explains. He also teaches Ariadne how to build a dream by showing her that the world can be manipulated by the mind. Scenes like collapsing buildings, curving streets, frozen time, and so on are materialized by special effects in order to present the idea of a programmed dream. There's a difference between reality and dream. Dreams (in Cobb's sense) are changeable, but reality isn't. That is why, after a while, Cobb admits: "Reality wasn't enough for me then."

Cue 3: Crosscutting. If we put the four layers dreams into a timeline, each dream layer is structured on top of the next layer. The events within each layer are taking place simultaneously. The figure below presents this idea.

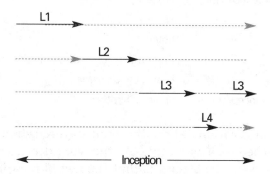

Figure 12.2. The Timeline of Dreams

To remind the audience that every layer of dream is taking place at the same time, the film uses crosscutting as a cue. From time to time, the film cuts scenes between different dream layers. This editing enables us to see what is happening in a different layer of dream. The time gap (the lines in Figure 12.2) that each layer has between the beginning and the end of the mission is thus explained and presented through the cross cutting.

Structure versus Structurelessness

The difference between Zhuangzi's dream and the dream in *Inception* is that the former is unstructured and the latter is structured. By using the structureless concept of the dream, Daoism allows us to see the structured dreams in *Inception* more clearly.

The narrative motivation in *Inception* can be understood through the model of reality/4 dreams/reality. Reality marks the beginning and the end. The multi-layered dreams in the middle represent the time when its narrative develops. Zhuangzi however, does not see any reason to separate dreams from reality. When he dreamt he was a butterfly flying happily around, it was merely his own imagination that created this dream. He was himself and at the same time the butterfly.

Flying as a butterfly is his own experience, in no way different from the experiences he has in his real life. Through his experience of flying as a butterfly he forgot his self-being, he really *became* that butterfly! In this sense, dream is just another experience of life. In *Inception*, on the other hand, dreams need to be marked out because of their importance to the narrative structure. Why can't Cobb transform into a butterfly as Zhuangzi did? Because he's the hero of the story, he has a mission to fulfill, and a goal to reach!

Who's dreaming in *Inception*? I am not sure if the protagonists are dreaming at all. They're not dreamers but narrators. *Inception* is not *about* dreams, but about a story *of* dreams that needs to be carefully controlled at all times as the story needs to make sense. However, the movie makes sense as a narrative structure only on the surface. If we look into the structured dreams in detail, there are many unexplained questions concerning how dreams can actually be structured.

All the team members need to be connected to the dream machine in order to share the same dream. However, within layer 3, when Cobb and Ariadne enter to layer 4 to save Saito and Fischer, how can four of them enter the same dream if they are not connected together with wires? (Cobb and Ariadne simply connect themselves with the machine but not with Saito and Fischer).

How does the team decide not to wake up when the "kicks" happen? In layer 4, why does Saito look so much older than Cobb, considering they are both in the same layer of dream? Why can't they save Saito in the same way they save Fischer? How did Cobb and Saito wake up at the end if they have missed the previous two "kicks"?

Presenting dreams in film through narrative does not reveal the nature of dream, especially within a classic narrative model. Dream cannot break free as long as it is subordinated to a structure. Coded dreams in movies are "meaningful," which is the reason why critics are able to investigate their meanings via these codes. We want to make the dream mean something because it exists in order to mean something. In that sense, the airplane means reality, the spinning top means dreams, the airport means reality, and people floating in the air means dreams.

In *Inception* both reality and dream have a meaning of their own each time we encounter them. In Daoism, on the other hand, meanings are not so important. The Daoist philosopher Laozi once wrote about the Daoist spirit:

> To know you do not know is the best. To pretend to know when you do not know is a disease. Only when one recognizes this disease as a disease can one be free from the disease. (Stepaniants, *Introduction to Eastern Thought*, p. 192)

Laozi's attitude overlaps with Zhuangzi's: Dreams are not supposed to mean anything, they are simply fragmentary and random experiences. Can these fragmentary dreams be presented in movies at all? The Russian director Andrei Tarkovsky has shown that this is possible. For Tarkovsky, as Botz-Bornstein puts it, "dreams take place in an intermediary domain of abstractness and concreteness, and dreamlike expressions represent neither the 'real' nor do they symbolize the 'unreal' but remain in the domain of the 'improbable' between symbolization, representation and *verfremdete* (alienated) expressions." Dreams "should not be introduced as 'technical' time shifts destined" (*Films and Dreams*, p. x).

Compared to the abstraction and distortion of time as it appears in the movies of Tarkovsky, the timeline of *Inception* is set up systematically in order to produce a coherent storyline (see Figure 12.1). Norman N. Holland has coined two terms, 'dream explaining' and 'dream worshiping' (*The Dream and the Text*). *Inception* is 'dream explaining', which aims to give meanings and values to dreams. In the opposite conception, Tarkovsky's films are 'dream worshipping'; they float as dreams themselves do, meaninglessly. In Tarkovsky's movie, *The Mirror* (1975), the images of memories, news footages and events simply co-exist like reflections in water, as a *whole*. Like the philosophers of Daoism, Tarkovsky believes that dreams don't need any explanation.

The Lack of the Whole

The idea of the *whole* is central not only to Daoism but to most Eastern philosophies. Laozi explains:

Dao produced the One. The One produced the Two. The Two produced the Three. And the Three produced the Ten Thousand things. The Ten Thousand things carry the *yin* and embrace the *yang*, and through the blending of the material force (*qi*), they achieve harmony. (*Introduction to Eastern Thought*, p. 191)

In Zhuangzi's 'butterfly dream', the harmony of the *whole* was also revealed through the transformation of him and the butterfly. There's no such harmony in *Inception*. There is only a battle between reality and dreams. Reality represents the good (it enables Cobb to return home and to reunite with his children), while dreams represent the bad (Mal's behavior in dreams). The conflict between reality and dreams creates its narrative. Cobb has to choose one of them.

At the end of the film, Cobb chooses the good, which is reality. However, the question is: Why can dreams and reality in *Inception* not unite and become a *whole* in the way proposed by Zhuangzi? Cobb returns to his children in reality, but does that mean that now everything will be all right? Is this the end? If we insist that *Inception* is *about* dreams, then we have to conclude that Cobb is just beginning to dream at the moment he returns home.

In Daoism, the biggest dream is reality. One needs to realize this in order to be truly awake. Furthermore, a "true person" (which means "The Master" in Daoism) no longer dreams because dreams and reality unite as a *whole* in his mind. In *Inception*, on the other hand, the separation of dreams and reality leads to a *lack* of the sense of the whole.

The End?

In *Inception*, the "dreams" are not dreams. The "dreams" are rather just another experiment of a *meta-space* narrative that plays with the idea of the mind in a relatively superficial fashion.

Nolan first established this idea in his short movie *Doodlebug* (2003), in which a man tries to kill a bug in his room. Next we see another, bigger version of this person who tries to kill the smaller version of him. This narrative is repeated three times in the movie. The unlimited expansion creates different layers as well as a *meta-space* for narration.

The numbering of layers is not crucial here, but the distinction between each layer certainly is (each character is bigger/smaller than the next character). The narrative progresses through the distinction between each layer. If all layers were identical to each other, there wouldn't be any progressions within the narrative.

Meta-space narratives require a notable change for progression. This space exists in *Doodlebug* as well as in *Inception* (borders between dreams or borders between dreams and reality) while in the Daoist concept of the *whole*, there are no such layers. A dream within a dream is one dream, and reality is also a dream. Changes shouldn't be notable while we're dreaming. Everything should stay on the same level even though the dream itself processes towards deeper and deeper layers. In Figure 12.3, the circle on the left presents the Daoist idea of dream and reality as a whole. The multi-layered circle on the right presents the idea of a *meta-space* narrative which creates certain patterns and claims to be a configuration of dreams:

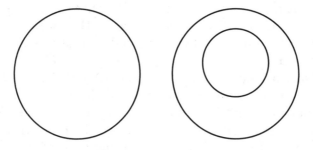

Figure 12.3. Dreams and Meta-space / Meta-level Narratives

The Daoist understanding of dreams and nature might not be universal. However, films that contain classical or post-classical models somehow are. Like many other Hollywood productions, *Inception* is a worldwide success.

Who's dreaming? I suppose everyone is.

Level 4

The
Most Resilient
Parasite

13
Dream Bigger, Darling

JOSHUA RICHARDSON AND ORA MCWILLIAMS

Over the summer of 2010, movie theaters across the entire world played host to a detailed philosophical debate. The source of contention was *Inception*, a movie sometimes referred to by its fans as an existential heist film. The uninformed spectator might be forgiven for wondering what the big deal was. What makes *Inception* a movie that lends itself to this kind of framing, as opposed to, say, *The Expendables*?

In *Inception*, we see philosophy and film intertwined to the point of inseparability; therefore, no understanding of the film can be complete without examining it both as a movie and as philosophy. Neglecting either side of the equation runs the risk of creating a false picture of the film.

But how can we examine a work as two things at once and maintain the balance between them? Well, just as the characters of *Inception* dive through the levels of the human mind to accomplish their seemingly impossible mission, we're going to dive through the levels of meaning in the movie itself.

Reality—the World of *Inception*

I thought the dream space would be about the visual. But it's about the feel of it.

—ARIADNE

During the primary heist sequence, the first layer of the film that the viewer experiences is that of reality. This layer presents the physical facts of the filmic world in itself. The combined effect of these various physical facts is to create a set of beliefs about the world, or what is sometimes referred to as an "ideology." Since *Inception* is a film about reality, we can say that its ideology is an ideology of reality itself.

The idea of touch is important to the film, as is evidenced by the opening scene. The film begins with Leonardo DiCaprio's character, Cobb, being jolted "awake" by the touch of the cold ocean. The viewer later learns that this is not reality, but a kind of dream referred to as "Limbo," in which another character has been lost for decades of subjective time. This scene is echoed later when Cobb's wife, Mal, looking up on the seashore; a voiceover from Cobb says, "We woke up on the shores of our subconscious, we lost sight of what was real."

The beach motif recurs again at the end of the film when Fischer and his projection emerge from the van and wash up on the rainy beach. The thread throughout these segments is the untrustworthy nature of strong sensation; several characters participate in these beach experiences, but none of them are feeling something objectively real.

An important claim made by the movie is that sensory experiences of various types are potentially universal; sights, sounds, and touch are shared between various characters, indicating a world that can be experienced by all of its inhabitants. An example of this occurs when Ariadne enters Cobb's dream of the hotel room and steps on the champagne flute on her way in the door, the same way Cobb did in the flashback to the original "real," event. The experience is shared between the characters across space and time through the dream world.

The exposition of the characters within the movie suggests that persons can travel seamlessly between the dream world and the real world, through a method referred to in the film as "shared dreaming." This process functions similarly to a computer network, in that information from the dream is shared into the various users and routed through a hub, a dream machine. The characters can exchange experiences in the same way someone would distribute a music file, with the software used to read that experience being the experiential realm of the dream world.

René Descartes thought about the idea of sensory experience as it relates to dreaming. He concluded that empirical evidence (evidence gleaned from observation and experience) was largely unreliable. In his thought experiment, he examined a piece of wax that had been solid and was then melted and reformed ("Meditations on the First Philosophy"). In each instance, his sensory perception of the wax seemed to inform him what he expected to perceive. The empirical data, what we see and feel, would lead us to believe that we're dealing with different objects, but in fact all three states were merely different forms of the same wax. So the evidence of our senses may be unreliable.

There's at least one sensation that the characters can trust, that of falling. David Hume stated that "all our reasonings concern cause and effect as derived from nothing but custom; and that belief is more properly an act of the sensitive, than a cognitive part of our natures." This is illustrated in the movie when the characters explain that the sensation of falling is what can bring them out of the induced dream state; it's the combination of the sensation and the belief that there's an effect that allows this escape. The characters relate this to each other through their dialogue; these conversations become a vehicle for the idea to become first social custom, then the own internalized belief of the characters as well.

These sensory experiences, although not perceived in the "real world" of our waking lives, become the basis for beliefs within the dreams in a manner similar to how we come to understand the real external world. The sensation of falling is the experience that wakes the dreamer. This first occurs in the movie after Cobb gets kicked into a tub of water during the double-dream extraction attempt; the effort to wake him up becomes integrated into the second-layer dream and manifests as water rushing into the fictional home of Saito. Another example happens during the revolution dream; slapping Cobb in the fake 'real world' throws him backwards in the second-layer dream world.

Throughout the movie, the text stipulates that sensory perception cannot be trusted. During its multiple extended dream sequences, sensory input from previous layers becomes integrated into the new layer as if it were a part of that layer. For example, the van dodging gunshots in the "car chase layer" translates into earthquakes in the "hotel layer." This is much like when someone calling a sleeper's name becomes integrated into the dream they are having, leading to the dreamer imagining a character calling their name in the dream. Knowing this, we realize that the sensory input that we receive within the dream cannot be trusted.

Pain, an extreme variant of touch, plays a vital role in the movie's events. Throughout the film, the sensation of pain and death is what actually returns the characters to the real world. In the dream world Cobb makes the point, "And a face full of glass hurts like hell, doesn't it? While we're in it, it's real." The characters in the dream world can perceive pain, but are awakened by death. This is reinforced when Mal states, "Killing him will only wake him up. But pain, pain is in the mind."

Sociologist Erving Goffman speaks of this idea of being "shocked" into different worlds. The dreamer deals with both a shock in and out of the dream world because there is no frame mechanism, such as a curtain call, to inform the dreamer they are in the dream. Cobb and Ariadne discuss this in the café scene when Cobb asks Ariadne to remember how they got there. And she cannot. When Goffman spoke of being shocked into those worlds there are moments of disorientation when the dreamer is unsure of reality. In *Inception* the characters remain constantly unsure of their reality because sensory perception is unreliable.

Cobb makes the point that when layering dreams, it's difficult to tell whether we're back in reality, or trapped in a dream state. Each of the characters has their "totem," a personal object which they use to ground themselves and test reality. The main characters are instructed to make it a point to know the weight and feel of these totems in order to "know" if they are in reality. Cobb's totem is a top, Ariadne's a chess piece; other characters have poker chips or dice. The characters are charged with assuring that they do not share knowledge of their totem with anyone to ensure that it cannot be forged in the dream world.

All of the totems are related to games. The key is in the flashback to Mal and Cobb's time together in limbo, when her totem is locked in the safe, hidden inside a doll house. By putting her totem there, she locks away the key to her reality. Reality is a game to be manipulated and toyed with in the inception-dream world; Mal chooses not to play, and instead picks a reality. Plato examined this in the allegory of the cave.

In this allegory, soldiers can only know the reality they can immediately see: shadows against a wall. This is the only world these soldiers know. When they're exposed to actual reality there is uncertainty. Some may even choose to return to the old reality of shadows, as Mal does.

With further reference to the totems as well, all the pieces are broken (or perverted) in some way. Cobb's top won't stop spinning, Ariadne's chess piece has a hole in it, Arthur's die is loaded, and Eames's poker chip cannot be wagered. The broken-ness of the game pieces makes them unique, but since the totems represent the characters it marks them as broken people. The broken-ness of Cobb is apparent in his loss of Mal, his loss of home, and his alienation from reality. The emptiness of the rest of the other characters is not really examined with any depth. However, although they are the protagonists and doing the inception for the "right" reasons, they are still willing criminals, which separates them out from social norms.

For Saito in the extraction heist, memories of his familiar surroundings work the same as the totems. Saito, thrown by Cobb to the carpeting, speaks of how much he hates that rug. However, his familiarity with the texture of the material, after he touches it, allows him to discern that he is still dreaming. The dreamer has created the wrong texture, polyester instead of wool. The use of touch instantly tips Saito off to the fact he is in yet another dream.

All this focus on sensory data and tactility is comforting—it provides us with the idea that there is something that can be experienced external to ourselves. However, not all philosophers would agree with that. There has been a long tradition of doubt as to the reality of the outside world in philosophical writings, and one of the schools of thought to address it most directly is the one most often name-checked in reference to *Inception*—existentialism.

The First Dream—The Existential Heist

The subconscious is ruled by emotion not reason.

—COBB

The car chase dream sequence, during the attempt at performing inception on Fischer, connects the experience of the film with existentialism and pragmatism. The sense of reality within this dream is marked by the obstruction of a traffic jam. The characters push and pull in many different directions, and are even hit by a train, before truth can be revealed, through the faith that the fall will jolt them back into reality.

The scene begins with the characters winding their way through traffic and discussing the heist. As they progress further, the two cars get caught in traffic jams. Their attempt to accomplish their mission is interrupted; a group of assailants generated by Fischer's subconscious has located the team and is attacking them. Not a typical commute to work! At the end of the car chase the characters mull over the situation, contemplating how various instances of incompetence and secretiveness have brought them to this point.

Cobb makes his existentialist leanings known when he tells the group: "Downwards is the only way forwards. We have to carry on." Cobb supports action, rather than inaction. Saito's shooting further motivates the action; it's established in this layer that the heavy sedation would not allow the dreamer to wake up upon death, leaving the victim to fall into an interminable Limbo state. In this layer the film comes more in line to traditional film thinking about death in dreams. One character suggests that he will just wait out the dream. Cobb tells him that's not possible. Inactivity is not an option, because the army will get the team.

In life there is so much waiting. Waiting. Waiting. In existentialist playwright Samuel Beckett's *Waiting for Godot*, the two main characters are waiting for a third character; the audience watches as the two play games, bicker, and go about a bizarre version of a daily routine. They stress the phrase over and over that they are "waiting for Godot," and yet, ultimately, Godot never shows. The two characters of the play occupy a limbo like the one that Cobb describes to Saito after he's wounded, becoming "an old man filled with regrets, waiting to die alone."

Existentialist Karl Jaspers considers that being human is taking in the breath of existence and knowing our place within that existence. "We are indeed truly human only to the extent that we always grasp what is nearest at hand, according to the standard of ideals that have become lucid up to that moment" ("Philosophy of Existence," p. 139). Jaspers also comes up with the idea that being alone allows us to notice the nothingness and "makes existence volatile" (p. 139). As a result when Cobb describes Limbo he describes it as fragments and loneliness. Cobb and Saito describe it as dying as old men alone and full of regret. Jaspers's way out of the despair is through encounters with someone else, and this is *Inception*'s way out of limbo too.

Dialogue reveals that Fischer was most likely trained to watch for extractors, but was never trained in how to harness his dreams properly. Since he sends an army after the incursion of the inception crew, Fischer subconsciously knows he's dreaming. Yet, he never lets himself leave the "dream world." The dreamer is taken in by the ruses of Cobb's team. This is evidenced by the fact that the dreamer never creates total chaos within the dream; order stays in effect throughout the entire dream period. The only hint of chaos is that which Cobb brings into the dream, through the inclusion of a freight train and his dead wife Mal.

When the characters are about to wrap their mission and need to finish their tasks, their handlers play music. American philosopher Charles Sanders Peirce spoke of two elements of consciousness that can be compared to musical composition. The composition is made up of notes and "air" or pauses. He spoke of sensation as a "continuity of consciousness," where the notes need the pauses, and the pauses need the notes, to create a perception of time. Peirce suggested that one could play a prolonged note continuously for an hour or a day, but without a pause (or change) the past is imperceptible. In the film, this passage of time is similarly marked by the passengers of the car slowly inching over the cliff. The perception is prolonged, while in other dream layers the passage of time continues with changes.

In the pharmacy scene, the movie claims that excessive dependence on the dream-sharing technology creates a situation in which people can no longer dream without machine aid. In that scene, the elderly man watching over the sleepers in the "pharmacy" states, "they come to be *woken* up . . . the dream has become their reality. . . . Who are you to say otherwise?" The dream IS reality. This is the pragmatics of the dream. The pharmacy's customers, like Mal, find the dream state more fulfilling and ultimately more "real" than their day-by-day existences, just like for many unfortunate souls who choose to lose themselves in fictional worlds rather than dealing with their problems. The existentialist and the pragmatist would have to disagree with this choice; the existentialist would wish you to encounter the real world, whereas to the pragmatist, if the dream world functions in the same way, the distinction becomes academic.

Cobb is ideologically an existentialist. He prefers action to inaction, rejecting the static world of the perpetual dreamers for the chance to see his children again in the real world. Although he enjoys spending some time in the deep dream of limbo with his wife, in the end, he needs to escape, so he can return to having real experiences. Cobb says, "It's not so bad at first, being gods. The problem is knowing that it's not real. It became impossible for me to live like that."

The previous two lines about reality and staying in the dream space also show the parallels of *Inception* with other movies such as *The Matrix* and *Vanilla Sky*. The difference is that *Inception* inverts the idea. The lesson of the dreamers in the pharmacy is the ambiguous lesson that Cobb learns at the end. One interpretation is that Cobb enters Limbo and experiences the life that has invaded his dreams; the presence of his children makes it close enough to the real thing. In this instance, Cobb is like Cypher from *The Matrix* when he eats the steak, stating "You know, I know this steak doesn't exist. I know that when I put it in my mouth, the Matrix is telling my brain that it is juicy and delicious. After nine years, you know what I realize? Ignorance is bliss." Both of the characters are aware of their placement in their respective 'dream machines' and enjoy their respective pleasures. Tom Cruise's character in *Vanilla Sky* is offered the opportunity to stay in the simulation and remain happy, but he turns it down in favor of the real-world experience.

The Second Dream—Film Theory

In modern society, many lessons about the world are given to us without our noticing. One such lesson is how to make sense of movies. Although few people would view themselves as conversant in film theory, most citizens of industrial societies in the twenty-first century have a vast, internalized set of perceptual filters that allow them to stare at flickering images on a white sheet and understand them as representing events.

This body of knowledge is generated not through deliberate effort, but rather through the process of being exposed to moving images from a young age.

This presents a problem to film theorists attempting an understanding of all the various things that go to make up a movie. How can we come to understand something so innately tied to ways of unconscious perception? Clearly, the method of doing so is tied to our distance from the movie in question. It's easier to step back from some films than others. *Inception* is an excellent case study, as its structure is highly reflexive—that is, it serves as its own commentary on the medium of film.

The reflexivity is reflected in *Inception* repeatedly, in a variety of forms. The first is the narrative flow of the heist setup. During the preparations for the inception attempt, we see members of the group assume various roles, similar to those assumed in the pre-production process. The function of certain team members can be related to production roles. Ariadne, the "architect," functions like a screenwriter, preparing a scenario for the others which to enact. Arthur can be viewed as a producer, working behind the scenes to get all the elements in place to facilitate the team's success. Cobb, the lead man on the job, serves as the director, central to all the events, leading his fellows on their journey. This view of film is quite "auteurist," which is to say that it follows in the tradition of French film theory that ascribes primary responsibility for the artistic content of a film to the singular vision of its director.

Another reflexive element of *Inception* is the use of "paradoxical architecture." The example called out directly in the film is the looping staircase which Arthur and Ariadne practice dream design. The pair walk up a seemingly endless set of stairs, passing the same person repeatedly, which confuses Ariadne. Arthur eventually reveals the truth—a quick camera move shows that they are on an Escher-esque creation, a fact which was hidden in the overhead views we have previously seen the stairs in.

Like Escher's drawings, this sequence relies on visual illusion caused by the fact that what is being observed is actually a flat image. Due to the viewer's experience understanding film and visual images as representative of three-dimensional space, the audience is taken in, perceiving the flat picture plain of the overhead shot of the staircase as representing a normal set of stairs. Only once the camera has flipped is the truth revealed, calling out the artificiality of the environment, and perhaps indicating to the viewer that what is seen can't always be trusted.

The movie's relationship to the passage of time creates a third point of reflexivity. Early on, the dialogue between the team members establishes that time passes at a different rate in various layers of dream, due to increased brain activity. So, in the extended inception sequence that is the film's centerpiece, the action occurs at different rates on different levels of the dreams. This is represented by cuts back and forth between the various layers; however, it's unclear whether the film actually uses an absolute reference of time, as the cuts camouflage the passage of time by omitting portions of actions.

Stephen Prince, writing about a slow-motion sequence in Sam Peckinpah's *The Wild Bunch*, describes how images of two bodies falling are matched even though they could not be occurring simultaneously in the real world: "The editing imposes a false parallel between normal time and decelerated time ("The Aesthetic of Slow-Motion Violence in the Films of Sam Peckinpah," p. 195). In other words, the art of editing can be used to match actions in ways that would not be physically possible. This process relies on the ways of perception that filmgoers have developed over time, a way of understanding images wherein we know that two seemingly disjointed scenes, such as a man getting out of a car and the same man entering a building, can be linked to create a sequence, through the tacit acceptance that the two things are linked, that the film does not need to show us every detail of every action of its subjects. In *Inception*, we see a direct acknowledgment of this process through the temporal discontinuity of the multiple layers.

So we can easily view *Inception* as a movie about movies. However, such a view creates yet more questions—what do movies themselves signify? Does the film form have a correspondence to anything in human experience?

The Third Dream—Dreaming Itself

Film is a medium frequently associated with dreaming. Edward Small, in *Direct Theory*, points out the reliance of experimental cinema on internal and dreamlike images as a characteristic of the form. While *Inception* is hardly classifiable as an experimental film, it shares an aptitude with the major genre that Small discusses in its connection to dreaming. In what ways does the structure and format of film relate to dreaming?

Two of the concepts we've already looked at, paradoxical architecture and temporal discontinuity, stand out. Paradoxical architecture in the movie works because the image being shown to the audience is two-dimensional; in dreams, it works because the space being dreamed has no physical existence, and therefore needn't correspond to physical laws. Temporal discontinuity is another frequent feature of dreams, referred to in *Inception* as not being able to remember how one has arrived in a situation. Like the characters in a film, the characters of a dream have no existence outside of the medium in which they exist. Nothing precedes the actions occurring therein, and nothing follows it.

The linkage between these two conceits is the notion of unreality. Although both dreams and films have some variety of physical form (as electrochemical brain processes and celluloid frames, respectively) this form has little to do with how they are ascribed significance by those who experience them. The meaning of a movie is found in the viewing of the projected movie by an audience, and the meaning of a dream is found in the way it is experienced by the dreamer. Both dream and film are often said to be interpreted by those who examine them. Meaning is found not in their substance, but rather in the way people think of them.

The Fourth Dream—a Theory of Mind

ARIADNE: Are you destroying those parts of his mind?

COBB: No, of course not. They're just projections.

With dreaming and problems of reality, ultimately it always boils down to one question: phenomenology. Phenomenology is defined by the *Stanford Encyclopedia of Philosophy* as

> the study of 'phenomena'—appearances of things, or things as they appear in our experience, or the ways we experience things, thus the meanings things have in our experience. Phenomenology studies

conscious experience as experienced from the subjective or first person point of view.

In the case of Cobb's dreams, the fact that his children's faces are obscured from him relates to his inability to sustain a relationship with them, due to his exile. Here, the dream world acts as a representative of the meaning of things. Another example from Cobb's dream is Mal's anger at Cobb. Cobb imagines that Mal would be angry at him for planting the idea in her head, and as a result Cobb projects her as bitter and angry at his betrayal. This shows the divergence between Cobb's view of the world and the truth; the film's flashbacks suggest that, before her suicide, Mal was more depressed than angry.

Cobb's sense of reality has become distorted; much like the dream addicts in the pharmacy, he seems, at first, to have decided that the dream world is better than his real life. Within the dreamscape Cobb is able to solely interact with his subjective interpretations of events. He spends much of the film there, chasing ghosts and his past.

Arthur's dream, set in the hotel, serves as a contrasting view. In the movie's opening sequence, Mal (or rather, Cobb's projection of Mal) says "judging by the décor, we're in your mind, aren't we Arthur?" The setting of the first scene, the large house, shows some similarities with the later hotel dream, which is also engineered by Arthur. While Cobb's dreamscapes are filled with violence, self-doubt, and betrayed lovers, Arthur's mind is a calm and orderly place, an otherworldly playground through which he swims effortlessly in response to the shifts of the van in the first dream. Arthur uses the dreams to accomplish a job, but doesn't lose his sense of self in them.

In comparing the different dreamscapes of the two men, we can see that the dream worlds of *Inception* can serve different purposes. To Cobb, the dreams are simultaneously a nightmare and an opportunity to get back what he once had. To Arthur, they're a playground to be negotiated in the course of work. Similarly, dreams can serve different functions to us in the real world. They can be welcome respites, or nightly torture sessions, reviews of past deeds or inspirations for the day ahead. To philosophers, though, they can offer a unique opportunity to compare daily experience against, in an attempt to filter out what we can know and what remains unknowable.

The Kick—Back to 'Reality'

Inception ends with the rapid ascent of its principal cast up through the layers of dream that have been built up during the preceding two hours. This ascension proves tricky, however, as it raises doubts in the viewer as to the veracity of any set of events. After all, the existence of any of those dream layers is no more convincing to the audience than any other; all are flat images flickering in front of sets of eyes. Why should we trust reality, if there's no easy way to distinguish it from illusion and dreams?

René Descartes wrestled with just such concerns in his search for a philosophy based on first principals. In his *Meditations*, he tells us that we cannot trust our perceptions of the outside world, because we have no innate proof that anything beyond ourselves exists. (Although he ultimately concludes that we *can* sensibly know objects). The only thing we know, he says, is that we have some form of existence ("I think therefore I am").

Dreams are an excellent method for pointing out the problems in our persistent belief in the external; Descartes makes this very point in *Meditations*, using the existence of the dream state as a way of showcasing the possible falsity of existence. If Descartes is right and we cannot ever know that anything external to ourselves exists, than the very meaning of reality is up for grabs.

Goffman described dreams as a form of "self-delusion" (*Frame Analysis*, p. 112). The movie ends on an ambiguous note as to whether Cobb forgave himself and gave up the self-delusion. The film folds in on itself and seemingly the characters go about their lives, including Cobb, who is seemingly given absolution. Descartes, Plato, Jaspers, Peirce, Small, Beckett, Prince, and Goffman could argue about the meaning of the top at the end of the film for hours, without ever resolving the question. However, the film allows us the opportunity to explore the projections within our minds and the minds of others.[1]

---

[1] Ora: Thanks to: Rachael Rost, Nikki Trooien-Smith, Jon Seagrass, Micki Dietrich, Dr. Elizabeth Cooke (Creighton), Dr. J.J. Abrams (Creighton). Josh: Thanks to: Dorthea Fronsman-Cecil (for preliminary editing), Chuck Berg (for inspiration), Lisa, and Dylan.

14
Shared Dreams in Virtual Worlds

MATTHEW BROPHY

At the close of *Inception*, Cobb finally walks away from reality, ultimately letting the simulacra of his children salve his broken heart. Increasingly, many people are walking a similar path. Multitudinous dreamscapes tempt the user with a more meaningful, less mundane existence. Such users feel plugging into the shared virtual dream is not dreaming: it is waking up.

Shared dreaming already exists. Not across slumbering minds, but within cyberspace. Computer users jack in, populating worlds created by programming architects. Already, forty-three percent of virtual world "residents" report that they feel as strongly about their virtual community as they feel about the real world. And nearly half believe the events that happen in their computer-created world are as significant as the events of the real world. Over fifty percent of these members log into their virtual lives more than once daily.

What I'm saying is that virtual realities, such as those in computer games, are fantasy worlds much like the dream worlds of *Inception*. Advancing technologies keep on amplifying the siren call of the dream-like fantasy worlds, which become steadily more enticing.

Ultimately, we're all going to be tempted—just as Cobb was tempted—to relinquish reality for a dream.

Do Gamers Dream of Electric Sheep?

Cobb's deceased wife, Mal, challenges him about his supposed reality: "No creeping doubts? Not feeling persecuted, Dom?

Chased around the globe by anonymous corporations and police forces? The way the projections persecute the dreamer?"

Mal is right: does this sound like a normal human life, or does it sound like a dream? But wait, doesn't Cobb's reality sound even more similar to a computer game?

The story of *Inception* matches neither the mundane reality of a normal human life, nor the slapdash surrealism of the slumbering. Organic dreams—existing in one's unconscious—tend to be fantastical and illogical, a chaotic patchwork more akin to an anthology of short stories by some surrealist author. The sustained plotline and action within *Inception* resonate closer to a spy novel: a rogue agent sneaking around the world, always on the run from vague goliath organizations, eluding bland agents tasked to hunt him down, assembling a team for a heist of the century.

If *Inception* as a gamer's "dream" seems far-fetched, take this as initial evidence: COBOL—the ominous corporation hunting Cobb—is the acronym for one of the first computer programming languages: **Co**mmon **B**usiness-**O**riented **L**anguage. COBOL is a computer programming language primarily applied to business, finance, and administrative systems for companies and governments. So Cobb's corporate arch-nemesis is named after a fundamental computer programming language. Coincidence?

Communal Dreamscapes in MMORPGs

Cobb and his crew manifest in shared dreams. The landscape of these dreams are created by an architect. As Cobb's team seeks to implant an idea in Robert Fischer's mind, for instance, the substrate is supposedly the mind of Ariadne.

Yet the notion of "shared dreaming"—occupying another's mind—threatens a metaphysical paradox: How can we occupy one another's dreams? I can't access your mind, and you can't access mine. You're trapped within your own mind, as am I inside mine. It is our "egocentric predicament." I can never know how chocolate tastes to you; I can never know if blue to me is blue to you; I can never even be sure you *are* thinking, as I can only be directly aware of my own consciousness. Thus, the only place we can interact is "out there" in some place beyond the mind.

Perhaps Cobb's crew journey in the "mind" of a computer. Virtual dreamscapes are created by "servers," the substrates that host such popular virtual realities as *Second Life*, *Everquest*, and *World of Warcraft*, among many others.

In Massively Multiplayer Online Role Playing Games (MMORPGs), the virtual world is created by a programming architect. The world exists on a server: one or more computers hosting the world, into which computer users log in. These users manifest as avatars: a three-dimensional character that the user controls. These avatars interact, often collaborating as a team to achieve some objective. For instance, in *World of Warcraft* and *EverQuest*, two popular sword-and-sorcery MMORPGs, users often form a "raiding party" of avatars to (for instance) go slay a dragon and loot its trove.

Another well-trodden MMORPG is *Second Life*, where avatars tend not to be elves, dwarves, orcs, but simulacra of human beings. Computer users control avatars typically more attractive than the user would be considered to be in the real world—avatars approximating the good looks of some dashing actor, like Leonardo DiCaprio, or an ethereal beauty, like Marion Cotillard.

Architecture of the Imagination

Architects of these gaming worlds, like Ariadne, need a high degree of technical proficiency to construct bridges from their imaginations onto the server substrates, where such worlds subsist. Ariadne is a natural, creating and altering the architecture of virtual Paris with her will, causing two city grids to fold in on themselves, meeting at a ninety-degree angle, each maintaining its own discrete gravity.

A similar architect in skill and vision to Ariadne is known as Furia Freeloader. In *Second Life*, she built in the "Escher Relativity House." Furia explains her creation:

> This house was created as a statement of what is possible when you free your mind from real-life constraints. Aside from being a three-dimensional rendition of Escher's famed work, "Relativity," this house is a fully functional, livable, interactive home.

The relativity house presents three different gravity directions, depending on where you are in the house.

Escher's genius appears realized repeatedly throughout *Inception,* most explicitly when Arthur shows Ariadne a version of Escher's "Penrose Steps," the infinite staircase, that allows architects to "cheat architecture into impossible shapes," to create closed loops so that the world seems infinite.

In *Inception,* the dream world was not an expansive globe, but was a finite grid that somehow looped in on itself. In virtual worlds, similar grids exist, relying upon similar tricks to make it appear that the world is without limit, as a globe would prove too complicated regarding physics, astronomical markers, and so forth. One way MMORPGs mimic a spherical reality is by designing their grids into a "toroid": a donut shape where an avatar can always vertically travel around the ring of the world, reappearing at the initial position by walking in a straight line, or travel horizontally the long way around the donut. Another way is to by allowing invisible walls, or creating insurmountable geography, which oftentimes may be in the surrounding oceans of a virtual continent.

The worlds of MMORPs are geographically expansive. Recent estimations put *World of Warcraft*'s world of Azeroth around the size of Manhattan. The world of *Second Life* was estimated, as of 2008, at the size of Cedar County, Iowa (approximately 579 square miles). And growing.

Shadows of the World

"Never recreate places from your memory," Cobb warns Ariadne. "Always imagine new places . . . because building dreams out of your own memories is the surest way to lose your grip on what's real and what's a dream."

Yet some virtual realities do just this. *Second Life* hosts a virtual copy of the entire A&M college campus. Joe Terrell, a Texas A&M student, describes his experience:

> During the time I had before class began, I would stroll—or fly— around the island the college is built on. Many famous University landmarks have been faithfully reconstructed, including the Academic Building, Cushing Library, the Memorial Student Center, Fish Pond, the clock tower, and most poignantly, the Bonfire Memorial. All of these locations can be entered and explored, just like their real-world counterparts. This feature is most appreciated when you enter the

MSC and find yourself in a spot-on replication of the MSC Flag Room. It has to be seen to be believed.

Such verisimilitude is portrayed in Jorge Luis Borges's short story, "On Exactitude in Science," which presents—as if history—some Empire, where cartography is so detailed and exact, that it lays a map atop of the actual landscape, matching point to point. As our technology progresses, like this verisimilitudinous map, so that the detail and physics of a real-world location is indistinguishable to virtual dreamers, will the dreamer know when she's asleep or awake?

In Borges's story, the Empire crumbles and all that is left is the map. In postmodernist Jean Baudrillard's version of the story, it is the map in which people live, the simulation of reality becomes the reality, whereas the reality is crumbling away from disuse.

Joe Terrell describes how one virtual "landmark" of the Texas A&M campus includes the Texas A&M beach, which contains a giant blue waterslide. He quips that he hopes "as soon as the MSC restoration is finished, that this online portion of campus will be considered for immediate real-world implementation." Terrell's ironic comment betrays the sentiment that the simulacrum has become the preferred level of reality, and actual reality may soon become a decaying shadow.

Already, some tech-inclined professors deliver their lectures in virtual-reality classrooms. We might imagine Professor Miles, Cobb's father-in-law and mentor, to be such an avatar situated in such a virtual classroom—a classroom Cobb hacks into, looking to co-opt a gifted student from Miles, to help guide Cobb through the labyrinth that lies ahead.

A Butterfly, Dreaming . . .

Cobb's life captivates us. It's full of action, thrills, adventure, struggle, failure, and triumph, colored by car chases, gunfire, fist-fights, daring escapes, forbidden romance, tragic temptations. It seems epic and meaningful.

Real life is not like that.

To respectfully disagree with Macbeth, while life may be a tale told by an idiot signifying nothing, real life falls short in the sound-and-fury department. Perhaps it's easy for a make-believe king situated in the virtual setting of a Shakespearean drama to characterize it so. Macbeth's make-believe reality is riddled with ghosts, witches, visions, homicide, suicide, sex, betrayal, and madness. Such stuff as dreams are made on.

But for the rest of us, life is characterized more by the mundane, the repetitious, the senseless. Not even something as existentially heroic as the Sisyphean shouldering of a boulder to its zenith compares to the meagerness of our lives. Ordinary life, version 1.0, is characterized by commuter traffic, data entry, TV dinners, sedentary sitcoms, difficult relationships, unrealized dreams, and not much meaning to shore against our ruin.

Virtual existence tempts users with what life lacks: drama and direction on an epic scale, tribal community and belonging, tangible and immediate meaning. After a day of 8:00 to 5:00 in one's cubicle, followed by a freeway stop-and-go procession home, the user can jack-in to virtuality to become a virtuoso: resuming his reign as a noble and chivalrous knight, mounting up with his cavalcade, to ascend a treacherous mountain in order to slay the Giant King who has been terrorizing peasants in villages below. Which of the two realities would the user prefer? Which identity allows the user to feel purposeful with his activities, positive about his own self-esteem, satisfied with his existence's meaning?

The computer user might prefer to be the dynamic butterfly rather than the human caterpillar confined in the cocoon of the mundane world. With a few clicks, a user can become an elegant princess sparkling with ornate jewelry; a fierce barbarian colored with tribal tattoos; a paladin gleaming in full plate armor; or an anthromorph—half-human, half-animal—flying through the skies of *Second Life*. The only limits are our imaginations. And when a user's life and identity online becomes more satisfying than their life offline, they may relinquish one reality for the other.

Sleeping to Awake

"They come to be *woken up* . . . the dream has become their reality," chastises the elderly man to Cobb, an elderly shepherd over a basement room of sleeping dreamers, "And who are *you* to say otherwise?"

Similar rooms across the globe, known as "internet cafes," teem with sleepy dreamers. These "dreamers" pay by the hour for their computer console, which allows them to "wake up" to their virtual reality. Internet cafes abound with "addicts" similar to the addicts in the basement room of dreamers. This "gaming addiction" is so powerful that it has been linked to several deaths.

One of the most tragic deaths is the suicide of a young boy in China, Xiao Yi. The thirteen-year-old leaped from the top of a twenty-four-story tower in his home town. Prior to his suicide, Xiao had spent thirty-six consecutive hours playing the MMORPG *Warcraft III*. His suicide notes spoke of his hope of being reunited with fellow cyber-players in heaven. The notes were written from the perspective of his avatar. His parents were not mentioned in the letters. For Xiao, it seems he tragically imagined that dying would be a way to permanently "wake up" into the real world of his gaming life.

In *Inception,* dying allows a "waking up" to reality. Mal takes a literal and figurative "leap of faith" in throwing herself from the hotel window in order to supposedly "wake up" from their "dream." She tempts Cobb to do the same, urging him to take a "leap of faith," suggesting to him that their real children are waiting, somewhere above his purported reality, which she assures him is a mere dream.

A Dream within a Dream

"A dream within a dream—I'm impressed," chuckles Saito, face pressed into polyester carpet, a slight missed detail that betrays Cobb's doubled ruse. Saito realizes that his "waking up" from the previous dream was not an awakening to reality but merely an awakening into another dream.

"Waking up" fails to verify reality. There are dreams within dreams. Similarly, there can be games within games. In such computer games, to "wake up" is simply to exit from the game world into another world. This "higher-level" world needn't be the real world, however: it can merely be another game, at the higher level.

Assassin's Creed, a popular computer game, poses one such game within a game. The main story involves a bartender, Desmond Miles, who is captured by megacorporation Abstergo

Industries. Desmond is forced by Abstergo to go into a machine known as the Animus in order to relive his ancestors' past, so he can recover artifacts. So the gamer at his computer is playing Desmond in a "genetic memory" machine, where Desmond is playing one of his ancestors.

There are three levels: first level, the reality of the gamer sitting at his computer; second level, the virtual reality of Desmond the bartender trapped in an evil scientist's lair, and third level, the "genetic memory" of the ancestor assassin avatar in whom Desmond manifests. The two game levels can cause some frustration for gamers, as one such gamer vents in a gaming blog, about the difficulty of exiting the game. The gamer curses in self-censored expletives:

> My ****ing GOD. What does it take to exit this ****ing game? You exit the 'memory' then you're back in the stupid evil scientist lair and laying on the table. . . . Then you bring up your menu and exit again—do you want to exit the game? Yes . . .

The possible multilayered regress of virtual reality is lampooned in a video by the satirical news channel, *The Onion News Network,* which covers a supposed sequel to *World of Warcraft*, called *World of World of Warcraft*. In *World of World of Warcraft*, the gamer plays the character of a geeky gamer sitting in his basement playing an avatar in *World of Warcraft*. The geeky basement avatar is clicking on the mouse and keyboard, mimicking what you, the real gamer, are doing.

How would I, as a player of *World of World of Warcraft*, be assured that I am the reality-level player, and not just an avatar in a game (perhaps *World of World of World of Warcraft*)? Like Desmond in *Assassin's Creed II* who cognitively merges with his ancestor assassin avatar, so may the real gamer of the near future cognitively merge with his *World of Warcraft* character. Yet even to "wake up" as the gamer, how do you know that the "reality" you've woken to is the principal level of reality? Perhaps you're like Desmond: you think you've woken up to reality as Desmond, yet the truth is deeper—that Desmond is merely your avatar within a further dream from which the real you has as of yet to wake up.

ATTENTION: You're Already Living in Virtual Reality

You sitting there, reading this chapter—you're unwittingly trapped in a virtual reality. Everything around you is computer-generated, even your own body. You're but a conscious simulation inside a computer program. This assertion is not skepticism of the mad, but the reasoned probability of Nick Bostrom, Oxford philosopher, and PhD from the London School of Economics. After some intricate arithmetic and calculations, Bostrom places the odds at "maybe better than even" that we are in a computer simulation already. Bostrom reasons:

> I think it's highly likely that civilization could endure to produce those supercomputers. And if owners of the computers were anything like the millions of people immersed in virtual worlds like *Second Life*, *SimCity*, and *World of Warcraft*, they'd be running simulations just to get a chance to control history—or maybe give themselves virtual roles as Cleopatra or Napoleon. (Quoted from John Tierney, "Our Lives Controlled from Some Guy's Couch," *New York Times*, August 14th, 2007).

We laugh off the possibility that we're currently living in a computer program. The notion seems like the fantastical ravings of a madman. Yet we know of no compelling reason to reject such a raving as a real possibility. A future looms near where veridical and immersive virtual realities are likely. Venerable futurist, Ray Kurzweil estimates that we will reverse-engineer the human brain by the mid 2020s, by the end of 2029 computers will be human-level intelligence, and by 2045, the quantity of artificial intelligence created will be approximately a billion times the sum of all human intelligence that exists today.

Concurrently, environmentalists also prognosticate ecological doom in the twenty-second century, if not sooner. If the environment is no longer suitable to sustain comfortable living—if there's not sufficient resources nor infrastructure for an enjoyable existence for the ordinary person—it's reasonable to expect many of us will opt for virtual realities, if available. An essential sacrifice that an individual must give up in order to fully assimilate into a more pleasant and hospitable existence in virtual reality, is to forget that it's a dream. Cobb admits: "The problem is knowing that it's not real. It became impossible for me to live like that." How could we, like Cobb, enjoy a virtual reality if we know it is but a shadow?

And so perhaps the future is already here, and we are already living in the simulated past. By electing to become ensconced in virtual reality, we would thereby shield ourselves from the reality of the ecological doom blighting the landscape.

By the time this future is here, virtual reality will by all accounts be immersive and veridical: that is, we won't sit at a keyboard, staring at a monitor, controlling our avatars with mouse clicks. We will assume the place of the avatar, cognitively melding with the avatar: seeing through its eyes—now our eyes; feeling stimulus in the simulated environment as if it is our own body; transversing the dreamscape as if truly running through space. Details of this simulated reality will be veridical to actual reality: the differences undetectable to human observation or inspection.

Skepticism aside, perhaps this—the book in your hands for instance—is true rather than simulated reality, and Bostrom miscalculated. Or, perhaps, at the end of our lives, when we're old, and maybe filled with regret, each of us will individually shuffle off our virtual coil. And finally, we shall wake up.

Spinning Tops and Lotus Eaters

Mal walks away from reality. Cobb laments, "At some point . . . she decided to forget our world wasn't real." Temptation to abandon reality harkens back to Greek mythology. In Homer's *The Odyssey,* Odysseus' crew are tempted to abandon their lives as crewmen—lives of isolation, repetition, hard labor, and lonely heartaching for home—in order to become lost in euphoric sedation.

Homer describes the lotus as "so delicious that those who ate of it left off caring about home, and did not even want to go back and say what had happened to them." Odysseus forces those of crew having ingested the lotus, "weeping bitterly," back to the ship where they "took their places and smote the grey sea with their oars."

In the twenty-first century, this temptation to abandon reality persists: imbedded in the human condition, as we find ourselves situated in difficult lives in an imperfect reality. So we're tempted to seek a better reality, identity, and life. Who hasn't dreamt of a lost lover—passion rekindled, divorced parents remarried, a forfeited family home reclaimed, a deceased loved one that we miss, back to life? Virtual reality offers all of that: everything lost can be regained, or at least the offerings of virtual reality can make us forget our regrets with its distractions of fresh woods, and pastures new.

Though not everyone, today, will succumb to the lotus flower of *World of Warcraft*, or the siren's call of *Second Life*, imagine the near future, when the lotus petals of virtual realities are more prevalent, more veridical and immersive, and more seductive. Such temptations will be hard to resist.

Already virtual-reality users are tuning in to virtual worlds and dropping out of reality. *World of Warcraft* is a leading cause of college dropouts, according to the FCC commissioner in December 2008. *World of Warcraft* is played by twelve million people, globally. Many users play *World of Warcraft* for fourteen to sixteen hours a day, at times, without breaks.

Stories abound of parents severely neglecting their children in order to immerse themselves in *World of Warcraft*. In 2007, a husband and wife in Reno, Nevada, were charged with "child neglect" for becoming so engrossed in online games that they almost starved to death their two babies (twenty-two-month-old boy and eleven-month-old girl). In 2009, a South Korean husband and wife left at home alone their prematurely-born three-month old infant, so that they could go to the Internet Café to play *World of Warcraft* for twelve hours straight.

Dropouts, neglect, teen suicide, and accidental death—all because of World of Warcraft—should at least give us pause to consider the engrossing magnetism of online virtual worlds. Participants in virtual realities are the Lotus-Eaters of today drowning out their troubles with the intoxicating flowers on virtual islands, becoming increasingly addicted to the escapism, and languishing as their real lives fall apart.

Ultimately, Cobb finds himself unable to resist the lure of the lotus petal. Eating of it, he—like Odysseus' crewmen—can forget that he's leagues from a home he may never see again. So instead, he can dream of it and forget the woes and mundanity of hard, stark reality—a dimensionless grey sea that each of us is sluggishly inching through, seeming to get nowhere. We're tempted to allow ourselves to abandon our boats, so as to wash up on the shore of fantasy.

Unweaving a Tangled Web

To think about the story of *Inception* is to pick up the threads which can lead us out of the labyrinth into reality.

Cobb is a high-level avatar, the virtual manifestation of an addicted gamer. The gamer, veiled from our movie-going eyes, has his identity so wrapped up in his character, Cobb, and his associated dashing, dangerous, creative and vivid life, that this virtual identity and world *becomes* the gamer's life.

Cobb's wife, Mal, is his real-life wife, who once played along-side Cobb in various levels of virtual reality. But Mal realized that their virtual existence wasn't real. She realizes that her "in-game" children are but simulacra: "They're projections, Dom. Your dreams. I'm their mother—don't you think I can tell the difference?" Her virtual existence became unfulfilling, and so she left the game, deliberately deleting her own character via her in-game suicide.

After her "leap of faith" back to reality, Mal returns to the real world without Dom. In essence, Mal has become what is popularly denoted as a "gamer's widow." Mal, having woken up from the game, is now truly with their real children, and is yearning for Cobb to come to the surface. Mal is angry at Cobb's refusal, his inability, to relinquish his gamer reality, and come back to true reality. He has abandoned her and their children.

The game being the only reality that "Cobb" now knows, Cobb is trapped in a reality bereft of his beloved. And so he creates simulacra of Mal here and there (such as in their hotel room) to reunite with her, talk to her, and try to get past his emotional guilt and emptiness. The real Mal, however, occasionally shows up in his world, creating an avatar by which to lead him home, even if by force. She seeks to ruin his plans, to kill his avatar if need be, in order to have him reunite with her and their children in the real world. Unfortunately, Cobb categorically dismisses her as Mal-ware: a manifestation of his guilty conscience. Some incarnations of Mal are indeed just that. But the real Mal shows up from time to time in the film as an avatar in his virtual reality, imploring him to "wake up."

Mal later challenges Cobb, "You keep telling me what you know . . . but what do you believe? What do you *feel?*" Mal suggests that the true thread out of the labyrinth, through the hall of mirrors of dreams within dreams, out of the cave and into the sunlight, is an inerrant thread woven of feeling and intuition. While an idea can corrupt the mind, it cannot corrupt the heart. The heart knows what the heart knows, even if the head has forgotten.

An Old Man, Filled with Regret . . .

Cobb is right: "An idea is like a virus, resilient, highly contagious, and an idea can grow to define or destroy your world. . . ." Mal finishes for him, "The smallest idea, such as . . . '*Your world is not real*'."

What Cobb doesn't realize is that this smallest idea is the shadow of another idea, an inverted twin virus that can just as easily plant and grow and define one's world. Namely, that your world *is* real. Cobb has succumbed to forgetting that he's in a game: the game is now his reality. To have Cobb, the character, die would be much like real death for the player behind the curtain (whom we never see), as his real identity has been eroded and supplanted by this other identity in virtual reality. To "wake from that. From decades lived. To be old souls thrown back into youth" and thrust into mundane reality would be too much for Cobb to bear.

And as Ariadne cannot stay away from the unbounded freedom and possibilities of dreamspace, Cobb—a veteran addict—cannot quit his dreamed reality. Cobb assures Arthur of Ariadne's inevitable return, "She'll be back. . . . One reality won't be enough for her now." Cobb speaks from experience: one reality can never be enough for the chronic dream addict.

Common among heist movies, there is the "long con" where it is oftentimes the audience has been conned, a twist which is not revealed to the audience until the end, if at all. The long con of *Inception* is hinted at with the last shot, focusing on Cobb's spinning top: it is that the *real* inception is not the planting of an idea in Robert Fischer's mind. The real inception was planting an idea in Cobb's mind.

Robert Fischer is but a gambit to misdirect the audience into investing their attention to the unfolding plot of a superficial father-son story. Why else would the "mark" of Cobb's con share the same name as notable Chess Grandmaster Bobby Fischer, perhaps the greatest chess player on record? A good heist plot always stays twelve moves ahead of the movie viewer.

The *real* inception is planting into Cobb's head that the reality at the end of the film, where he's finally "reunited" with his children, is actually real rather than just another dream within a dream. In the final minutes, as we see Cobb walk seamlessly from scene to scene without sensible transition—from baggage area right into the living room of his old house—where he finally abandons his spinning top, his litmus test of reality. He embraces his never-aging children *as* reality. The seed that was planted has bloomed. He's now a willing prisoner of a dream, blissfully forgetting that it is a prison.

The cruel irony for Cobb is that someday, the real Cobb will wake up to reality, to discover that his real wife and children have left him. To find that all he has to show for his time, his sound and fury, is an avatar, signifying nothing. He will have awoken to find himself an old man, filled with regret, waiting to die alone.

15
The Movie as a Thinking Machine

THORSTEN BOTZ-BORNSTEIN

Inception produces a special kind of dream cinema in which dreams are not separate worlds, nor are they seen, as in Ancient Egypt, as messages from God. In *Inception*, dreams are simply programs that can be hacked into.

Inception does not rely on blurred images or other stylizing devices nor does it create a dream logic distorting actions by making them incoherent. Instead, *Inception* presents movie dream in the form of a complex, but logically consistent dream system. In this sense, film has become a "dream machine" able to "think" different levels of reality.

Within the three levels of dreams, events like "the fall" are synchronized in a mechanical fashion by orchestrating, for example, the explosions in the hospital and in the hotel room as well as the van's fall into a river or by using a musical countdown for synchronization. The combination of Fischer's safe is a phone number or a hotel room number in the other layers; the swaying of the van makes the elevator sway . . . The dream machine co-ordinates contradicting layers of time and space and the movie itself can appear as a "brain" or as a "reality processor" whose activities are similar to those of computers.

A Dream in a Dream

Inception abounds with flashing insights about dreams, many of which have been borrowed from philosophers. Cobb affirms that "our dreams feel real while we're in them. It's only when we wake up we realize things were strange." This echoes the statement of the French philosopher Henri Bergson that "waking life, much more than dreams, asks for explanations." Cobb also explains that "you never remember the beginning of your dreams, do you? You just turn up in the middle of what's going on." This is reminiscent of the view of another specialist of dream, the French writer Paul Valéry, who held that in dreams "there is no perspective" and "everything appears to be word for word."

In spite of these occasional allusions to a variety of philosophical views on dreams, the dream model of *Inception* is mainly cognitive. It explores the possibilities of film dream as a cognitive machine. There isn't much Freudian, analytic splitting up of symbols in *Inception*, but the dream movie excels through its organic, synthetic quality based on a peculiar "dream in a dream" structure.

In film and in theater, the "dream in a dream" technique is unusual. It goes back to the Swedish writer August Strindberg who, in his *Dreamplay* (1901), deconstructed traditional forms of theater by putting a play into a play. Strindberg's intention was to produce a stage-dream by expressing the dreamer's lack of self-awareness. Later, Ingmar Bergman would develop this approach towards dream by experimenting with the authoritative status of a film, attempting to leave entirely unclear who the author of the narrative is (a technique used, for example, in Bergman's movie *Persona*).

Inception uses the "dream within a dream" model, but executes it in a highly mechanical fashion: on the one hand, it suggests a lack of awareness because some subjects begin to lose control of what's real and what isn't. On the other hand, *Inception* avoids such a lack because the different realities are clearly distinguishable (they play in entirely different environments) and don't fuse.

It's essential to keep dream and reality apart. For example, Cobb advises Ariadne to avoid using existing elements from memory in order to not "lose hold of what is real and what is a dream." *Inception*'s "dream in a dream" model follows cognitive models of deduction, that is, it establishes dreams in terms of classes and subclasses whose relationships remain well defined, at least in theory.

Cognition and Psychoanalysis

The film's big idea, "inception," is inspired by meme theory, a branch of cognitive science. Memes are memory items or portions of information that are stored in the human brain. Through replication (the production of perfect copies) these memes can develop into large cultural networks, similar to genes in the area of biology. Biologist and popular science writer Richard Dawkins coined the term meme (from the French *même*, meaning the same) in 1989 and evoked the possibility of the existence of a gene-like unit of imitation in the realm of culture.

Memes can be

> tunes, ideas, catch-phrases, clothes fashions, ways of making pots or building arches. Just as genes propagate themselves in a gene pool, memes propagate themselves from brain to brain through imitation. (*The Selfish Gene*, p. 192)

In *Inception* the spread of memes is most explicitly adopted for an age of terror and acquires dramatic dimensions when Cobb explains: "The smallest seed of an idea can grow to define or destroy your world."

Another idea linked to the manifestation of ideas or images that stick in the mind has been borrowed from the Stanislaw Lem–Andrei Tarkovsky film *Solaris* (more recently a remake by Steven Sonderbergh). In both movies, *Solaris* and *Inception*, the "real world" is depicted as an idyllic, sunlit, family-life world that forms a marked contrast with the "Ocean Solaris" or with the somber sphere of dreams through which the protagonists of *Inception* travel like cosmonauts. The Earth scenes in *Solaris* present a dacha and a Russian landscape and in *Inception*, the "reality" scene is a typical American home.

In *Solaris*, a biomagnetic current that looks like a gluey mass or fog acts upon the minds of cosmonauts while they're traveling through outer space. The result is the appearance of strange visitors on the space station: living persons who are since long dead (for example Kris's wife who has committed suicide) but who have "survived" as ideas or memes in the brains of the cosmonauts.

In *Inception*, the same thing happens to Cobb (though not only to him) when he perceives his wife and children as "projections" in various situations. The "projections" theme from *Solaris* is combined with that of the spreading of memes through imitation because in certain situations, the projections can "converge on you," meaning "they attack like white blood cells fighting an infection" (Cobb). Cobb explains this to Ariadne and while he is doing so several people around them stop and echo Cobb's attitude, look hostile, and finally attack Ariadne.

Inception gives us a combination of horizontal and vertical dream structures. On the horizontal level there are the different dream realities that the spectator perceives more or less simultaneously in the form of organically linked stories. At the same time there's a vertical pattern, which aligns the different levels of dreams by suggesting a hierarchy within the mind of the person who will be subjected to inception.

The movie describes the journey from the highest to the deepest levels of dreams as the journey down towards the profoundest layers of the person's mind. The most basic structure of the film shows us a simultaneous use of horizontal and vertical arrangements: of the three levels of dreams, two have been installed in a larger overall dream. There is a fourth level, which is Cobb's dystopia from his fifty year in Limbo.

In Buddhism the "dream within a dream" model is known as a contention suggesting that any truth about reality is hidden "deep" inside a person's mind. However, in the first place, this pattern is psychoanalytical in that it supposes any "truth" to be hidden in the deepest layers of the subconscious. The "dream within a dream" model supports this vertical scheme. In *Inception*, the Freudian themes are announced somewhat surprisingly when Eames declares that "various political motivations, antimonopolistic sentiment and so forth" aren't deep enough to be used to implant an idea in Fischer's mind. What's needed for a successful inception is to get to the level of Fischer's relationship with his father.

The combination of cognitive insights with psychoanalytical elements is highly unusual. Cobb and his people don't implant ideas into the subjects' consciousness in their waking life, where they would spread and develop "horizontal" social dimensions that would indeed be identical with structures of memetic distribution. In *Inception* the ideas are implanted into the peoples' subconscious by way of their dreams, which gives the cognitive model a vertical dimension, which brings it closer to cultural hypnosis.

Some of the ideas that have been planted into peoples' dreaming minds will even persist once they awaken. Even more, a meme can get out of control and develop a dynamic of its own, a possibility not very much considered by classical meme theory. In *Inception*, memes develop a "depth dimension" because, as Cobb says, "the seed of the idea we plant will grow in this man's mind. It'll change him. It might even come to define him." Cobb discovers the auto-dynamic aspect of memes when Mal becomes unable to abandon an idea he has implanted in her, a mistake which finally leads to her suicide. Cobb comments: "I never thought that the idea I'd planted would grow in her mind like a cancer."

Film as a Thinking Machine

In *Inception*, Chris Nolan doesn't stylize reality into a dream. Instead, he lets the movie think the dream. The devices he uses aren't a matter of style but of film thought. Slow-motion, for example, isn't the sign of a dream but of the film thinking in slow motion.

The French film theorist André Bazin explained in the 1950s that the use of slow motion for a dream sequence is highly inappropriate because it does not produce a "dream reality" but merely announces "attention: dream." Bazin's point, in itself a classical idea of film theory, is to oppose all standardized signs in film in order to become more realistic: "The director who uses slow motion in a dream sequence . . . might not really be convinced that we are dreaming in slow motion. At the same time he might not think that his deformation of the temporal level is without any link with the dream reality itself. He might still believe that dreams are very well expressed through slow motion" (*What Is Cinema?*, III, p. 28).

In *Inception*, the Bazinian opposition of a stylized dream reality versus a "realist" dream reality is neither possible nor necessary because the question of if the reality of the dream is "really" slow or if it's only slow due to the director's decision to use slow motion as a sign announcing "attention: dream," has become irrelevant. In *Inception*, slow motion has become a matter of cognition because the film doesn't produce or reproduce a reality. It's merely a certain cognitive pattern.

Nothing could be clearer than Cobb's explanation: "When you dream, your mind functions more quickly, so time seems to pass more slowly." By reproducing this constellation, the film becomes a thinking machine as opposed to a machine that attempts to reproduce a (real or imagined) reality.

"Film thinking" has fascinated film theorists for almost a century, starting with Sergei Eisenstein and refined by film theorist Jean Mitry and philosopher Gilles Deleuze. Most recently, Daniel Frampton has insisted, in his book *Filmosophy*, that film does not narrate or show things, characters, or actions, it thinks them: when watching a film we observe a thinking process. Frampton attempts to grasp the cinematic thinking process with the help of newly coined concepts such as 'film-thinking' and 'filmind' and assigns to 'filmosophy' the task of "conceptualizing all film as an organic intelligence" (p. 7). Film-thinking isn't a metaphorical way of arranging reality: "The filmind has its own particular film-phenomenology, its own way of attending to its world" (p. 91).

So far, thinkers have forced themselves to perceive moments of thought in film, but with *Inception*, film has (for almost the first time) been designed as a thinking machine from the outset. *Inception* provides an organic aspect in the most consistent fashion as its focus is on the systematic aspect of a film reality that has been designed like a thinking machine. The idea of film as a thinking machine able to produce a reality that is different though still logically structured has been most clearly expressed by the early French avant-garde filmmaker and theorist Jean Epstein (1897–1953).

In *The Intelligence of a Machine*, Epstein defines cinema as a "robot brain" (p. 71) able to transcend typically human physical and mental limits because cinema "permits the synthesis of discontinuous and immobile elements into a continuous and mobile whole" (p. 9). For Epstein, film isn't a text or a writing, but a machine able to produce a dreamlike reality by overcoming human reason and by unhinging the most basic rules of time. Comparing film with the microscope, Epstein anticipates contemporary computer reality or virtual reality. Epstein observes how cinema stretches and condenses time letting us feel its variable and relative nature. The conclusion is that cinema does not present but think time, that it's a "partial mechanical brain" able to develop a "rich philosophy full of surprises" (p. 71).

Epstein's definition of cinema as a "machine for producing dreams" (p. 55) is opposed to realist theories of any sort. At the same time, Epstein fights what he calls "irreality" in cinema. Neither realism nor irrealism recognizes cinema's inherent thinking capacity. Epstein sketches the history of cinema in the following way: The beginnings of cinematographic art were clearly "anti-philosophical" as the inventors of cinema believed they had created a recording machine. They had no idea that film could also be a machine able to "think" attributes, categories, relations between space and time, or series of causations, in the same way in which they are thought by humans.

However, equally anti-philosophical is the attitude that classifies cinematic reality as unreal and insubstantial for the simple reason that it's imagined. Epstein explains how, during its further development, cinema would undergo the same stances that other sciences had undergone much earlier. Cinema had to learn how to split reality into parts and to recompose those parts afterwards. Epstein shows that throughout history (starting with the pre-Socratic philosopher Democritus who held that matter is made of atoms), human thinking has increasingly contested primitive visions of a continuous reality and formulated atomistic theories able to interpret reality as constituted of particles.

This is why, in the end, cinema would also become able to see "reality as the sum of irrealities" and would attempt to present such an overall time composed of countless "ultra-particular times" as a new cinematic reality. In cinema there is no "time as such" but time and space "are constituted through variable relationships between successive or simultaneous appearances" (p. 21). Film as a "Machine to Think Time" "stretches or condenses duration, which shows the real nature of time" (p. 17). Cinema shows that reality isn't an elementary continuity, but "a collection of grains of reality" (p. 67).

Second Life and Third World

Inception follows Epstein's predictions most clearly, but why does this happen right now in 2010? One reason is that the dream as a machine that can be hacked into has become a reality. Scientists have announced that the technology able to electronically visualize brain activity has been invented and that "dream reading" might be possible one day (Pallab Ghosh, "Dream Recording Device 'Possible' Researcher Claims").

Another reason why *Inception* presents cinematic dreams in such a mechanical way instead of working with well-established phenomenological or stylistic devices, is that our approach towards reality (and therefore also towards dreams) has changed. Computers have created a new way of experiencing texts and images. Today, instead of blurred images and fades, the dream experience is much more likely to be conveyed by entering into labyrinthine structures that appear as constantly moving and changing virtual worlds.

The formal structure of *Inception* is reminiscent of that of an interactive hypertext: it follows the process of non-sequential electronic reading and writing, which has become most useful for websites such as Wikipedia. In a hypertext the reader clicks on a word and a new text opens up in which she will find other words to click on: "As one moves through a hypertext, one has the sensation that there's an almost inexhaustible reservoir of half-hidden story material waiting to be explored. That isn't unlike the feeling one has in dreams," writes cyber-theorist Christine Boyer. This is the structure of *Inception*.

Another reason why the journey through dreams takes on the form it does in *Inception* is that in the contemporary world "traveling" has acquired extremely experiential connotations. For the contemporary consumer, tourism is supposed to open up a new set of sensory experiences with adventures lurking around every corner. The presentation of dreams in film has to take these expectations into account: tourism is conceived of as a sensorial and liberating encounter with a dreamscape that includes changing ambiances as well as different psychological conditions.

As Matthew Brophy shows in Chapter 14, the entire concept of *Inception* is reminiscent of the worlds of computer games, most specifically *Second Life*, a virtual world in which players can interact with each other through avatars. In the film, the possibility of entering dreams is said to have been developed as a training program for the military "where soldiers could strangle, stab, and shoot each other," and "then wake up." During the fifty years that Cobb and Mal spend in Limbo, they are believed to be "playing God" because they aren't only almighty, but the world they build isn't bound by rules of reality: "We both wanted a house, but we both loved skyscrapers. In the real world we had to choose. Not here." Cobb summarizes this life as "interesting" though—unfortunately—"not real."

Epstein predicted the production of scientifically established worlds of introversion through the medium of cinema but, as it turned out, cinema had to wait until the day computers would change our expectations of cinematic reasoning. Epstein saw that "science pretends to possess the extroverted mode of knowledge *par excellence* but, contrary to its pretensions, it evolves in the direction of abstraction, that is, of increasing introversion. Through rationalization, it becomes a mathematical dream, whose relationship with human reality . . . is incoherent" (p. 57). Today the introverted dreams, still results of the Democritic atomization of the world, are "thought" by a computer and cinema attempts to follow this model. This is how, in the Epsteinian sense, film became a dream machine as much as a thinking machine.

Within the atomized dreams of *Inception* we perceive pictures of the real world, but this world remains "outside." The "real world" impressions are like streaming media images that can be switched off at any moment. The political turmoil that takes place in the chaotic Third World country in which the team is operating approaches the shabby hotel and enters through the door right at the moment when Piaf's "Je ne regrette rien" announces the end of this dream sequence.

Soon Saito discovers the fake quality of the carpet and recognizes that all this is a dream. Though the rioters are smashing and burning, this world isn't supposed to be real (the script announces that the scene "feels like a different time"). The film shows political realities such as torture whose media reports we're accustomed to digesting like fiction. In Yusuf's basement, well hidden behind a steel door, twenty interconnected people are sleeping a Matrix-like sleep with tubes in their wrists. Yusuf explains that they come in every day "to share the dream." They aren't organ donors but mind donors who lend their minds like computer hardware to Yusuf who installs a dream. They don't only dream, but they live in a dream, which lets their real world appear as a dream. Is this a metaphor for the "Third World," that is, for ramshackle Mombasa which is supposed to be not real?

Obviously, Mombasa is a reality for them but not for us. The atomized presentation of real world images in *Inception* very much overlaps with our perception of reality as they occur in the media. French sociologist Jean Baudrillard has most famously said that reality most definitively absorbed the energy of fiction when 9/11 became an absolute media event. The repeated images of airplanes flying into the Twin Towers were ritually shown from many different angles as if the imagination of Hollywood had been turned into images of reality. Through the detached level of representation, the images of the Twin Towers attained the playful quality of movies or of computer games. Cinema has to take into account this new way of presenting reality or this new way of formulating any relationship between imagination and reality.

Architecture and the Dream Machine

The thinking machine also gives rise to a new way of presenting architecture, which will have to be "thought" out by a machine. Again, films and computers begin here to play similar roles. Virtual reality has immensely influenced our expectations of architectural dreams. This isn't an entirely new phenomenon as the perception of architecture went through similar stages when being confronted with the newly invented cinema. In the 1930s, the German philosopher Walter Benjamin pointed out the effect that the invention of cinema would have upon architecture:

> Our taverns and our metropolitan streets, our offices and furnished rooms, our railroad stations and our factories appeared to have us locked up hopelessly. Then came the film and burst this prison-world asunder by the dynamite of the tenth of a second, so that now, in the midst of its far-flung ruins and debris, we calmly and adventurously go traveling. With the close-up, space expands; with slow motion, movement is extended. (pp. 236–37)

Similar to Benjamin, Jean Epstein would meditate upon the influence that cinema as a thinking machine can have upon architecture. Cinema transcends the human scale and the "truths for the National School of Bridges and Roads" (*Intelligence*, p. 27) don't apply to what Epstein calls "the new architecture":

> Today Euclid's postulates of whose validity our reason never doubts are only true on the scale of human architecture. . . . Once they are transposed to the global scale, they will have to be multiplied by tens of thousands of kilometers and not of meters, and when we reduce objects for the fraction of a ten millionth these clear truths become false. (p. 27)

For Epstein, cinema gives us a vision of pure creativity, which is exactly what Cobb the architect has written into his agenda. Cobb does not want to engage in "attic conversions and gas stations," but wants to let his creativity run freely: "If I mastered the dream-share I'd have a whole new way of creating and showing people my creations."

Ariadne finds that the entire inception job is "pure creation" because this architecture isn't bound by functional imperatives and practicality but only by perfection, uniqueness, and aestheticism. Architecture's main driving force isn't to build shelters and facilities for people but, as Cobb puts it, "cathedrals, entire cities—things that have never existed, things that couldn't exist in the real world." This is an architecture not made by engineers, but by dreamers and its main function is to satisfy the vanity of the builder.

In *Inception*, architecture plays a primal role. Architects create the structure of dreams. As Cobb says to Ariadne, "You build the world of the dream. We take the subject into that dream, and let him fill it with his subconscious." The film abounds with architectural metaphors: there are mazes and a whole building is made up of different, piled-up realities that can be reached through an elevator. Mazes are also needed when it becomes necessary to hide from the attacks of projections. In *Inception*, dreams are made by architects which means that time is translated into architecture: the stories of the building become stories in the sense of histories. When Ariadne bends the streets, she becomes the specialist of the architectural dreams that Epstein had anticipated.

The most expressive architectural dreams appear in Limbo,

an unconstructed dream space made by sheer imagination. Everybody dreams, but "architects are supposed to make those dreams real," says Miles. More precisely, unconstructed dream space is made of "raw infinite subconscious." This architecture is even less material than a thought (which can't be infinite) but revels in the realm of the eternally undefined.

In their fifty years of Limbo, Cobb and Mal create space in order to kill time. The result is a space reminiscent of computer games. When Cobb and Ariadne access this space years later, we see tall, crumbling buildings symbolizing a dysfunctional Third World modernity that is different from the labyrinthine old Mombasa, but equally hopeless. Behind those buildings arises a New World, absolutely modern, sterile, and impersonal, in which the nostalgic and melancholic childhood home and the old apartment look like architectural projections. The entire space is deserted and uncanny, apparently meant to represent the wasteland of a failed utopia.

It can't be a coincidence that Cobb's dystopia looks so much like contemporary neoliberal "paradises" such as Dubai. Being a victim of hasty speculation and global crises, the newly built skyscrapers of this Gulf emirate remain eerily empty and Dubai has become a "city in limbo" as well as an emblem of the arrogance and vanity of its builders. As the city provides an oversupply of office space, many newly built buildings will probably be destroyed in the near future.

Christopher Hawthorne in the *Los Angeles Times* writes that "many of Dubai's skyscrapers were conceived and designed primarily as vessels to store excess liquidity. If the endless rows of stalled towers now resemble mere shells, perhaps shells are all they were ever meant to be." Mike Davis describes Dubai as an "eerie chimera" and as the "hallucinatory pastiche of the big, the bad, and the ugly," and architect Hisham Elkadi speaks of an "etheralization of culture" that results from pervasive electronic mediation leading to "killing the present time by isolating it from its here and now."

Strictly speaking, any etheralization of architecture is counterintuitive because normally, architecture is the non-ephemeral art par excellence, distinct from theatre or dance by its capacity to produce lasting expressions. However, Dubai, just like Cobb's dystopia, has been anticipated by specialists in cyberspace. Twenty years ago, Michael Benedikt forecast, in his Introduction to *Cyberspace*, the existence of "gilded dreamworlds," which aren't "real" cities but mere nodes of communication.

For Benedikt, the "ephemeralization of architecture and its continuing capitulation to media" (p. 28) is a continuous process that started a long time ago. "Thinking architecture itself as an abstraction" has a tradition reaching back to ancient Egypt and Greece and the meeting of mathematical knowledge with geometry. In a way, architecture is always about "transcendence, about a desire to go beyond," an idea that finally led to the "ephemeralization and self-dematerialization of architecture, as buildings became light, hollow, and transparent" (p. 15).

At the end of this development emerges cyberspace as a liquid medium. This explains why sights of Dubai look so much like computer generated images, exposing the "cyclopean fantasies of Barnum, Eiffel, Disney, Spielberg, Jon Jerde, Steve Wynn, and Skidmore, Owings and Merrill" ("Sand, Fear, and Money," p. 51).

Inception responds to these new architectural paradigms by presenting architecture as a dream device. Neoliberal paradises are like programs that can be hacked into. In the end, the world itself can appear like a complex but logically consistent dream system. Did Jean Baudrillard not say that Americans "built the real out of ideas"? *Inception* does no more than announce the next stage. Now, within this system, tourists can hack into places that look similar to Cobb's dystopia. In this sense, the dream machine of *Inception* has become an allegory for the globalized world.

16
Where Time Stands Still

INDALECIO GARCIA

> Hladik began a shriek, a syllable, a twist of the hand. He realized he
> was paralyzed.
> Not a sound reached him from the stricken world.
> He thought: I'm in hell, I'm dead.
> He thought: I've gone mad.
> He thought: Time has come to a halt.
>
> —JORGE LUIS BORGES, "The Secret Miracle"

There is in *Inception* a place where time seems to stand still, to
become an eternity. This place is Limbo—an infinite space, or a
space without precise limits. Even the limits of time seem to
disappear there:

> ARIADNE: How long would we be stuck there?
>
> YUSUF: You couldn't even think about trying to escape until
> the sedation eases.
>
> EAMES: How long?
>
> YUSUF: Decades—it could be infinite—I don't know! Ask
> him—he's the one who's been there before!

The term 'limbo' was originally used by Christian theologians
to designate a place where souls wait when they can't go
directly to heaven. They could stay there either for a period of
time or for eternity. (In Dante's *Divine Comedy*, Hell, canto IV,
Limbo is populated by the souls of poets and philosophers). The
limbo in *Inception*, however, has a different nature.

In order to plant a thought in the depths of Fischer's mind, the members of Cobb's team take a sedative. This drug is so intense that if someone dies in one of the dreams he won't wake up but rather fall down into Limbo:

EAMES: So what happens if one of us dies?

COBB: That person doesn't wake up. Their mind drops into Limbo.

ARIADNE: Limbo?

ARTHUR: Unconstructed dream space.

ARIADNE: What's down there?

ARTHUR: Raw, infinite subconscious. Nothing there but what was left behind by anyone on the team who's been trapped there before. On this team, . . . just Cobb.

Though it can be interrupted, the temporal slide into limbo can be endless for those who fall down there. This fall into temporal infinity, which could be called 'eternity' because of its indeterminate length, is carried out by the mind. In dreams, the mind performs modifications on time, the most dramatic of which is seen in Limbo.

In *Inception* the characters, or their minds, descend to ever deeper levels of unconsciousness. In each new level time expands again. The reason for this extension is the intensity of the mind's activity during sleep. But what type of mental activity can perform such a modification? How is that possible in dreams?

Inception raises questions about the relation between the mind and temporality—even between the mind and eternity—such as: how do we know time? If time is something that can be modified by the mind, what guarantees that such modifications don't occur while we're awake? What distinguishes our perception of time in dreams from our perception of time when we're awake? Can we assert that we perceive the real extent of time when we are awake? Further, how can the mind comprehend eternity?

Slow Time

Mind and time are brought together in the movie after Ariadne's first training session as the new architect:

ARIADNE: We were only asleep for five minutes? We talked for an hour at least. . . .

COBB: When you dream, your mind functions more quickly, so time seems to pass more slowly.

Although they have spoken for almost an hour, Cobb says that in dreams time "seems" to pass more slowly, because the time measured by Arthur, who observed Cobb and Ariadne while they were sleeping, has been just five minutes.

However, what Cobb says isn't quite accurate. Cobb and Ariadne were in fact not only asleep for five measured minutes, but also in fact they spoke for about an hour, as measured by a clock in the dream. To them, in the dream, time didn't seem to move slowly: time as they experienced it passed as it would for someone who was awake. Moreover, the perception of time on each level of consciousness is measured by clocks, which, it can be assumed, function as any other clock in the realm where someone is awake.

Even if time doesn't pass more slowly when we compare it at each level of consciousness, the period of time in which the characters were speaking in the dream was longer than the period of time that passed while they were asleep.

The problem is, then, that a longer time period may be included in a shorter one. How could this happen? It can be clarified if we consider a more general problem: how do we know time? The philosopher Aristotle has something to say about this.

Timeless Sleep

There is no object in the world that we can point to and call 'time', nor are there objects corresponding to its parts: present, past, and future. Rather than assume that time is something in itself, or an independent reality, it seems more likely that time is some aspect of something.

Aristotle considers time this way, and defines it as "(i) a number of change (ii) in respect of the before and after." For Aristotle time isn't an independent reality, but rather occurs within movement: time is an aspect of movement. It exists precisely because there's movement: if there were no movement, there wouldn't be time. This linkage is evident in perception.

When we perceive movement, we say that time has passed. To perceive any movement means to perceive time, which is the measure of the movement.

This is shown by Aristotle through an example similar to what we see in *Inception*. There's a myth, Aristotle claims, that certain men fall asleep in Sardinia. While they are sleeping they don't see any change or movement. Once they awake they believe that no time has passed. Those sleepers have joined the now in which they have fallen asleep to the now within which they are waking up because apparently there's no change or movement in between these two events.

If, as it happens in the film, the sleepers had dreamed of different movements, or had perceived successive different movements while sleeping, most certainly they would think a long time had passed. However, this isn't the case, for Aristotle says that the sleeper's soul has remained in a single state: they have neither perceived anything external, nor become aware of having dreamed.

Therefore, our knowledge of time comes through our perception of motion. If time is modified when the mind dreams, this modification must have to do with our perception of motion in dreams.

Perception and Time

The problem that we have thus far considered is how time in the dream can be one hour longer than the period of time during which Cobb and Ariadne have been sleeping. Considering the relation between the perception of motion and the perception of time (time is perceived only when motion is perceived), then we can assume that in sleep the mind can create movement, whose succession is equivalent to a period of an hour for those who perceive it. The movements would occur very quickly, but since the activity of the mind is higher than normal, the subject would perceive them as he perceives movements when awake. In Cobb's words, during sleep the mind "creates and perceives a world simultaneously. So well that you don't feel your brain doing the creating."

Since according to the first part of Aristotle's definition, time is the number or measure of motion, the perception of time will vary if what is measured in dreams in *Inception* is a greater amount of movements. The extent of time will also be greater. Cobb's explanation would be: 'because your mind functions more quickly, the movements created by the mind seem to occur slowly, even if they are very fast'.

The question now is: couldn't the mind always create such movements in reality just as in dreams?

The Reality of Time

We might assume that time in dreams differs from time as we perceive it when we're awake, because while we're awake the perception of time depends on the nature of the observed movements, not on the mind itself. Arthur, who is timing Cobb and Ariadne's sleep, observes the same changes or movements that we would observe in five minutes: Cobb and Ariadne breathe, the light in the room flickers in this or that way, some noises come in from the street, and so on. These events are measured by him through his watch, and he has no influenceon them.

For its part, in dreams the mind creates movements and simultaneously perceives them. How many of them occur and how they occur is determined by the mind itself. The mind doesn't depend on something external to create them. Therefore the speed or extent of such mental or dreamed movements isn't restricted to the normal speed or extension of the movements that we perceive when we are awake.

Nevertheless this distinction between natural movements and created movements is problematic. The unconsciousness that occurs in dreams, where the dreamer isn't aware that his mind is creating something, could be extended to our perception of the movements while awake. We know all movements through the mind, both when we're dreaming and when we're awake. When we perceive something, we think that it's external, because we haven't done anything in order for the perceived event to occur. The problem is: maybe we haven't, but our brains do. When we perceive, for example, an external image, this image is actually a process in our brain.

Many processes in our brains happen unconsciously. If it were the case that the mind created all movements that we perceived, without an actual external influence—just like in dreams—we wouldn't know it. So the distinction between imaginary movements and real or natural movements seems to be arbitrary, because we wouldn't know which influence has the mind in it. In any case, if the mind creates all movements, and time is an aspect of movement, time would also be just a mental product.

The second part of Aristotle's definition of time makes it possible for us to distinguish the time that is created in dreams and the time that we perceive when awake. Although the movements that occur in dreams seem to be measured just like we measure the movements when we're awake, what happens in dreams isn't really temporal. Dreams don't have an intrinsic before and after.

Eternity in Time

By defining time, Aristotle speaks about before and after: before and after are essential to time. To understand what Aristotle means, we can use an analogy with movies themselves. When we're in the cinema watching Cobb being chased through the streets of Mombasa, we see that persecution as a continuous movement: it isn't interrupted by something, it forms a unity. Nevertheless, when seeing how the chase unfolds in the film, we perceive only separate frames, in which there's no movement. there's only Cobb in this or that place. A frame on its own isn't movement, but requires the other frames. In order to constitute a movement, each frame has to develop out of an earlier one and give way to a subsequent one. (First and last frames are a different case.)

When Aristotle says that time occurs in relation to before and after, he's claiming that what is temporal—in Nature— doesn't take place according to separate moments or nows, as in the case of the still frames of movies. On the contrary, it always comes out of something and evolves towards something, it's continuous, unitary, and has a before and after.

This continuity of time, referred to in the second part of Aristotle's definition of time, is precisely that which dreams don't have. The mind creates movements that can be measured in dreams. So it seems that the dreams are temporal. But *Inception* does not only show this: it also shows that the mind can break the temporal succession—a succession based on the before and after—by introducing something like eternity in time.

Mind, Eternity, Limbo

In order to reach Fischer's subconscious core, the characters in *Inception* are forced to create dreams within dreams. Thus, by the end of the movie we can see three different dream levels (the Limbo isn't included here as a level, for it wouldn't be a dream, but a possible permanent state of consciousness.) The way in which time is perceived in each level is explained as follows:

> YUSUF: Brain function in the dream will be about twenty times normal.
>
> COBB: And when you go into a dream within that dream the effect is compounded.
>
> ARIADNE: How much time?
>
> YUSUF: Three dreams . . . that's ten hours, times twenty, times twenty, times twenty. . . .
>
> EAMES: Math was never my strong suit.
>
> COBB: It's basically a week one layer down, six months two layers down—
>
> ARIADNE: And ten years in the third level. Who wants to spend ten years in a dream?

The period of time at each new dream level is multiplied by twenty. At each level the mind produces more successive movements, which, also due to the speed of mental activity, will be perceived by the dreamers in the same way in which they perceive any natural movement. ('Natural' means here 'independent of the mind'.)

However, since the Limbo is something like the deepest level of consciousness, the extent of time in dreams tends to infinity, as Yusuf says: in Limbo time can be infinite, the temporal sequence can be endless. What this implies for mental activity isn't made clear in the movie. We can understand simply that the mind of someone who dies in a dream while being sedated falls into Limbo; and even though he can wake up, his mind will remain trapped there. Maybe it will there create and perceive movements frantically.

Those who visit Limbo in the film are Cobb, Mal, and Saito. Cobb and Mal enter Limbo voluntarily. They spend fifty years there, building a world representing a blend of the world of their memories and the world they always wanted to live in. Through their death in Limbo they interrupt this long period of time and wake up. It can be assumed that they weren't sleeping more than a few hours, though this is not mentioned in the movie.

Saito falls into Limbo after he dies in a dream. By the time Cobb finds him, he is already an old man, maybe a hundred years old. He aged in Limbo, just as he would have aged in reality.

We know too little about the world that Saito may have created. He has armed men at his service and lives in a fortress. We get to know better Cobb and Mal's world. And this world is what allows us to discuss the strange elements that are present in the Limbo.

Before thinking about what Cobb and Mal have done in Limbo we will specify two senses of eternity which seem to be mixed in 'Limbo'. Eternity can be understood:

1. as an infinite temporal succession: endless time. This is the time that can be called properly eternal, for its succession does not necessarily have an end. Limbo is eternal in this sense though only as a possibility (since, as it's shown in the movie, it's possible to leave the Limbo).

2. as a property of something that lies outside of the temporal succession: it no longer moves or changes (this is the eternity normally ascribed to God).

Whilst building a world in Limbo, Cobb and Mal seem to experience eternity in the way in which it is described in #1. There are no temporal limits, Cobb and Mal have the possibility to create indefinitely and remain indefinitely within their creation. However, such an eternity is just a possibility. Finally, they decide to leave this place:

ARIADNE: And when you finally woke up?

COBB: To wake from that. From decades lived. To be old souls thrown back into youth. It was hard.

So a possible eternity is interrupted. But this isn't the only eternity that we find in limbo. Cobb's description of what he and Mal have built suggests that limbo contains elements that are timeless in the sense described in #2:

COBB: This is our neighborhood.

ARIADNE: From what city?

COBB: No. Our neighborhood. That was our first apartment . . . then we moved to that building . . . we got that small house when Mal became pregnant.

ARIADNE: You reconstructed them all from memory?

COBB: We had time.

Certain objects which do perhaps no longer exist but are part of Cobb's and Mal's memories are imported into Limbo where they will appear as present. These objects are completely detached from the sequence of movements, which were their cause, as well as from the succession of movements which caused their disappearance.

That's why Limbo shows that what is experienced in dreams isn't actually temporal. It's an ideal world and in this sense it is permanent. It involves no change, no movement, and therefore it involves no time. However, while timelessness is evident in limbo, a certain timelessness also occurs in the other dreams. The temporal succession in dreams is anomalous, for it includes some elements that also possess an eternity as described in #2.

Dreaming Timelessness

Typical events in time happen according to the before and the after: what happens now is necessarily preceded by something that happened before. When we talk about the perception of time, we talk about the perception of that order: about a state of something which moves, about one state in succession to another.

If something is moving, the diverse states that it acquires are temporal because these states happen articulately: the now which corresponds to a particular state of something that moves, bears always reference to something before and to something after it. Something independent of the order of the before and after wouldn't be temporal, but it would rather be something eternal in the timeless sense described in #2.

Things or events detached from something that happened earlier and something that happened later is what can be particularly well observed in limbo as well as on several occasions in other dreams: there are remembered places in conjunction with invented places; for example, a remembered train appears abruptly in the middle of an invented street, without rails and so on.

It's true that the actions carried out by the characters in dreams follow an order of a before and an after, but those actions are interrupted by, or occur in, timeless realities which have no relation to anything before (from where they come) or with an afterwards (into what they will change).

What is it that doesn't happen in accordance with the order of before and after? The answer is: Past things or events, which are perceived as if they were present. If the past becomes present, temporality is negated, for in dreams that which is present has nothing to do with anything by which it was preceded nor has it any future (since it doesn't change).

This timelessness occurs in all the dreams shown in *Inception*. This is especially obvious when we see what populates Cobb's subconscious. For example, his two children come and go, reproducing the same actions over and over again as though they are caught in a loop.

Also when Ariadne, being allowed inside one of Cobb's dreams, looks into a building built with his memories, we see something like moments that remain forever the same: Mal is on the beach with her children; Mal talks lovingly with her husband; and Mal is hysterical because Cobb didn't commit suicide along with her. Cobb's dreamed perception is trapped by eternal nows. Being deprived of proper temporal successions, these remembered objects don't change. there's neither a before nor an after. Moments occur simultaneously.

Thus, in the before and the after, which are mentioned by Aristotle as being essential to what time is, we find a criterion to differentiate the temporality of dreams and the temporality that we perceive when being awake. In the mind, any order of a before and an after can be altered or negated. In nature this isn't possible.

Mental Time and Real Time

COBB: We were on a job. Exploring dreams within dreams. But we didn't understand how your mind can turn hours into years. How you can get trapped. Trapped so deep that when you wash up on the shore of your subconscious you can lose track of what's real.

In an interview with the *New York Times* (30th June, 2010) Christopher Nolan talks about "The Secret Miracle," the story by Jorge Luis Borges, that partially inspired the story of *Inception*. A man sentenced to death asks God to grant him a year to complete his play, *The Enemies*. It seems that God concedes him this time. The precise moment when Jaromir is executed is prolonged for one year. Jaromir, or more precisely his mind, takes advantage of this prolongation and completes the drama. He creates, edits, and concludes the work all at the same moment: the moment when the bullets are fired, somebody cries, a drop of sweat runs down his face.

In Borges's story there seems to be a similar way of understanding time to that shown in *Inception*: there are different temporalities. In "The Secret Miracle" the physical temporality is represented by the movements that stop at the instant of the execution. But the mind isn't linked to this kind of temporal succession. It may have another kind of temporality, which would be based on changes in thinking. Jaromir's work represents this mental time: in the same unique instant, his consciousness considers in detail the diverse parts of his work, and the different corrections that must be made.

A similar distinction is made by Aristotle between the mental now (or, in his words, the now in the definition) and the now in relation to the thing that moves. To understand what Aristotle means, it's helpful to consider what is shown in the movie. We see in *Inception* how Cobb has built a dream world, where moments are chosen and linked arbitrarily. Generally, when the mind determines periods of time, it does so by means of 'nows' which are the limits of those periods. The determination of these periods, and of the limiting nows, is arbitrary: you can choose a previous now that exists more or less closely to the present now, or you can show one which is far away. In that sense, all the nows, as well as the time are at the mind's disposal.

These mental nows are multiple and stay in memory. They don't move by themselves. If they change, they do so through the intervention of the mind. The physical temporality is something different because its determination isn't arbitrary. Neither the continuity of the movements nor the actual state that the moving thing reaches can be modified by the mind. The physical temporality is caused precisely through the relation between the continuity of the movement and the actual state that the moving thing attains. Also the real now will be no more than the current state attained by the moving thing. This state causes the distinction within the continuous movement between the before and the after and can be described as a now because it lacks duration. It doesn't persist. The physical now is merely the boundary between a state of the moving thing which is gone and another one which is achieved.

Precisely this lack of duration shows a difference between what happens in *Inception* and what happens in Borges's story. In the latter, Jaromir's mind undergoes many changes, all of which take place in the same now. In *Inception* changes don't take place within a single instant, but they do always occur within a period of time—in and outside dreams. Therefore we can give an account of the time in the movie through Aristotle's theory of time. According to Aristotle's theory it's impossible that many changes occur in the same now, because the now, being merely the boundary between the before and the after, lacks extension. Only periods of time are extended or can last.

Eternal Iteration

There's yet another way in which Borges's story is related to *Inception*. If time were constituted only with mental nows, we could imagine a kind of closed or circular temporality, in which the before and the after would be apparent. For if they are circular, all nows will be simultaneously before and after to the others. A good example is the story of John Connor in *Terminator I*, who sends his father to protect Sarah Connor. Obviously the beginning of this mission is posterior to the

John's birth, but John is conceived during the mission. As a result of John's birth, or because of John's existence, his father performed the mission. But because of his father's mission, John is also born. John's life is trapped in a circle.

Within such a circularity there's no time in a strict sense, because everything persists. And perhaps the whole temporality in *Inception* is closed or circular because it would be determined by the 'eternal' nows of Cobb's dreams.

In the film a totem is an instrument which helps to know when someone dreams or is awake. Cobb uses a Mal's spinning top:

> **COBB:** This one was hers. She'd spin it in a dream and it would never topple. Just spin and spin . . .

If he's awake, the totem necessarily will fall. At the the end of the movie it seems that Cobb's totem won't fall, and could remain forever in the same state. The totem seems to be outside the temporal succession. Everything that we've seen in the movie as real time can be questioned. The encounter with his children can be only another dream created by Cobb's mind.

In all levels of *Inception* atemporal items happen. Cobb's story could be like the play that Jaromir, who is executed, desires to finish, in which an insane man is trapped in a certain timelessness:

> The incongruities gradually mount up: actors who seemed to have been discarded from the play reappear; the man who had been killed by Roemerstadt returns, for an instant. Someone notes that the time of day has not advanced: the clock strikes seven, the western sun reverberates in the high window panes, impassioned Hungarian music is carried on the air. The first speaker in the play reappears and repeats the words he had spoken in the first scene of the first act. Roemerstadt addresses him without the least surprise. The spectator understands that Roemerstadt is the wretched Jaroslav Kubin. The drama has never taken place: it is the circular delirium which Kubin unendingly lives and relives. ("The Secret Miracle," pp. 146–47)

Level 5

Downwards Is the Only Way Forwards

17
Dreams, Mourning, and Desire

NICOLAS FLOURY

> The absence of time—this is something we dream—what we call
> eternity. This dream consists of imagining that we wake up. We spend
> our time dreaming, we do not only dream when we are asleep. The
> unconscious is precisely the hypothesis that we do not only dream
> when we are asleep.
>
> —JACQUES LACAN, *Le moment de conclure*

According to Jacques Lacan, the definition of the neurotic subject is that he does not desire what he wants and that he does
not want what he actually desires. *Inception* presents us with
a single unique dream, that of a neurotic subject.

The movie is about the dream of one man, Dom Cobb, who
has a dream of a wanted but undesired grief. The dreamer's
desire is not only to mourn the suicide of the beloved woman he
lost, but it is also the will to power, it is the hallucination
enabling the dream to continue as the dreamer lives intensely
and eternally in the presence of his wife.

Christopher Nolan's film presents the aspect of the
Freudian unconscious with all its twists and turns. The film
portrays the unimaginable grief and melancholy associated
with the inability to desire the desire itself. This is well illustrated by the Russian doll structure of the film: a dream within
a dream within a dream . . . until it reaches the state of Limbo.
Can Limbo, that is, the unconscious and the navel of dream so
dear to Freud, be staged in a movie?

From my point of view, everything is dreamt from the very
first images of the movie. Everything starts with a disconcert-

ing dream shot which gives this movie its particular aesthetic quality. Cobb is washed up on a beach. He can see his son and his daughter from a distance. His eyes are half-closed and he seems somnolent. From the start, we're plunged into an atmosphere of strangeness. Oracular sentences are pronounced, whose sense we can't grasp, exactly like in a real dream. So the movie explicitly shows the absurd side of certain dreams.

Freud has said that it is necessary, when interpreting dreams, "to neglect the dream's apparent coherence because it is suspect and to give instead to clear and to obscure elements the same amount of attention." We will thus start with a simple assumption. Throughout the film Cobb has only one single dream. He falls asleep in the aircraft. All the characters in his dream are fellow passengers or people he met at the airport.

The dream is a dream through which Cobb is supposed to solve his neurosis and his melancholy. With this dream, he will end the mourning of his loved and lost wife. Let's say that Cobb, when he falls asleep, is battling against the counter-will of the desire defining the neurotic subject. He wants what he does not wish and at the same time he wishes what he does not want. To make this clearer, he wants to go on living as if Mal is still alive and at the same time he wants to be able to continue his life without her.

Like any dream, Cobb's dream is the place where a desire is fulfilled, but in this case the desire is nothing more than a sorting out of his own conflict. Eventually Cobb will solve it. His problem is solved at the moment he is able to produce a steady desire. A *steady* desire means that he eventually wants what he wishes and that he really wishes what he wants.

Desire and Counter-Desire

Cobb has the *desire* to carry out the mourning of his wife. However, his *counter*-desire tells him that he wants to go on living with her, standing by her, as if she were still alive. Cobb is in a conflict with himself. When his wife emerges in the dream, that is, in his "subconscious," Cobb becomes unable to control anything; he's in the grip of the counter-will of his desire and everything wavers. Saito asks him if he wants to go home to his children. "You can't fix that. Nobody could," answers Cobb.

Here's the conflict: Cobb wishes to go home but this home is the home which existed before the death of his wife who is no longer alive.

"During sleep the brain can do everything", says Cobb to Ariadne when they're sitting at the terrace of the café and Cobb explains to her what her "mission" is going to be. Obviously, when we're dreaming we can carry out all our desires. But at the same time—and this is what the whole first part of the film is dealing with—Cobb wants to return to reality, to wake up, to live his real life. He can do this only once he has carried out the mourning of his wife. All this is symbolized by the joint dream, dreamt together with other characters inside the dream itself. Cobb would like to be reconnected to others, he would like to quit the community of his alter egos and his melancholic isolation, which is like the universe of an extremely egocentric person locked into her own self.

Still, in the end, the counter-desire of the dream will override Cobb's desire. I believe that this is the movie's message. It would be interesting to know whether Christopher Nolan made this film as a "sublimation exercise," enabling him to overcome some kind of grief.

The dreamer has to use a powerful sedative developed by an expert chemist, Yusuf, in order to let the counter-desire grow so it will eventually become a *steady desire*. This process is not without risks: potential failures will cost the dreamer dearly. What could be more difficult than to accept the reality of the death of the beloved, lost wife? On the one hand, he will leave the cherished object behind, but on the other hand he will find a steady desire. In the first part of the movie, Cobb lives this situation as a betrayal, and he will get rid of this feeling of guilt with the help of a powerful sedative which represents the *steady desire* that he needs. It will take Cobb the entire film to reach that point, which probably corresponds more or less to a dream lasting only a few minutes for a dreamer. And the dreamer is Cobb sitting in the seat of the aircraft that brings him back home.

In principle, the dream (which is the entire film) represents a conflict between a counter-desire and a desire; and eventually this counter-desire will dominate. Cobb's primary desire is stated on several occasions: "In my dreams we are still together," he says when he talks to Ariadne in the elevator. This is the reason why it is so important for him to dream. "You're keeping her alive, you can't let her go," retorts Ariadne. Ariadne might be no more than a double of Cobb. She very well understands that he doesn't really want to achieve the mourning, at least not for now, while he's dreaming. This means that within Cobb's dream there is a dialog, a dialog of Cobb with himself. In the same sequence, when he is walking around with Ariadne in Mal's house, he says that he's dreaming in order to be able "to grow old together" with Mal and "to see again the faces of my children."

To stand by his wife would be for Cobb the same as spending the rest of his life asleep, entangled in dreams, and to remain forever locked up in the existential condition of living while being dead. Very slowly Cobb begins to refuse this. Cobb has been in limbos, in phases of deep melancholy. In my opinion, this is the meaning of limbos: they are states of melancholic dullness where you're completely detached from the world. Cobb built his own dream world although he was awake. Melancholy is a life without desire, a life under the seal of death, a life spent scrutinizing memories of the past without perceiving any possible future.

The chemist's task is to clarify all this when he shows Cobb the twelve people who take a sedative in order to be able to remain in their dreams forever. An old man tells him that "they come to be woken. The dream has become their reality." Cobb prefers an imaginary dream world to hard reality and he *wants* to continue doing this though he *wishes* at the same time that he could stop.

But fortunately for Cobb, the counter-desire emerges: "We yearn for people to be reconciled, for catharsis," explains Cobb to his team when they are planning to implant an idea into Robert Fischer's mind.

A Way toward Redemption

Fundamentally, the much discussed question of the "levels"— the dream in the dream in the dream, up to the limbos—is not really a problem. Level 1 is where Cobb is in the hands of his desire, where he wants to continue living as if nothing has happened, with his wife still standing by him, just like before. Level 2 is the level where the counter-desire starts to intervene. Cobb no longer wants what he desires, but he needs "time to understand." Then appears Ariadne, and scenes evolve towards violence and death. This is the level where Cobb is battling against himself, or at least against his primary desire.

At this moment he can hardly control things, and his wife reappears together with her phobia of trains. The following level is the one where Cobb will slowly accept his counter-desire as his only desire. This desire will help to resolve the neurotic conflict of the dream: it represents the choice of life and the final achievement of mourning. This evolution happens while Cobb is in diverse limbos, which represent the last level. Of course all these levels are not really distinguished, they are superimposed and proceed simultaneously. Finally we can assume that there is, during the whole film, only one reality and one dream.

Somehow the film reaches a critical point when Saito is wounded, and the mission is about to fail. This is how a new "level" is attained. Cobb is plunged in the middle of snow-covered mountains. A true war will occur, of which we do not know many details. The first task to be solved is to plant a desire in Fischer's mind in order to make him dismantle the financial empire he has inherited from his father. But in principle, the war is only a metaphor induced by Cobb's dream-work. This dream-work is a battle that Cobb is leading against himself. However, this desire is—at this moment of the movie or dream, since the whole film is only one dream—again in the firm grip of the counter-desire of the will. And it is here that the intensity of the battle reaches its climax.

We're shown a real war with tanks, large guns, an excessive number of soldiers, and other trappings of armed combat. Here the internal conflict lived by the dreamer Cobb reaches its climax. And this is precisely the moment of the dream where Cobb shoots Mal. This is clearly a sign of the overcoming of mourning. But Mal seems only to be wounded and not yet dead. Slowly she will become able to occupy the place of a lost object. Therefore, we can presume that Cobb is on his way to admit the reality of her death.

The Choice of Mourning

Everything will be cleared up in the limbos, and Cobb—not without the assistance of the young and brilliant architecture student Ariadne—will make his final decision: he will accomplish the mourning of his wife. This decision takes place unconsciously.

Ariadne will try to convince Cobb to remain in his initial position, in which he was living as if she was still alive. She's trying hard to persuade him not to end his mourning. With Ariadne, Cobb visits the city that he and his wife had imagined in former times and which is no more than a fantasized memory distorted by the dream-work of his ancient life. It represents his life at a time when he was living close to Mal. "We had time," says Cobb. This sentence quite obviously expresses nostalgia.

"Your ideas are confused," says Mal in order to convince Cobb, telling him that he must stay in limbo if he wants to go on living with his children, James and Philippa. Cobb is confused, but he is about to give up his guilt to stop living with his remorse. Cobb makes up his mind while sleeping: his desire is going to become the primary counter-desire of the dream, but this time it's a steady desire. He chooses to return to reality, to life. His dreamed dialog with Mal occurs as a plea addressed to himself.

Cobb believes he caused the suicide of his wife and we have every right to assume that this is true: Mal obviously did commit suicide. Moreover, in a scene which is about the labyrinths she's building, Cobb tells Ariadne that he can't go back home because "they" think he killed her. Cobb probably believes himself that he is at the origin of his wife's suicide. This is well illustrated by the scene inside the helicopter, when Saito asks for an "inception to be carried out." Though this seems to be impossible, Cobb affirms that he has already done it. This means that he could have pushed his wife to commit suicide while planting an idea in her mind against her own will.

From then on, guilt will prevent him from ending his mourning. The kind of mourning that he undergoes is quite impossible. In the dream he hears, for example, Mal telling him: "You can still save yourself by staying here in the world we built together." However, this world is no more than Cobb's melancholic self-enclosure: he lives in this world in the way in which a person who is living, but at the same time dead lives in the past.

"No, I don't regret anything," is the title of the famous Edith Piaf song that is repeatedly played in the film. For me this signifies that Cobb is making progress with his mourning and that it will soon be accomplished. The tune is also chosen as a signal for the return to the level of reality. At the same time, it helps Cobb to choose life and to give up regrets and remorse. "I do not stay;" "She does not exist, so how could I stay with her;" "I would like" to stay with you, "but I can't recreate you with your whole complexity, your perfection, all your imperfections;" "You are nothing but a shade, the shade of my true wife;" "You are the best I could recreate but, I regret that it is insufficient. . . ." Once these sentences are uttered, Cobb, undergoing a real Freudian dream-work, chooses to live without his wife. He decides to leave his imaginary life of melancholy made of the past and memories.

The storyline proceeds from level to level, and each time he reaches a new level, this is a sign that Cobb has woken up. "Waking up" means that he is eventually coming back to real life, to a life in which Mal is dead. This is also true in a more literal sense: he will wake up in the airplane, that is, he will return to a reality that he had actually never left. This means that he has merely been passing from a state of sleep to a state of being awake. This is true even if, as Lacan says in the epitet to the present chapter, we are all constantly dreaming even when we are awake. We can't know anything about the reality that we're in. We can keep in touch with reality only through the skylight of our phantasms. Even when we're awake and immersed in reality, we see the world only by means of our projecting imagination.

The Question of the Body

What remains relatively real, however, is the presence in the physical world of Cobb's body. In order to interpret Christopher Nolan's movie philosophically and psychoanalytically, we should assume that Cobb is sitting throughout the whole film in his seat in the airplane that brings him back home.

This is certainly a materialist point of view, assuming that the physical world is unique and that there are not various levels of reality in the film. Instead, there is the insertion of dreams into the dream, a constellation that can produce the false perception of a variety of dreams. At many points of the film, at the beginning for example, it is possible to read the film in this way, especially after the chat between Cobb, his associate Arthur, and Saito, when everything starts shaking and crumbling after Arthur has been killed; or when the characters are totally weightless and are tossed in the air. This could be air pockets that the plane is going through causing Cobb's body to experience the shaking while he's dreaming.

If there is only one physical world, and if the film presents only one unique dream, there is no passage from one world to another. This is why nothing in Nolan's film comes from the realm of science fiction. On the other hand, the Russian doll structure upon which the whole film is built can be interpreted in the following way: when we dream that we are dreaming we very often like the second dream to remain only a dream. That's at least what I think. This could explain the pattern that permits this continuous ascendance "level by level." Because Cobb's ultimate dream, dreamt right before the awakening that saves him, consists in the desire to be together with Mal.

Cobb wants the moments associated with being unable to let Mal go belong to the realm of the dream. And the entire film leads him towards this aim. Cobb wants to come back to reality, and this happens when he ascends, level by level, to the state of being awake.

Epilog

In the epilog of the film, Cobb wakes up in the plane just after talking to Saito. He has grown much older, and Cobb tries to convince him to come back to reality in order to resume his youth. Perhaps Cobb is speaking only to himself, convincing himself, for a last time, that it is necessary to join "live life" and to give up his melancholic state of dullness. Just like in James Joyce's *Finnegans Wake*, the beginning of the film reappears at the end.

Moreover, while Cobb is talking to Saito, his weapon and his spinning top are on the table, which might show that the fact of leaving the dream has been a means to buckle the loop. The mourning is done, and Cobb won't need to repeat the dream.

In the next sequence we see Cobb opening his eyes in the airplane. This gives us the key to the entire movie. At least, it proves to us that there is only one single dream, Cobb's dream, which represents the whole film. Cobb leaves the state of sleep and approaches the only level on which reality really exists and which, as a matter of fact, he had never left. Freud says in *The Interpretation of Dreams* that one always uses the images of the day before in order to build a dream. Cobb finds all the protagonists of his dream in the airplane. They are the passengers sitting next to him or the people he had noticed in the airport before the plane took off.

His passport is okay and he can come back to America; in the dream this had been impossible. Coming back home had been impossible and the dream has made it possible through a metaphorical actualization. Coming back home means to come back to his real self and it means that the weight of mourning has been removed.

Cobb's father-in-law (and a father figure) Miles is perhaps the only element that symbolizes something like a "life instinct" in the film. Cobb visits his father-in-law because he is looking for a good architect and Miles clearly tells him: "Come back to reality." The image of Miles appears in the first part of the film and is quite benevolent. Miles seems to push Cobb to do his mourning. For Cobb, Miles probably represents that part of his will that drives him forward. Miles is the little voice inhabiting Cobb, pushing him to reach out for real life, to give up the past, to confront himself, to be youthful, and to look towards the future. All these elements allow us to consider Cobb's dream as "a dream of redemption."

The spinning top does not tumble when Cobb comes home. But on the basis of our assumption that the whole film is one single dream and one single reality, we can conclude that this is not really important. Its meaning is merely metaphorical and should probably be understood as a link connecting Cobb and Mal. The function of the spinning top is clarified for the first time when Cobb explains to Ariadne why she should create her own totem. This totem has to be absolutely unique and its details should be known only to its owner. Only then will it allow her to know if she is in another person's dream or not. The spinning top is also presented as Mal's former totem. What sense does this spinning totem have? Several interpretations are possible. For me it is merely an element allowing Cobb to build his own dream; it isn't used in order to discriminate between "real reality" and dream.

On another hand, the spinning top was Mal's creation, it was her object, and Cobb appropriated it afterwards. Consequently it remains her object, her totem, her guide. In the last sequence of the film it continues spinning on its own as if it belongs to nobody, as if it is completely detached from Cobb's psyche and from his "subconscious." The top could be a representation of the beloved and lost Mal, which has eventually been expelled, and which allows Cobb to come back to life. The object of grief is neither erased nor forgotten, but it has been put into its right place, where it is unable to block Cobb's will to life.

Something needs to be said about the children. At the beginning of the dream, the image becomes fuzzy and develops towards a dream aesthetics. Are the children real or did they die together with their mother? Did they ever exist? We can assume that the melancholic state of Cobb prevents him from living with his children and that he needs to alter this psychological state. The discussion with his father-in-law in the amphitheater could support this assumption, especially when he says to Cobb: "It'll take more than the occasional stuffed animal to convince those children they still have a father." This implies that Cobb has been away from his children as a result of his melancholic state and that he has not been able to take care of them. But we shall leave this question open. Let's simply say that the children are the umbilical point of the dream, mentioned by Freud, that they are an element whose sense cannot be grasped. They are the element that makes it impossible to interpret a dream in its entirety. The reason is that throughout the film there are plenty of seemingly absurd elements, exactly like in a dream. We have to read these elements as the author's intention to recreate, with great subtlety, a dream universe of rare precision.

Perhaps the attentive reader has noticed that this chapter has been constructed so that its successive individual elements are not necessarily connected in terms of a logic that is visible at first sight. It's just like a dream.[1]

---

[1] This chapter was translated from the French by Pascal Coulon.

18

The Undiscovered Country Called Experience

JASON J. HOWARD

There are lots of things in life that people are uncertain about, whether it is relationships, employment, or stock prices, but few are unsure about whether they're dreaming or awake. Such basic distinctions, like that between our waking perceptions of the world around us and the dream worlds we encounter while asleep, are not the kinds of things that people confuse on a regular basis.

Where would our love life be if we couldn't distinguish the memories of our ex-lovers from the ones we are presently with—and from those we daydream about? Talk about trouble! Yet the apparent confidence we have distinguishing what we experience when awake from what we experience in a dream doesn't solve the question of how it's possible, it only confirms that we can do it.

To answer the question of what distinguishes waking perceptions, memories, and dreams, we need to look at our own subjective experience in a new way. For that we require a guide, an architect of dream space, who can lead us through the undiscovered country called experience. *Inception* is that guide.

It's easy to miss the complexity of human experience. *Inception* draws our attention to this complexity through the novel way it invites us to question the reliability of human experience, undermining the traditional distinction between dream and reality. As Cobb explains: "Well, dreams, they feel real while we're in them right? It's only when we wake up that we realize something was actually strange." And it's precisely in this sensitivity to the question of how the world appears and feels to us, that *Inception* stands out. Rather than approach this issue from a purely skeptical standpoint, collapsing the distinction between dream and reality in its entirety, *Inception* also explores the differences between our dreams and waking perceptions of the world, suggesting both the continuity and discontinuity between different levels of human experience.

One of the central insights of the movie is that our dream experience is constructed or constituted. Our mind experiences dreams as an independent reality yet this is so only thanks to the creative activity of our mind as it unconsciously builds a world for us to discover. As Cobb explains: "Now, in a dream, our mind continuously does this. We create and perceive our world simultaneously. And our mind does this so well we don't even know it's happening. . . ."

In its emphasis on how people unconsciously construct or constitute experience in uniform and identifiable patterns, seeing the mind as an active source in the creation of meaning, *Inception* assumes what some philosophers call a phenomenological perspective on experience. To look at experience phenomenologically is to pay close attention both to how subjective consciousness organizes experience and to how our experience feels different depending on our mode of awareness, whether we are dreaming about something, remembering something, or perceiving something. *Inception* plays on these points in subtle and sophisticated ways in an attempt to explore how Cobb and his crew can steal into someone's dreams in order to not only 'extract' information, but also 'plant' ideas.

Inception as Phenomenological Philosophy

People have been interested in understanding how human experience works for a long time. Phenomenology is a branch of philosophy, founded by Edmund Husserl (1859–1938) that attempts to identify the different elements that structure and organize human consciousness, describing how these elements cohere to form a common world of experience.

Phenomenology describes lived experience with as much precision as possible, while ignoring more abstract theoretical questions like 'What is consciousness made of?' or 'Where does consciousness come from?' or 'What happens to consciousness when we die?'

Phenomenology focuses on specifying the multiple levels and modes of organization that make up all the invariant features of experience, the majority of which are largely implicit and so are rarely obvious. How can experience yield evidence of the world and ourselves? How can subjective processes generate objectivity? Phenomenology's fundamental insight is that consciousness is intentional, which means that "all consciousness is consciousness of something."

We don't just have beliefs, but beliefs about certain things; likewise, we don't simply have emotions, but emotions directed towards people and events, and the same holds for perceptions, dreams, memories, and anything else that forms a meaningful element of our experience. To have an experience is for consciousness to be directed towards some object in a particular way; it is to be attentive to what exists and the manner in which it exists.

Inception shares much of this standpoint with its interest in the architecture of dream construction and the relationship between dreams, memories, and waking perceptions. *Inception* introduces a number of crucial distinctions that not only make for great entertainment, but also provide real insight into how our consciousness organizes experience.

Although it's hard to pin down, meeting someone in a dream feels different from meeting someone in waking reality. Likewise, remembering your ex-girlfriend is different from dreaming about her, yet the content of the experience is the same in either case, your ex. It is a mark of Nolan's perceptiveness both as a writer and director that he exploits the very same categories that have been of fundamental importance in the tradition of Husserlian phenomenology for understanding the continuities and discontinuities between dreams, memories and perceptions. Nolan uses these categories to explore the ways in which dreaming, remembering and perceiving all 'feel' slightly different, even when such states are directed towards the same objects.

To borrow language from Husserl, the modes of givenness or degrees of evidence that structure our experience will vary when we move from perceiving a real Japanese castle, to remembering that castle the next day, to imagining a Japanese castle we have never seen. Our awareness of the castle, how strongly we believe in its reality, will be different in accordance with how we are conscious of it, whether as perceived, remembered, or imagined. This doesn't mean that people can never be mistaken about what they perceive, or that we can't confuse our memories with our dreams. The point is just that such cases are the exceptions rather than the rule, otherwise our experience would be so unreliable we could never make predictions, corroborate information, or even speak about a shared world of events and people.

Ordinarily our waking perceptions, dreams and memories remain quite distinct from one another, each one providing us with a different window of awareness. Of course if you have a device that lets you construct dreams, which you can then trick other people into believing are their own dreams, allowing you to steal inside their subconscious, the line between dreams and reality is going to get blurry!

According to Husserl, "Every subjective process has a process 'horizon', which changes with the alteration of the nexus of consciousness to which the process belong" (*Cartesian Meditations*, p. 44). Minus the jargon, Husserl is drawing our attention to something that's very easy to miss, and that Nolan spells out so very well: every distinct mode of conscious awareness is distinguished by a horizon of expectations, anticipations, and assumptions that uniquely characterizes the type of awareness. Dreaming is different from waking perception because the experience itself is structured differently, things are verified differently, the horizon of expectations and anticipations is organized according to different criteria, and this is not a conscious choice, but an intrinsic feature of the specific mode of conscious awareness. If it weren't for such differences poor Cobb would be trapped in dream time forever.

What Do You Mean It's Only Been Fifteen Minutes?

One important way that dreaming is distinguishable from other kinds of conscious awareness is that we experience duration very differently while in a dream. Time passes in a surreal way in a dream, simple actions and events that should take no time at all, say going for a walk, appear to stretch on for weeks, or in Cobb's case for decades.

This point is emphasized by Arthur: "Five minutes in the real world gives you an hour in the dream." In addition to such temporal dilation, the experience of duration itself feels disjointed. What's more, the more involved one is in the dream, the more expansive is the subjective experience of duration. The ten-hour flight from Sydney to New York that Cobb uses to hijack Robert Fischer's dreams ends up feeling like ten years in dream time, enough to drive someone insane who is trapped there long enough (poor Saito!).

What's instructive here isn't whether the time differential between the dream world and reality actually is five minutes for every hour, but the insight that time does flow differently in our dreams—something each of us is familiar with even if we don't usually notice it. Cobb puts the point this way: "In a dream, your mind functions more quickly, therefore time seems to feel more slow."

This experience of time dilation and disjunction is simply accepted within the subjective consciousness of the dreamer. One minute we're on the beach with our kids, and the next we're celebrating our anniversary in a hotel with our wife, and this fluctuation in the linear sequence of time is not experienced as abnormal in any way, at least not while we are in the dream.

One of the first things that Cobb asks Ariadne in their initial training session is to recall how she got to the café. Not surprisingly, she can't remember, because she didn't really 'get there' at all in the traditional sense; she's simply dreaming she's there. As Cobb clarifies: "You never really remember the beginning of a dream do you? You always wind up right in the middle of what is going on." In waking experience we can almost always quickly and reliably state why we are where we are and how we got there.

Now it's true that intoxication and intense traumatic experience can disorient us momentarily, but we usually recover from such events, most of the time by the middle of next day's hangover. When we dream, this is different—the present simply begins without a past. This is a crucial point that Husserl uses to explain the phenomenological difference between imagination and the conscious experience of remembering, a point Cobb himself is painfully aware of.

On numerous occasions Cobb empathically insists to Ariadne that she not populate her architectural dreamscapes with actual memories. "Never re-create places from your memory. Always imagine new places. . . . Building a dream from your memory is the easiest way to lose your grasp on what's real; and what is a dream." The images we see when we dream, even if they are of familiar events, are not internally linked to any linear temporal sequence, while actual memories are always linked to specific moments. Husserl defines memory as "consciousness of the past" or "re-presentification" of what was once present.

Memories are not simply random images, but intentional transformations of what is present to what is no longer present. All actual memories are linked to events in a temporal sequence of before and after and this is an intrinsic feature of what constitutes memory; this 'remembrance of things past' is an internal feature of what it means to remember. Although it's true that I can be mistaken about my memories, such mistakes can be corrected, at least in theory. I can find other people who witnessed the same event, try to remember what had just happened prior to the event and match this with other memories of the same period, or perhaps seek counseling or therapy. None of this makes sense in terms of what we dream about, since the dream doesn't directly correspond to any reality, past or present.

Technically when memories from our past occur in our dreams they are not actually memories, since they are not consciously being accessed through an act of remembrance; rather we have images that rise up sporadically throughout our dreams. Those dream-images may be of events that actually transpired or they may not, but it's not essential that they reliably reflect and fit into the dream world, whereas the same can't be said of the images we recall when we consciously remember something.

Between remembering and dreaming, the type and degree of awareness is different in each case, even when they are about the same thing and even if the difference between them commonly goes unnoticed. This distinction is not something we are taught but persists as an invariable feature of consciousness. As with the case of perception, this doesn't mean that people can never confuse actual memories with the content of their dreams, but that this is the exception rather than the rule. It is precisely because we all intuitively sense the difference between dreams and memories, that deliberately confusing them causes serious problems. For most of us this is a point that isn't explored or tested much outside the field of mental illness. *Inception* provides a way into the issue through its idea of dream architecture.

Once an architect populates a dream world with her actual memories, the phenomenological distinction between dream image and perceptual reality is threatened, since the temporal sequencing that is an intrinsic feature of memories is temporarily disabled. We take lived events that necessarily have a specific halo of time and place, a temporal signature of sorts, and sever that connection by trying to enlist memories into different forms of subjective awareness where temporal continuity has no special priority. The result is that consciousness becomes deeply disoriented and loses sense of what is real and what is merely imagined.

In Cobb's case, he's unable to dream without relying on his memories, which is why he no longer builds dreamscapes. His sense of grief and guilt over Mal, compounded by the time they spent together constructing their own shared dream world, has overridden his natural ability to distinguish his dreams from his memories. Cobb's concern over the need to distinguish memories from dreams is a genuine phenomenological insight that plays on the intentional differences between what was once perceived (and now is only memory) and what was never perceived.

To Leap Tall Buildings in a Single Bound

Time is not the only thing that is experienced differently depending on our type of intentional state. Much of the general rules of physics simply don't apply within our dreams, or at the very least they don't apply consistently. This point is something that is readily verifiable by just about anyone who can recall their dreams.

What's phenomenologically interesting about this fact is that such irregularities are rarely ever noticed while we are dreaming. The reason for this is that our dreams conform to a different pattern of evidence and confirmation than does waking experience. As Husserl puts it, "the subjective alteration of manners of givenness, of manners of appearing, and of the modes of validity in them . . ." differ depending on our intentional state (*The Crisis of the European Sciences*, p. 146).

We expect a certain continuity to our waking perceptions of the world—that objects won't randomly appear and disappear into thin air and that when I turn around to look behind me, my gaze will fall on the same world as the one I perceived in front of me. We also intuitively assume any object that we see can be seen by other people. No one chooses to think about perception in this way, nor is anyone ever taught these elemental truths; such cognitive assumptions are necessary components of our perceptual states. Just imagine how strange it would be to hear the following exchange between a father and son: "Now James, always remember to look both ways before you cross the street, and don't forget that any object that you see, other people can see too." Talk about wasted fatherly advice!

It was Husserl's genius to unpack all of the complex intentional states that are necessary ingredients of perceptual life, and that so few before him had ever really noticed. The guiding insight here is that the unity of perceptual experience, the confidence we have in it, is something that can't be explained at the level of sensory stimulus alone, but rather consciousness must play a role in synthesizing these elements.

Undoubtedly, external sensory impulses are essential and without them there is no perception, yet the structuring of raw sense data in terms of the expectations we have about them and their degrees of reliability can't itself come from the sensory data, but is an unconscious interpretation about the *meaning* of the data. Simply put, if not for intentionality we would be locked in a perpetual present, stuck in sporadic moments that have no necessary continuity and from which we could draw no inferences and make no plans.

Dreams and perceptual experience are both intentional modes of awareness, and each undoubtedly has much in common with the other. The defining difference between them is that waking perceptual experience is guided by actual sensory data which severely limits how this data can be interpreted, whereas the same is simply not true of our dreams. Dreams never make immediate contact with any raw sensory data from the external world, but remain reconstructions. This point about the reliability of perception and its difference from dreams is something explored to great effect by *Inception*.

There's a reason Cobb carries that spinning top wherever he goes!

Most of us have no control over whether we will confuse our dreams with our waking perceptions of reality. This is a choice that is ruled out for us on the basis of the intentional state we happen to find ourselves in. To dream is to accept certain characteristics of the dream world and to perceive is to accept certain characteristics about the perceived world. The two refer to distinct intentional states of consciousness, each one with its own rules of evidence and horizons of fulfillment. Through its idea of dream architecture and the accompanying idea of hijacking people's dreams, *Inception* confuses this distinction in very subtle ways, yet it never entirely collapses it.

Regardless of how vivid our dreams may be, we always eventually wake up from them, and with this comes a corresponding change in intentional state. This basic fact of life undergoes some radical refinement in the movie. Cobb and his crew are essentially stuck in their target's dream until they are forced or pulled out of it in some way. As a consequence, many of the natural safeguards that we have against crisscrossing different intentional modes of awareness are sidelined by Cobb.

Despite this fact, the difference between dream and reality remains a centerpiece in the film. The reason that everyone carries an object totem with them, whether a loaded die, chess piece, or spinning top, is to ensure they have access to some piece of evidence that can confirm their true intentional state. Each of the totems is affected by gravity or some other law of nature. Objects that we see in waking perceptual experience must conform to certain laws of nature or else our experience is immediately called into question, whereas the same is not the case for dream experiences.

If you have a spinning top and you spin it and it never stops spinning, this is an indication that something is not right! Likewise, if a train suddenly appears out of nowhere and goes barreling down the middle of a city street, or buildings curl upside down, you can bet that you are no longer in the shared world of waking perception; either that or you are having a wicked acid flashback!

Even when Cobb's crew of dream architects attempt to 're-create' a certain piece of the real world, say Saito's love shack, there are inherent limitations built into the dreaming experience that condition what can be achieved. Waking perceptual experience provides the most robust and durable evidence that we can have, both about ourselves and the world. Although sensations alone can't explain the continuity and objectivity of waking experience, there's no such experience without actual sensations to interpret and intentionally reconstruct.

Husserl makes this point in his insistence that waking perception is the most reliable mode of consciousness, and it is essentially its shared dependability that distinguishes it from other types of consciousness. Dreams not only follow different patterns of confirmation, but their content, what we dream about, is largely derived from the reality of perceptual experience. Our common perceptual world, what Husserl calls the *Lebenswelt* or life-world, is the ultimate touchstone of meaningful experience:

> ... the life-world, for us who wakingly live in it, is always already there, existing in advance for us, the "ground" of all praxis whether theoretical or extratheoretical. . . . To live is always to live-in-the-certainty-of-the-world. Waking life is being awake to the world, being constantly and directly "conscious" of the world and of oneself as living *in* the world, actually experiencing and actually effecting the ontic certainty of the world. (*Crisis of the European Sciences*, p. 142)

We can try and use our imagination to create a copy of the real world, but our dreams won't ever match reality. Even though Saito's love shack appears to be a perfect copy, which Cobb's crew re-creates in the hopes of tricking him, the copycat carpet in the dream world ends up giving Cobb away; it isn't made of the same material, and Saito recognizes this.

Inception's phenomenological savvy is repeatedly illustrated in the way it explores this discrepancy between dream and reality. For example, small details, such as the lettering on Cobb's watch, are off within the dream; it is backwards while in the dream world. At a more obvious level, Ariadne needs to employ special perceptual tricks to close the dream world off, the famous Penrose steps. Such closure is impossible within the life-world.

We can physically detain people, limiting their movement, but we can't literally determine for someone where the world ends and where it begins. Technically, there are no set limits to waking experience. So long as our vision is not obstructed, we see until the clarity of our vision fades into obscurity. And this speaks to yet another fundamental characteristic of waking experience, its openness to possibilities and limitless exploration.

However much Cobb loved the world that he and Mal created, however much they got to fuse together the best of everything, it was always deficient in one profound respect —it was not reality. Eventually Cobb came to realize that the limits of their own creativity and experience could never equal the vivacity of ordinary waking experience. A world of our own design is necessarily a world without any real surprises; it's a world limited by the insights of those who construct it. Although it may take some time, people who construct their own reality are going to run out of ideas, and what people will be left with won't be a dynamic statement of their own creativity, but a stale and one-dimensional copy of their own personality. Cobb finally comes to this realization, which is what allowed him to take the initiative needed to find a way back to the life-world.

Learning How Not to Wet the Bed

It's not just that our experience of objects is confirmed differently while dreaming, but our very experience of corporeality and spatiality is different. We may appear to have control over our bodies while dreaming and we seem to be free to move about and do as we please, but this appearance is deceptive.

Remember the old sleepover trick of putting your pal's finger in a glass of water in the hopes he'll pee his pants? Recall the last time you really had to pee while you were in a dream. Chances are you didn't register the need to urinate directly, but you did feel it some other way. Perhaps it started raining, as it did in Yusuf's dream, or perhaps you found yourself in an actual toilet, or maybe you were swimming. Stimuli from the waking world can condition what we experience in the dream. If we're hungry when we go to bed, it's not unusual to dream about eating. If we're anxious about something in our life, more often than not our anxiety carries over into our dreams. And so regardless of how liberating our dreams may appear, however removed they may be from waking life, the encounters we have while dreaming are often an extension of the stresses we have in everyday life.

How many of us have dreamt about strange lights and sounds, only to discover when waking that such experiences stem from our waking experience—lights were left on or the sound of traffic made its way into our dream. Whatever doesn't wake us up is often incorporated into the dream itself. In fact, one technique of lucid dreaming is to gear your dream experience to some outside signal. Lucid dreamers can buy headsets with adjustable lighting that can be set to go off with a certain frequency sometime during the sleeping session (I know this because my old roommate was a lucid dreamer, he got his headset from some sleep institute in California).

People can be trained to notice this fluctuation within the dream itself, and so realize they are dreaming and partially 'wake up' in the dream, and thus participate more actively in their dreaming. Cobb and his crew follow a similar strategy, except their cue isn't light, but music. We see the same effect when it comes to maintaining our balance. Typically, if our body changes location only slightly while dreaming, aspects of this change may be incorporated within the dream, but if our balance is really thrown out of whack, we wake up automatically, at least unless we are seriously sedated.

We remain embodied, even while dreaming, and our biological, physiological and emotional needs don't ever disappear. Being trapped in Limbo is a real concern in the movie partly because Saito's living body still requires attention and nourishment. Akin to being in a coma, if Saito can't wake up, his joints and ligaments will atrophy and his body will wither away if not constantly maintained. The connection with our lived bodies can only be delayed for so long before serious side-effects begin to take shape. This is true both mentally—we begin to confuse dreams with reality—as well as physically: our bodies decay if not properly attended.

None of this would make any sense if there weren't an intrinsic difference between intentional states. Dreaming, like remembering, is an innate mode of awareness, a capacity built into the intentional framework of consciousness, but the cognitive authority both hold is limited by design. When consciousness is operating properly, these modes do not usurp the authority of waking present life, they supplement, complement, extend, and perhaps even amend aspects of waking experience. It's when imagination and memory completely supplant waking experience that things go wrong.

Guilt Can be a Real Bitch

One of the most powerful themes of *Inception* is Cobb's struggle to return home and simply be with his children. All the time spent trying to extract and implant information in some alternate dream world are just so many hurdles on the journey back to the reality of other people. As Cobb finally confesses to Mal: "I feel guilt, Mal. And no matter what I do, no matter how hopeless I am, no mater how confused, that guilt is always there . . . reminding me of the truth."

Nolan's point here is as phenomenologically sound as it is simple: to be in the world is to live amongst other people, to love them and be loved by them. In Husserl's words, however we want to define reality it is inseparable from the inter-subjective community of other people. The life-world is a shared world and it is this commonality that ultimately grounds the confidence we have in it. Cobb's guilt operates as a veritable Ariadne's thread that circulates through the labyrinthine conflation of his dreams and memories. More than anything else, it's his emotional life that compels Cobb back to reality, even if initially it is this same emotional life that motivates him to flee it.

What we experience in our dreams as well as our memories are never actual people, but only a "shade" of actual people. As was the case with the imagined dreamscapes he created, Cobb's representation of other people in his dreams, as well as his memories, could never match or capture the reality of his loved ones.

Regardless of how routine our lives may become, or how predictable are those we love, others exist in their own right, indisputably. Our very sense of self-identity is built up over time through interaction with these others, and it is only through them that something like an objective world of nature, things, and culture appears at all. As Husserl explains, within intentional consciousness "there is implicit a *mutual being for one another*, which entails an *objectivating equalization* of my existence with that of all others" (*Cartesian Meditations*, p. 129).

Individual consciousness can't duplicate the complexity, perfection, imperfection, and personality of other human beings. Try as we might, the lives we imagine for these people will never match the lives they actually lead or have led for the simple reason that who they are is forever restricted by what we want them to be. *Inception* explores this insight in a powerful way.

Guilt is one of the most compelling emotions that we have. Inherent in this emotion is its directedness towards others. We feel guilty about what we do to others, not what we do to ourselves, for even when we do something alone in private that we shouldn't, feeling guilty about it implies the presence of others, that we have betrayed some value that is shared.

And so it is quite fitting that Cobb's confrontation with his own guilt is what allows him to finally abandon Mal to the world of mere memories, and seek out Saito in order to return to the present. Doubtless our sense of guilt can play tricks on us, as it did with Cobb, but the fact that we experience guilt at all points back to the guiding anchor of waking experience and our shared experience with others. To quote Cobb again, guilt reminds us of the truth. Our common vulnerability conditions who we are at the deepest levels, the traces of which are scattered throughout our memories and our dreams. Yet it is waking experience alone that allows us to affect this vulnerability, to engage with others and make our mark, whether beneficial or not. You can't offend a memory, nor can you betray an image from a dream.

Inception is an exceptional film on many levels, not least of which is what it shows us about the complexity of human experience. Instead of taking the theme of hijacking other's dreams into the domain of pure fantasy and idle speculation, Nolan treats it as an occasion to explore different layers of consciousness with a sensitivity and seriousness that few films can parallel. The idea of dream architecture works as an ideal vehicle to investigate what many of us simply take for granted, how it is that dreaming, remembering and perceiving refer to distinct and distinguishable intentional states.

What makes *Inception* so exceedingly clever is precisely that it does *not* collapse these distinctions into one long dream, but interweaves them. Does this mean that Cobb's top is going to stop spinning? That he did make it back to the real world and his family? From our phenomenological perspective, the ending of the film can remain as open as Nolan intended. The point is that the type of experience, whether of fantasy or reality, will eventually reveal itself, since dreams remain dreams no matter how much we desire to make them real. If Cobb finally recognized Mal as a projection of his own guilt, there is no reason to believe he won't eventually recognize his kids as one. But we'll leave that to another movie.

19
Inception's Faith in Everyday Life

CHRISTOPHE D. RINGER

Inception isn't possible. I know that hurts so let me be a little more specific. Inception isn't *philosophically* possible. The reason why however, is what makes *Inception* philosophically a rich, good piece of science fiction.

Inception quickly establishes Cobb's credentials as a master at stealing ideas from people's dreams (this is *Ocean's Eleven* of the unconscious life). If only it were that simple!

Inception's appeal rests on taking the viewer into the world of a "dream within a dream." The philosophical underpinnings of *Inception* are revealed when Professor Miles allows Cobb access to one of his brightest students, Ariadne. *Inception* claims that what makes the mind so special is what it does while dreaming. According to Cobb, the mind "creates and perceives a world simultaneously."

Everyday Wonders of Conscious Life

The branch of philosophy known as phenomenology describes the features and qualities of that which appears to consciousness. For phenomenology, there is a basic starting point: consciousness is always consciousness of *something*.

Given that Ariadne receives her first schooling in shared dreaming over a cup of coffee, let's have some Java and phenomenology. So, I'm conscious of the cup of coffee before me. I can't actually see behind the cup, its back side. However, due to my previous everyday use of such an item, my mind "fills in" the back of the cup. Philosophically we would say, the front of the cup is *perceived* and the back of the cup is *apperceived*.

In our normal everyday wide-awake conscious lives, perception and apperception are not experienced as two things but one. They are given to consciousness, or appear to consciousness, simultaneously. That is, until I grab the coffee that some producer from MTV's *Punk'd* has put super glue on! After having my hand stuck to the cup and going to the emergency room (not wanting to lose all of my skin), I finally have the cup of horror removed.

Since I am a die-hard coffee lover, I'm not easily deterred. I go back the next day, bandages, gauze, and all. However, when I reach for the cup of coffee, I hesitate, and slowly grasp the top of the cup and turn it around, to check to make sure there is no super glue. In that moment, I *perceived* the front of the cup, but what I *apperceived* was no longer based upon my overall experiences of cups throughout my lifetime. I no longer simply assumed that all cups are round and smooth. Rather, I recalled the experience of my hand being super glued. So, I paused and turned the cup around to make sure that this cup shared all of the wonderful qualities of every other cup that makes having coffee such a wonderful experience. Thus, apperception may include an act of recalling a memory or an act of imagining. In the words of Cobb, the ongoing complexities of conscious life in the most mundane matters, such as drinking coffee, are done "so well that you don't feel your brain doing the creating."

In the coffee shop scene Cobb draws two arrows on a napkin that illustrate perception and apperception. And it is between those two arrows—the front of the coffee cup you see and its back that you also "see"—where *Inception* lays down its philosophical anchor. This aspect of consciousness not only applies to parts of coffee cups you see and "see." It also applies to everything that exists within your social world. It is apperception that allows the everyday experiences of the social world to become invested with your personal experiences, expectations, hopes, fears, anxieties, loves, culture, and history.

Perception allows you to literally see the world, but it is apperception that allows you to *see and have* a world that is meaningful. And this is why Ariadne keeps coming back. The chance to build "cathedrals, entire cities—things that have never existed, things that couldn't exist in the real world" and of course, what's "real" is precisely what needs to be kept track of so you can get back to it. For phenomenology and *Inception,* the wide-awake world of everyday life is not the only reality; however, it is the "paramount reality."

For the phenomenologist Alfred Schutz (1899–1959), paramount reality is the world of everyday life governed by pragmatic motives such as going to work and earning a living in order to have food to eat. In addition, pragmatic motives include carrying out various projects that are meaningful and have an effect on the social world around you. However, there are other realities or provinces of meaning. There are realms of meaning in which people speak in tongues, play jazz, and attend sporting events where it's perfectly *normal* to be half naked with your body painted green and yellow with a giant slice of cheese around your head.

Various realms of meaning have their own "cognitive styles," which give them consistency and coherence. Thus, dreams and fantasies are "real" in their own way while we are attending to them. Indeed, Mal is right when she says "Admit it Dom, you don't believe in one reality anymore. So choose. Chose your reality like I did. Choose to be here. Choose me." The idea that we can choose our own reality certainly is attractive. Soon, however we'll see that such choices have limits and sometimes require a leap of faith.

Philosophy for Breaking into Fischer's Mind

So, what exactly does Cobb want Ariadne to do? Ariadne would "take over the creating part" and build the world of the dream. This is where *Inception* as a science-fiction movie really shines. One key difference between dreaming consciousness and the wide-awake world of everyday life is solitariness. When you're dreaming, you're always alone, even if you don't know it. You have to wake up in order to share your dreams.

Within the dream world, consciousness does not engage in genuine apperception. There is no actual external world for you to be able to act upon. There's no spatial reality which your consciousness may fill in. In other words, in the consciousness of everyday life, you really do need to know the difference between a regular flight of stairs and one that you'll walk on forever in an infinite loop.

However, Cobb's right. While we're in the dream, it feels real. Anyone who's been jolted out of a nightmare with fear driven rapid breathing can attest to this fact. It's exactly this barrier that the technology of shared dreaming is designed to overcome. Thus, shared dreaming allows for the experience of another recognized genuine actor within the dream.

Here's where things get tricky: the technology of *Inception* makes shared dreaming possible, albeit in a particular way. In *Inception* people do not share dreams in the same way children share a fantasy world of imaginary play or the way fraternities, churches, and temples share a set of meanings. Rather, this technology allows for *one* person to be the *dreamer* and another to be the *subject*. And it is the thoughts, perceptions, and memories of the subject's subconscious that fill the world of the dreamer. Talk about hospitality!

The catch is that the subject *feels* as if it is their dream. Again, while dreaming there is no reason to think it isn't real. As Ariadne finds out rather quickly, the strangers walking down the street are not the strangers of everyday life. They're projections—acts of Cobb's subconscious that he can't control. Of course, there's the rub. The key to being good at stealing or implanting an idea is not to let anyone know you're actually in their dream as *you* but to let them suppose you're only there as a projection created by *them*.

This is why, when creating a dream world, it's critical to include a safe or a bank vault that the subject thinks is their creation. In case the subject suspects it's not their dream, they have a 'safe' place to put their most cherished thoughts. It's an interesting twist on the heist genre. Don't worry about breaking *into* a safe, just dream one up and they'll fill it with exactly what you want!

In order to successfully crack into Fischer's mind, we'll need more than technology that allows us to experience a dream within a dream. We'll also need to draw a philosophical distinction between experience and meaningful lived experience. Pure experience is the ongoing, coming and passing away of every moment of conscious life. The metaphor of "streams" has been a favorite of philosophers even since Heraclitus (535 B.C.–475 B.C.) remarked that "You can't step into the same river twice."

Thus, living within the stream of experience called "pure duration," we're aware only of the coming to be and passing away of conscious moments. Whether gleaned from various religious traditions or your latest New Age author at Barnes and Noble, indeed all we have is *this* moment. Experience as such is a unity before we ever engage in acts of reflection. In the act of reflecting upon an experience, we attend to something that is already passed. More importantly, in reflection, we lift up a particular aspect of that experience.

It's similar to a camera lens bringing an object into focus. The already experienced is that which can become meaningful. The meaningfulness of prior acts always undergoes modification. Since this happens in the irreversible experience of time, this ongoing meaning modification of prior acts contributes to the narrative sense of our identity. A sense of "my story" or "my life." Something similar happens in everyday face-to-face relationships. It is only after I have finished having a conversation with someone that I can fully reflect upon it. The kind of face-to-face relationship may determine if I am reflecting upon a friendship or a marriage. More importantly, these various conversations and moments together contribute to the narrative quality of an enduring relationship. Speaking in a emotionally pain-drenched chuckle, Fischer drives this point home in reference to his father saying "We didn't have a lot of meaningful experiences together."

You may want to protest and say, Hey, reading this book is meaningful! Indeed it is, however in a particular way. Given the fact that you're not currently done reading, this would be a *meaning endowing* experience of consciousness. A meaning endowing experience of consciousness describes the attitude one takes toward a particular act. For the purposes of engaging *Inception*, any given act that is past, when repeatedly reflected upon, undergoes modification.

Let's say I went to the grocery store and bought a carton of milk. As I reflect upon this act, I might say "I went to the store in order to satisfy my thirst." However, I might reflect upon this act in light of my childhood experience of getting sick after drinking orange juice. Then I would say, "I went to the store and purchased milk because I will never get sick again!!" These are referred to as 'in order to' motives and 'because of' motives.

So, How Do You Know You're Dreaming?

Inception relies on the above distinctions within the world of everyday life to bring people into the awareness that they're dreaming. Cobb remarks to Ariadne in their first session of shared dreaming: "You never remember the beginning of your dreams, do you? You just turn up in the middle of what's going on. So . . . how did we end up at this restaurant? How did we get here? Where are we?"

In that moment, Ariadne cannot recall an already lived through meaningful experience that can serve as a 'because of' motive or rather, the basis for pursuing actions in everyday life. This is also the key question Cobb uses to awaken Fischer to the fact that he's dreaming. Fischer's attention is drawn to the strangeness of the dream when Cobb says, "The easiest way to test yourself is to try and remember how you arrived at this hotel." Sure, he may have been enjoying his drink and thinking about the blonde who approaches him at the bar. But he doesn't know why or how he got there. His inability to come up with a 'because of' motive suggests he's dreaming.

Now we're set to go into Fischer's mind and manufacture a good father-son drama that Freud would be proud of! First, after Fischer is kidnapped, there must be a way for Fischer himself to get the ball rolling, something that will later convince him that he's really in a dream. With a gun pointed to his head, Fischer shouts out numbers to a combination that he doesn't have, "Five . . . Two . . . Eight . . . Four . . . Nine . . . One!"

These arbitrary numbers have been given to Fischer in a way that will create an association between them. The team can now plan their scenarios in a way that mirrors the meaningful construction of our everyday life. When Mr. Charles enters the scene, he briefly draws Fischer's attention to the napkin with the same combination of numbers he has just spoken. Mr. Charles must be ever so subtle in bringing to Fischer's attention things already perceived in the prior stage of the dream. Cobb convinces Fischer that the first dream, the kidnapping, is really his awakened state. And Cobb is ready with a 'because of' motive as to why he associates "five, two, eight" with "combination." The room number where he confronts Browning is Room #528 with Arthur and Ariadne below in Room #491. In addition, Cobb is ready with an answer to the strangeness of this dream: the shaking they *both* experience is from the wide-awake reality of being in back of a van.

The deal is sealed. Fischer thinks that he's in his own dream and Cobb is a projection of his subconscious that will deliver him from the very real kidnapping taking place. Meanwhile, Fischer is sleeping like a baby on an airplane while his militarized subconscious fights the good fight on the first dream level.

I within an I

The technology in *Inception* that makes experiencing a dream within a dream possible entails a new understanding of the Self. In order to experience a "dream within a dream" you'll need to understand yourself as an "I within an I." No longer do you have to interpret the contents of your subconscious through psychoanalysts, dream interpreters, sages, prophets, or seers. You can have a genuine face-to-face conversation with projections of your own subconscious. Or if you wish, have a cup of coffee outside in an exotic location as your subconscious projections walk down the street. When the team is going deeper into Fischer's subconscious, we're witnessing the "step-by-step" construction of meaning. In reverse!

The possibility of a "dream within a dream" while experiencing ourselves as an "I within an I," creates a mirror image of how the social world is meaningfully constructed within conscious life. In Fischer's subconscious the more he goes 'forward,' trusting Cobb as his own projection, the further he goes 'back' into himself. In the wide-awake world meaning is built 'up', in the dream world meaning is built 'down'. Down so far as being able to potentially redefine who he is. That moment of meaning creation or the inception of an idea is so constitutive of our self-understanding it survives the transition between dreaming and waking.

Risks of Faith

Philosophers and theologians alike have long made a distinction between faith and belief. We believe things for which there is enough evidence to make them probable. I believe that the news on the front page of the morning paper is reliable.

I believe that a given statement or claim is true. I may even believe the reports of my dentist or doctor as it relates to my health. In this case I *trust* them because I don't have the training or tools to make a surgical incision or fill a cavity. However, this would subject faith to merely greater or lesser forms of theoretical knowledge.

For a theologian such as Paul Tillich (1886–1965), I may trust my doctor to treat me, but I would still not put my *faith* in them. Although trust is an element of faith, the term is reserved for matters of "ultimate concern." This was Tillich's translation of the great commandment given by God: "You shall love the Lord your God with all your heart, and with all your soul and with all your might" (Deuteronomy 6:5). For Tillich, the God who is of ultimate concern represents the promise of ultimate fulfillment when accepted in the act of faith. In addition, when preliminary concerns are treated as ultimate, the result is nothing less than demonic. If we were to use the classical theological language, we're talking about idolatry. When the everyday ordinary things of life are taken as ultimate, we no longer see them for what they genuinely are. We fail to see that they have a history; they can be subject to error. If you think about the atrocities throughout history committed in the name of a particular religion or race, you understand what happens when preliminary concerns are made ultimate.

There are many religious traditions that understand God not from what we take to be an object of ultimate concern. Rather they take any knowledge of God as having been revealed by God to humanity. For Tillich, however, this only returns us to the act of faith in which we acknowledge that revelation in a religious tradition is that which has been *accepted* as revelation.

Within the religious vision of *Inception*, the revelation comes from within, from the totem. In a classic postmodern twist in which movies routinely remix cultural understandings, the totem makes an unlikely return. The totem, once the primary symbol that Western culture used to define the religious practices of "primitive" cultures from which we have "evolved," now mediates knowledge of reality. The totem literally is sacred, set apart unable to be touched by another. The totem is shaped from the individual's experience of everyday life. Thus, the key is not whether or not someone else knows the meaning of it. Rather, only the individual can know "the weight and balance of it."

With the totem being untouched by another, presumably this would constitute a unique object within the dream world. To use our earlier example, someone else in the dream can create a coffee cup, but they could not create my totem, not even in their dreams. In religious terms, Mal and Fischer are people without totems, without Gods, and are susceptible to the tragic consequences of misplaced faith. For Mal, the consequence is death and for Fischer, a profound distortion of the reconciliation he so desperately desired with his father.

Within the world of *Inception*, it is indeed the world of everyday life that serves as the primary religious symbolism, that which is of ultimate concern. It's tempting to think that the world of everyday life is peripheral to the movie's dream-hopping; however, *Inception* reveals everyday life as the ultimate reality. Reflecting on what it means to live a 'dream within a dream' with Mal on the shores of the unconscious, Cobb remarks, "We created a whole world by ourselves. It's not so bad at first, being Gods. The problem is knowing that it's not real. It became impossible to live like that." There on the beach, Mal and Cobb, with echoes of the Genesis story of Adam and Eve, create with their hands the giant structures pictured behind them. The huge castles fall away just as easily as their hands push through the sand. On the shores of their subconscious, Cobb and Mal live moment-to-moment and thus do not genuinely grow old together. As such, nothing they create endures in order to accumulate meaningful lived experiences.

When awakened, they were relentlessly thrown back into their youth by the reality of everyday life. More importantly, this was after Mal had chosen to accept the dream world as the world of everyday life. Thus, Mal placing the totem in the safe symbolizes a misplaced faith, a retreat from the reality of everyday life. Her dream becomes a profound idolatry the very moment she's unable to accept the dream *as* a dream. Mal's act of faith in the dream world is symbolized by her suicide, which she ultimately considered would reunite her with her children. A sobering thought for the question posed by the elder looking over the men in Yusuf's basement states, "The dream has become their reality. . . . And who are you to say otherwise?" Hey, don't take my word for it, ask Mal!

Inception has given us an exciting vision of the various possibilities with the technologies of shared dreaming. One thing's for sure: everything we know about who we are will be far more complicated. However, some things continue to remain the same. In the world of *Inception* even the strangeness of the dream does not slow our thirst for meaning. We will still take profound risks on what is real. Some commit tragic acts of misplaced faith based upon the serenity, joy or pleasure of a given experience. Many will surely be the victims of intentional acts of deception in which vulnerabilities of our deepest subconscious are exploited. Others will see the world of the dream as an untapped market that reaps financial benefits in the world of everyday life. There may be those like Cobb who whose failure to mourn will threaten their ability to discern the reality of everyday life. However, all is not gloom and doom. After all, we'll make cathedrals and things we've always dreamed of but could never exist in the everyday life.

Now you may be wondering when I'm going to do what I promised, and explain why inception isn't philosophically possible. But I already did. You don't remember?

20
Building and Dwelling in *Inception*

VALENTIN HUSSON

Inception thinks through images. An image is not simply a representation of reality but also shows, through its movement, a complexity, a difficulty, and a truth. The French film director Jean-Luc Godard describes it like this: "Photography is the truth. Cinema is twenty-four times the truth per second." Twenty-four is the number of images that appear on a cinema screen per second. Twenty-four times truth per second means that the film suggests, through its images, a truth. What is this truth in *Inception*?

Perhaps it is that living requires building and dwelling. Before you can dwell you have to build. Even animals mark their territory. Marking your territory means to prepare a place where you can dwell. A dog lifts his leg in an unknown space and thus makes it his own. The space that he has marked belongs to him.

A bird living in Australia, the *Scenopoietes dentirostris*, prepares its territory by dropping leaves it has cut off its tree. The contrast between the color of the leaves and the ground gives its territory an artistic dimension, which becomes particularly nice when the bird begins to sing certain complex patterns. For this bird, color and singing are enough to appropriate a territory and to live in it.

To build and dwell is thus not unique to humans. Dwelling in a place, a territory, a world, a space always amounts to creating it, building it. However, in *Inception* this transcends anything an architect can do. A dream, as Cobb suggests to Ariadne, "creates and perceives the world simultaneously," meaning that this is the point where creation and perception intermingle. In other words, the world creates itself, builds itself, becomes populated, and dwells within the very act of perception.

The act of simultaneously perceiving and creating is a matter of art. A painter perceives her work while painting just like a dreamer perceives her dream at the time of its creation. Nothing precedes the creation. This is actually the difference between craft and art: the craftsman develops what he visualizes (the object), whereas the artist creates works out of nothing. In principle, the movement of creation is the same as that of perception. I do not perceive my dream before having created it. Also, I do not visualize a painting before having painted it. Any artistic creation comes out of nothing.

When Cobb advises Ariadne not to create a dream world based on reality, he doesn't do this out of caution in order to avoid any confusion between dream and reality. Instead, he gives her an artistic condition. All art has to create itself out of nothing, which also means that all art is defined by its creation. By creating his dream, the subject dwells in it.

Ariadne's role is to intervene in the creation of a dream. She creates a world while letting the subject dwell in it. While they are sitting on the terrace of the café, Cobb says to Ariadne: "You build the world of the dream. We take the subject into that dream, and let him fill it with his subconscious." This means that Ariadne is supposed to insert her own person right between the act of perception and the act of creation. Normally, the subject of the dream perceives his dream without building it. But how is it possible that the dreamer dwells in a dream built by Ariadne? Is there not the risk of a gap opening between the dream and the reality, a gap through which the subject will become aware that the dream is not real? Is it not necessary for the subject to participate in the act of building?

Paradoxically, the act of building consists of two movements. Ariadne provides the element of durability through her architecture. She provides the buildings and the details of the environment. The second movement, however, is related to the subject of the dream who continues to build within the territory of this imposed architectural framework. We have to understand that the dreamer from whom a thought has been extracted, or into whom an idea has been incepted, ceaselessly continues to create in spite of the intervention of the architect. He does so for the simple reason stated by Cobb: the dream is a dream only because it is a constant creation. The dreamer who stops creating will also stop dreaming. From then on, everything takes place as if the dream is determined by the aforementioned twofold movement. The architect provides outlines and the dreamer populates them—fills them with life. For the dreamer, building amounts to dwelling.

It's only because he's still building his dream that he believes in it. The dream is paradoxical because it creates itself out of itself. The dream is imposed upon the dreamer by the extractors while the dreamer simultaneously creates it. To dwell thus always means to build a place in which one can dwell. Here, to build is not limited to the strict architectural sense. Building is not the privilege of an artist or a craftsman, of a genius or a creator. We all build by the very fact of dwelling. This is one of the paradoxical lessons that *Inception* teaches us: to dwell requires the dreamer's act of building. The proof is that once the extractors are spotted by the unconscious, they're in danger. This way, the subject of the dream remains in control of his dream. Suddenly, the people who stay in this imaginary world become skeptical and understand that the walls, the grounds, the carpets, and everything in this place are the work of another person, of a counterfeiter disguised as a creator or as an architect.

Isn't this the very demonstration of the fact that the dreamer can be fooled neither by his own dream nor by the things that he's building? Doesn't this prove that any dream creates itself out of itself, that it builds itself, and that everybody has to accept this? Cobb explains that any simulation can work only if the team manages to infiltrate itself into the process of building. In other words, they can cheat the dreamer only by thwarting the building process of the dream, by acting simultaneously with its creation and acting within that process of creation.

However, if building has nothing to do with architecture, what other meaning can this word have? And where does this non-architectural act of building come from? Who or what builds in a dream? The subject? Her subconscious?

Inception is an attempt to answer exactly these questions: the dream emanates from the subconscious. Its production, its construction, and its act of building have a non-conscious origin. The work of the unconscious consists, among other things, of producing dreams and disengaging itself from its fears. We dream of death in order to exorcize our fear of death. This is how the dream builds a cathartic world.

Guilt and Atonement

Cathartic? What does this word signify in this context? The word 'cathartic' comes from the Greek *catharsis*, meaning purgation. Aristotle, in his *Poetics*, says that catharsis is the main purpose of the theater. Theater serves to atone for the passions in order to release the spectator. To see the tragic hero defying death or to watch him fighting against an inevitable fate allows the spectator to purge himself of his own fears.

We observe the same pattern on the stage of the dream. Here everything is performed like a theatrical production. The dream sets up a world and purges the subjects of his anxieties or fears. This is how the extractors try to atone for Robert Fischer's resentment towards his father. To dream allows us to free ourselves from what harms, torments, and saddens us.

The dream is the catharsis of the repressed representations. They are repressed because they are forbidden, because they have been censored by the conscience: "The dream is the (concealed) fulfillment of a (repressed) desire," says Sigmund Freud (*The Interpretation of Dreams*, Chapter 3).

The origin of all this is the unconscious. However, the unconscious doesn't create a place or a location. When something comes from the unconscious, we can only say it comes. 'It' is the name used by Freud to signify the unconscious. If the dream—'it'—comes, then this is due to the fact that it is built out of a no-place, out of a silent, inconceivable and hardly penetrable origin. "The unconscious is that chapter of my history that is marked by a blank," says Jacques Lacan. It is marked by Emptiness. In this sense, the dream, as a production of the unconscious, is always poetic. Poetry, from the Greek word *poiesis*, means production in a very general sense. So, the dream being poetic means that it is the product of the unconscious by which it has been built and created.

This also means that all poetry is creation, and it is creation *ex nihilo* (out of nothing). Out of nothing means coming from nothing, coming from Emptiness. When poetry comes to dwell in a creator this is quite mysterious. "Poetry . . . call it Mystery," says Stéphane Mallarmé.

It is even a double mystery: there is the mystery of its creation and the mystery that it is going to be art. It is a creation out of nothing: poetry, like any art, is the art of a genius. Classically, art defines itself through a natural gift, through an innate gift. In a word, you can't learn to be a genius. To be a genius is not a technique among others but a natural offering that you can't acquire. This means that poetry, since it has been created by a poetic genius, comes out of nowhere. It's not just produced by knowledge or learning. We can note that it comes: this is true for both the poetic creation and the production of the unconscious. And it comes by sending itself right into another Mystery, into that of the evocation of the things that make the poetic language so somber and elliptical.

Somebody's sure to tell us that the created dream comes from an unconscious "structured as a language" (it's actually Lacan who tells us this), where any creation is merely made of signifiers loaded with a subjective sense. This happens, for example, in Diane's dream in David Lynch's *Mulholland Drive*, where Diane imagines being a young and promising actress called Betty, who went to Los Angeles to make a career. In Los Angeles, Betty meets Rita (who has the features of the real Camilla Rhodes) with whom she falls in love. However, Betty's career will be ruined by a strange affair of corruption. Camilla Rhodes (who is the signifier loaded with hatred and contempt) will be chosen for the role instead of Betty. In reality, Camilla is Diane's (Betty's) partner, whom she leaves in order to get married to a movie director.

I mention this dream because it contains the interesting duplication of Camilla's character. The signifier Camilla is loaded with Diane's hatred. Furthermore, in Lynch's movie the dream creates itself out of Diane's repressed emotions. It is a cathartic dream where passion starts all over with Camilla (Rita), and where guilt (in reality she hires a killer to murder Camilla) will be overcome by engaging in a new love affair. Here, the building of the dream flows out of a repressed content, out of empty signifiers.

All this is true, but will it lead us to concluding that the poet creates nothing, in the sense that he only cobbles together his poetry out of signifiers? Certainly not! We all know that a poet creates, if he is a great poet, out of nothing. Nothing, as we said before, is the Mystery of creation. Its origin is veiled, hidden, and withdrawn.

Heidegger says that the origin of the work of art is not expressible, that it has no foundation that could be pointed out or shown. The work of art simply "comes." And it comes out of nothing, out of Emptiness. Perhaps this Emptiness expresses the Mystery of the Mysteries: God, which is the name consecrated to express the mysterious in general, the unspeakable, the inexpressible.

Coming back to *Inception*, the only thing we can point out about the dream is that its origin, its creative movement is due to nothing, not even to the signifiers and the repressed contents. That is how *Inception* informs us about what is art: it is a Poem in the sense of "production." The dream is poetic, which means that the dream is produced from nothing, out of an unconscious which is structured, in the final analysis, by nothing and as nothing. It is very much like the Limbo into which Cobb goes to join his wife, Mal. This is a non-structured Emptiness, a space where nothing is. Limbo is the most immediate image of the Emptiness from which proceed both the unconscious and its signifier and the repressed content. This leads us to the conclusion that if the unconscious is structured as a language, the dream must be structured as a poem.

It becomes obvious that the fact of living in a world, no matter real or dreamlike, requires living in a place of a Mystery, in a place of Emptiness. It means to live in a place of miraculous creation whose origin remains hidden. This is similar to a situation where a person is standing in front of a great painting and wonders how the master has been able to produce this result. That is exactly what is meant by Mystery and by Emptiness: they occur at the moment when we are stunned by the beauty of a work of art, when we are absorbed by the incomprehension of its origin. "How did he do that?" one says when standing in front of Velázquez's *The Maids of Honor*. "Where did this idea, this inspiration come from?" Well, it came from nowhere, that is, from the Emptiness, from a brilliant flash of inspiration which cannot be learned, which depends neither on knowledge nor on technique. Its origin is bottomless, unreachable, and incomprehensible. The problem is that this is exactly what tends to mislead us in front of the beauty of art. As stated by Joyce in *Ulysses*, it is the very sense of beauty: always mysterious, always misleading us.

The dream tells us something similar: that all this arises from nothing and that to live in a dream, inside the creation of a dream, is to dwell in a place of Mystery, in the very place of what the dream deploys during its creation. We feel good in a dream because we dwell in a dream just as we dwell in any world. How much pleasure can we feel when living in a dream! As a matter of fact, weren't Cobb and Mal living too well? Mal refuses to leave the place she had built with her husband. This is why Cobb had to implant into her the idea that this place is unreal and that she has to die first if she wants to come back to reality. The plot becomes tragic when, once she's really back in reality, she can't give up the idea that this real world is unreal, and that leaving it will necessitate death. The step from a dream to a nightmare is often very small.

Dreams and Nightmares

Dream versus nightmare: the opposition is so weak that it should be of interest to us here. Isn't Cobb living the most perfect nightmare? Isn't he living in the middle of darkness, in the midst of his guilt? Ariadne doesn't stop appealing to his guilty conscience, just as she doesn't stop blaming him for risking the lives of their companions when projecting the threatening Mal into their dreams. This is Cobb's nightmare: in every dream roams a threat and dwelling has become impossible. The nightmare is the reign of the uninhabitable. It's the place where no one can dwell but at the same time, it's the prerequisite for any possibility of dwelling. As a matter of fact, Cobb lives in this nightmare until dwelling has become possible again. Reality or dream, the place has become habitable. Once he is freed from Mal, he can try to live close to his children.

If the nightmare is uninhabitable this is because it's also the product of an act of building. It is Cobb who populates his bad dream with the repressed content and the guilty conscience that he has contracted since the death of his wife. It is he who puts the life of his companions at risk as soon as the image and the projection of Mal begin roaming through his life.

Every dream contains the condition of the uninhabitable and every dream contains the possibility of a nightmare, which means: both the habitable and uninhabitable are due to an act of building which comes, as we have said above, from nothing. It comes from Emptiness. To dwell in a dream or to dwell in a world means: to build this dream or this world so that it becomes habitable. Or, if you like, to dwell in a world means to live in the place that you have built.

Living in the no-place of Emptiness means that the act of dwelling in the (no-)place of the creation makes it possible to build as a creation *ex nihilo*. It also means to dwell in a Mystery, a mystery from which, as has said Mallarmé, all poetry arises. To dwell is thus a poetic Mystery. This can be understood in the sense that any life, just because it dwells in the (no-)place of a Mystery, is poetic. *Inception* informs us of what it means to live as a poet.

Heidegger said that dwelling in a world is poetic since humans build their places of life by appropriating them just like an artist does through his creation. In the same way, a poet is a poet because she builds her dwelling. She is a poet because she builds places in which we can live. Heidegger says that "poetry builds the being of the dwelling. Poetry gives rise and gives a place to the dwelling as such because it mysteriously builds the dwelling place, the place to stay. To stay in a dream or in a world is to build this dream or this world so that it becomes appropriate for life. Poetry builds a space and raises it to the dignity of a dwelling place.

I've mentioned that the word 'poetry' comes from the Greek *poiesis*, which means production. As long as it produces, poetry builds. And by building, it gives rise to the dwelling. Heidegger says: "As it makes us dwell, poetry is an act of 'building'.". *Inception* informs us that to dwell in a dream and to dwell in a world make sense only as long as we dwell as poets. This doesn't mean that we have to be real builders (architects etc.) or even real poets. But we dwell because we have built our place and populated it with our affects. Just as Cobb populates his dreams with the projection of Mal. Cobb asks Ariadne not to reproduce in dreams those things that are familiar to her. He says this because he doesn't want her to confuse dream and reality. However, she doesn't take the dreamlike dwelling for her real dwelling.

This means again that any life is produced on the basis of a poetic Mystery. The poem's origin has no foundations: it is Emptiness. To dwell as a poet means to dwell in the Mystery that is able to transform a non-familiar space into a dwelling-place, into a place to stay. This process has a name: Poetry. "A silence is the strange source of the poem" according to Paul Valéry. It is a silence or an Emptiness from which the poetry arises.

If Cobb wants to live again in his dwelling place with his children, does he not have to learn again to dwell in his dreams and to release himself from his guilty conscience? Is *Inception* not an allegory on the poetic dwelling? A nightmare means that you have to go through the uninhabitable. The purpose of the mission confided to Cobb by Saito is to allow Cobb to see his children again. His own dwelling place had become impossible to live in because he had to flee the charges of murder. The movie is a modern *Odyssey*; however, it is no longer Ulysses leaving Ithaca and returning home, but Cobb running away from his dwelling place and finally coming back to it. It doesn't matter whether his return is imaginary or not. What matters is that dwelling has become possible again, either in the real world or in a dream. The film is a new *Odyssey* into which has been introduced the myth of Ariadne's thread. In this Greek myth, Ariadne helps Theseus to get out of the labyrinth, where the Minotaur would have devoured him. Theseus escapes thanks to a ball of thread she gives him that can be unwound. In *Inception*, Ariadne tries to save Cobb from his guilt in a similar way. She even goes with him into Limbo in order to make him return to reality.

Back from Limbo (or perhaps better, given the ambiguous ending of the film, back from the nightmares to which he was repeatedly submitted), Cobb is able to dwell again in a world. He is freed from his repressed desires.

The end of *Inception* suggests the following: if it is impossible for us to decide if the spinning top falls, this is because we are already taken in by the dwelling of a Mystery, like the dreamer from whom we try to extract an idea or into whom we try to incept an idea. The ultimate experience of *Inception* is the experience of passing though a Mystery. Moreover, the etymological meaning of experience is "ex-periri," that is, "going through a peril." In the film this means to go through the peril that appears to those who can't distinguish the dream from reality.

The fact that we are able to wonder if Cobb is still in his dream or if he is in reality means that we have remained in the Mystery. We dwell in a world as soon as we are taken in by an enigma. We thus stay in the suspense between dream and reality, in the suspense created by Emptiness where we have to create some sort of 'sense' and subsequently build it; just as we build a limbo in order to create a place of dwelling. In this condition, which is always precarious and fragile, as Hölderlin puts it "Man dwells poetically on Earth."[1]

---

[1] This chapter was translated from the French by Sarah Kaufmann, Marthe Teusch, and Thorsten Botz-Bornstein.

21
Dream Time

RANDALL E. AUXIER

Over-Confidence Is Like a Loaded Gun

At the end of *Inception*, when Cobb arrives home and finally sees his children, he spins the top and walks away. Does the totem finally tumble? We all know that's the question. Christopher Nolan has scoffed at those who expected him to answer it. People have exchanged theories *ad nauseum*, and most of you have probably decided there is no definite solution, so you might doubt it when I say this: I actually know the answer, with something like clear certainty.

The answer is pretty simple (so I claim), but getting there is a little tougher. It's sort of like the touching simplicity of Robert Fischer's believing that he planted his own pinwheel in his father's safe, and since Nolan miraculously succeeded in preventing that "Rosebud" moment from being anti-climactic, I'll aspire to the same.

But don't you dare skip to the end. That's cheating, and you're only spoiling it for yourself. Just remember the first rule of any well-written play: The gun you see in the first act always goes off in the third. You should also be forewarned that I'm attempting waking inception in this chapter.

Lasagna for Lunch

Our man Nolan is fascinated by the topic of time, especially the various ways we humans can experience it. And his curiosity is peculiarly drawn to what we can call the "pathologies of temporal experience"—where time goes bad on us for one reason or another, or for no reason at all. In *Memento*, Nolan explored the way time and memory become strange when a head injury to his main character breaks the link between the present and the past by destroying his ability to make new long-term memories—that is an example of a pathology of temporal experience. I want to talk about that in a minute or two, but first a word about dreams.

Time in dreams is also weird, but maybe not as weird as some other things about dreams (hang on to that thought boys and girls, and check out my other chapter in this volume). There's trouble with working our way through the layers of *Inception*. By the time we see the finished movie, Nolan and company have already analyzed all the time-stuff that interests them and have embedded their results back into the script and the images. We have to swallow everything whole, as it were. It's sort of a lasagna of ideas about time and dreams. I don't mind ingesting someone else's intellectual main course, but if I'm curious about the ingredients and the process of preparation, I may have to ask after the recipe (and hope it wasn't a close family secret).

On the other hand (and there always seems to be another hand, doesn't there?), it's no fun just to pull apart somebody's lasagna. Even if you could get a clue from looking at the resulting mess, you still might miss the secret ingredient. Is that cottage cheese from the store or feta from the Old Country? That's a fair question. Can't tell much from looking at the steamy melted pile of goo on the plate. And there is something to be said for using the best ingredients, but we also don't want to walk to Umbria to see what the goats eat. We know good cheese when we taste it, but it's also wise to find out at least where we can order some of it, you know? Such is the analogy with Nolan's lasagna of a movie.

So I promise not to make you feel like you have to eat on the run, or like a pedestrian on a slow tour of goat forage in the Old Country, but maybe we can share a table for a while and I'll just prompt you to notice some of the prominent spices and speculate with you about how the cook combined them. Anyone can see this is mainly about the pasta (time) and the cheese (dreams), and that one is soggy and the other is actually melting everywhere. But on one thing I'll tip my hand: like everything else in life, the secret's in the ingredients, but not just individually. This is about how certain kinds of ingredients blend and interact when they're baked. Christopher Nolan is quite the cook.

Part of the reason a lasagna comes to mind is that I saw an image on the web that reminds me of a Penrose lasagna (that, and I'm hungry). The image is sort of an Escher-esque staircase of the dreamers and their dreams and the kicks that catapult them from one level to another. The web address for this image is: <http://thecrapbox.com/wp-content/uploads/2010/07/ZZ79EABF11small.jpg>: Very cool. The more I study this image, the more I like it.

Mementoes and Totems

In *Inception*, the idea of a "totem" is an item that our professional dream-invaders keep with them, always and everywhere, especially in the dream world. It has to be something heavy and uniquely identifiable, and something they don't let others touch or handle. Its function is to provide a test that enables a dream-invader to know whether he or she is in a dream or just knocking about in the real world. You apparently make a deal with your own mind that if the totem feels and behaves in a particular, expected way, that's a sign that you're in the real world, while any deviation from that expectation indicates that you're in a dream. The idea is set up and justified early in the movie when Nash, the first (unfaithful) architect, fails to design the apartment in Saito's "test dream" with a carpet that smells right, and so Saito is tipped off that he's dreaming. The brief exchange between Nash, Cobb, and Arthur that follows is meant to show that even details as small as the smell of the carpet must be known to a dream architect (and considered in building a labyrinth).

So, the reason that our dream-invaders do not let anyone handle their totems is that such handling would allow any architect to duplicate its expected behavior in a dream and the invader could then be deceived about the dream-reality relation. "Totem" is a good word for such an item, sacred and untouchable as it is. Remember (for later) that one character does not let another handle his or her totem—to do so would require absolute trust or, dare I say it, a leap of faith. It's also good at this point to keep in mind that the totem needs to be substantial in weight and something the dream-invader always, always has with him. So the totem is supposed to be a sign or indicator of what is true about your external world, a point of connection between what you're experiencing within yourself (beliefs, perceptions, assumptions) and the way the world really is.

This is not the first time Christopher Nolan has dealt with the problem of connecting our inner experience with our outer world. *Memento* (written with his brother Jonathan) confronts the same problem. Both movies point to the devilish problem of temporality in experiential terms, and they pose the problem very nicely. The question is really about continuity and discontinuity in our experience, and especially the effect of discontinuity on our ability to know the truth about the world. All of us have gaps in our experience—and by the way, how did you get to be sitting where you are right now . . . Do you remember?

Memento teaches us the problem of discontinuity "from the inside out," or, what happens when we can't make the real world a permanent part of our on-going inner selves? We know that there is often a difference, a gap, between the way time passes in the world and the way we experience it—after all, time flies when you're having fun, and a watched pot never boils. Memory is the ability to make the world your own, and to carry it around with you as an accumulated touchstone for grasping whatever you're experiencing now.

In *Memento*, the story assumes that time is continuous and orderly in the objective world, but our central character, Leonard Shelby, has suffered a head injury and can no longer move his short-term experiences into his long-term memory. (Such injuries can and do occur, although their consequences have been slightly different than the Nolans present in their story.) There is no problem with Shelby's perception, but his higher order world effectively begins anew every five minutes or so, against the background of all he learned in life before his injury. So the past world, as Leonard knew it long ago, does remain "intact," so to speak, but as he tries to live a normal life now, that past world becomes less and less relevant to making his way in the present. Eventually he doesn't know where he is or why he's there. If he had stayed home and kept everything as it was before his injury, he might have been okay, but his complex circumstances made that impossible.

In order to live life in the present, Leonard has to find ways of arranging the objective world of the recent past and immediate present so that he can compensate for that crippling discontinuity in his higher mental functioning, and most importantly, he must discern the difference between the truth and deception in order to navigate the social world. Is there an adequate method of arranging the objective, changing world so as to compensate for a radical discontinuity in our internal experience of time? Leonard combines many methods, but the most poignant is tattooing on his body "true propositions," statements he regards as certainties. These supposed "certainties" get him into trouble, eventually, since it turns out that they may not all be true. But if we think about that too much, we will never get back to *Inception*.

My point is a small one. How Leonard remembers that the things on his body are "truths" is one of many problems the Nolans can't really solve (not without trickery), since it requires the continuity in Leonard's memory of the idea "the statements tattooed on my body are true," to hold from one radical break to the next in Leonard's experience. I assume his decision to tattoo himself with only true statements was made after his injury. The Nolans actually have to smuggle some continuity back into Leonard's inner experience. Without cheating, they have no story, no unified narrative. And here, boys and girls, is a lesson worth remembering: Whenever an author messes with the continuity of time, said author will have to cheat eventually to get it back into the narrative, somehow. Otherwise, the story falls apart in ways that don't sell tickets and books.

So, the "totem" idea is a sort of "continuity machine." It says to its owner: "No matter what you think right now, there is a continuous self somewhere (maybe here and now), and that one is the real 'you'. So, my dear Cobb, look for discontinuities and let them be your clue that you are dreaming. I, your totem, am the most trustworthy guide."

Like the Corners of My Mind

Misty and water-colored (so the song goes) are our memories. Memory is the way the past "gnaws into the future," according to the philosopher Henri Bergson (1859–1941). The past isn't really dead and gone. You may not be very much aware of it but your past is quite active in your present experience, even overrunning the present and stretching into the future. When you walk into a room you've been in a thousand times before, you really don't see it, you mainly remember it, and as you prepare to walk in, your memory runs ahead and tells you what to expect. That's why you may notice if something is out of place, say the pepper grinder, or the jars of dried basil and oregano (I always like to be generous with the basil, especially, but simple spice combinations are the best). You experience the change in position of the displaced item first as a gap between memory and present perception; only then do you work to try to identify and fill the gap.

But memory also accumulates. As we get older, our memories and our past experiences become so heavy upon us that they overtake the present, fill it with the past. You struggle against this as you get older, trying to stay in meaningful touch with your present experience, but it's a losing battle. In fact, there comes a point, and we've all seen it in our grandparents and other loved ones, when the past really eclipses the present, even before that person gets a fair chance to perceive the present. Part of the reason it gets harder to remember what you've read when you reach middle age is that in the process of reading you are, more and more, remembering other things you've read before that were similar.

Failures of short-term memory, such as we see in Alzheimer's disease, have the initial effect of invigorating the relationship of long-term memory to present perception. Thus, you can still have lively conversations about the old days with people who can't remember what they did a few minutes ago. Indeed, you certainly should have such conversations with your elders, with all the vigor and detail you can call up. This brightening of the more distant past continues until the expanding erasure of short-term memory begins to wipe out the awareness of where one is and who one is with in the present. Alzheimer's spreads backwards in time, increasingly destroying the active presence of what was, from most recent to the increasingly remote. The patient's finally left with an uninterpretable present devoid of anything familiar. Little wonder such people ask to be taken home, even when they already are home. They are asking for something—anything—familiar.

This variable intensity and the "trade-off" of memory and perception is something Nolan has noticed. Memory has an odd and covariant relation to present perception. So if you want to become an architect for the dream-invaders, you'll want to be sure to make your mazes by thoroughly rearranging and re-combining things you've seen before, and doing so in light of new possibilities. Let the novelties dominate. Don't, and I repeat, do not use your memory, unaltered. That is dangerous because it's too close to being continuous with your personal past experiences, and you need those experiences in order to interpret your present perceptions (whether dreaming or waking).

Our hero Cobb cannot be an architect any more because he's overtaken by memory—it's not just because he can't forget Mal, but also because he's getting older. Part of the reason Ariadne is a promising dream architect is because she's so young, with less total memory and more intense connection to her present perception (both in dreams and in the waking world). She also has more possibilities ahead of her and so her memories, such as they are, spill over into an open swath of possible futures, and these possibilities are the sources of her novel variations for building her dreamscapes.

It would be dangerous (not to mention unprofessional) for Cobb to mix his work life and his personal life, right? But that isn't the only problem he has. The difficulty goes deeper, and it is partly in the aging process. According to Bergson, all dreaming is remembering, but it isn't necessarily the remembering of my personal past. I can also "remember" (in dreams) the collective past of my family, my species, of life itself—it's all still active in there. Long before *Inception*, Bergson not only suggested the possibility of group dreaming, he showed how it occurs—memory is embodied and your body carries forward in time the traces of all the bodies that contributed material to generating your body (or even just patterns of order and processes). The memory of the species lives in your active body. It isn't easy to get at, but it's there. You need the right kind of chemist or a hypnotist to help you tap in.

But like Cobb, the older I get, the more my general, impersonal "species memory" is made inaudible and invisible to me by the vivid intervention of my personal past. Children of four dream the dreams of the species, of the collective mind. I have come to the point that I don't so much dream as re-enact, with variations, my own life. The more I do that, the fewer are the gaps between my dreamlife and my waking perception. So the advice Cobb gives early on to Ariadne, "never use your memories," can be rephrased as such: "Introduce gaps when you create your (professional) dream spaces so that you can find your way home, by rediscovering the gaps." The gaps are Ariadne's thread to follow out of the labyrinth. If Cobb can't introduce gaps any more, and he can't, then he can't be an architect, and he can't (sort of—he's still got a few twists left in the old noggin). But there's too much continuity between his waking and dreaming, and that gets worse as he gets older because memory fills both sides.

Yet, to introduce gaps between your dream and your real world is to invite discontinuities into your experience of time. When we mess around with the idea of time's continuity, whether it's the continuity (or at least the accumulative tendency) of our internal time consciousness, or the assumed continuity of objective time in the world, things get strange in a hurry. And now I must make an assertion: It is not actually possible to make narrative sense of radical temporal discontinuity.

Thus, Leonard Shelby really does accumulate experience, whether the Nolans make a point of it or not, for without this accumulation, there would be no arrow of events. Even though *Memento* is presented in reverse chronological order, to help us feel some of Leonard's confusion, still, the accumulation of experience is built into the way Leonard perceives his world. In spite of the discontinuity in his higher order experiences, he remains a living, biological being. Not only is he aging, but in fact each new physical experience is conforming to his previous experiences. And he knows that. Otherwise, he wouldn't bother to tattoo himself with true statements. If he gets a superficial injury on his body (like a new tattoo), the injury will still be there after he can't remember getting it, and will still heal gradually, regardless of whether he remembers where it came from. There is plenty of continuity in Leonard's experience of time, it's just that Leonard isn't able to gain access to what his body has experienced.

A Selective Physics?

One wild thing about dreams is that they can seem so continuous with waking experience (and ordinary time). The relation is even closer in lucid dreaming. Part of the reason for the continuity is that stuff from the waking world does seep into our dreams. Music especially has the power to retain its own form as it pervades and accompanies sleep. That's why music is the marker for our lucid dreamers at whatever level they are dreaming, and unlike the rest of the dreamscape, the music does not undergo time-expansion as it shoots down the levels of unconsciousness. Ten seconds of Edith Piaf music is still ten seconds, even at the third dream level, where time is radically expanded.

The outside, the waking world, definitely gets into our dreams, whether or not it undergoes temporal expansion or transmogrification. What a great scene it was when Cobb was being awakened by a bathtub-dousing in one dream while water impossibly shoots into every opening of Saito's mountain fortress in the deeper dream. But water is still water from one dream level to another. It raises a question—perhaps even a doubt. I've heard people say that the physics in *Inception* is "selective," and they elaborate by claiming that the gravitational effects that slosh over from Yusuf's dream (the kidnapping/van/bridge) to Arthur's dream (the hotel) ought also to have carried over into Eames's dream (the snow-fortress).

I disagree. In fact, Nolan really has this right, in my view. But to make good on this claim, I'll have to drug you and take you on an airplane flight, or at least feed you something Italian. To see why, we have to understand time better.

The More Things Change . . .

There is a type of philosophy that specializes in the nature of time called "process philosophy." Henri Bergson, whom I mentioned earlier, is a "process philosopher," but the "Christopher Nolan" of process philosophy is a guy named Alfred North Whitehead (1861–1947). He specialized in trying to understand change.

Of necessity, process philosophers practice their arcane arts in the midst of change, since change is one of the main ingredients of every process. Remember I was riffing on ingredients earlier—I haven't forgotten, so you don't forget either. "Change" is an ingredient of time. Nothing on Earth is wholly exempt from change, and you and me least of all, so it makes sense for us to try to understand change, to discern its patterns and meanings. But it isn't easy to get a grip on such a topic when nothing consents to sit still. The best you can do is to compare the things that change slowly to those that change more quickly.

Fortunately, understanding change is aided by two basic kinds of expression. The first is "narrative," learning to tell a kind of story we make up about what's happening, and the second is visualizing a whole series of changes as if they all existed at the same time, in a co-ordinated "space" created just for those changes, and adapted to our ways of envisioning changes all at once. That lasagna-looking image I brought up at the beginning is an example of such a "space."

The "space" thing may sound fancy, but this is really just common sense. If you want to make dinner, say, lasagna, you need to be able to "see" what will be on your plate when dinner is made. The plate is the "space" you imagine, where your dinner will be all together, existing at one time (and lasagna is a pretty complete meal, by the way, especially if you pack some veggies in, like fresh baby spinach, so if you just want to imagine that lasagna on the plate alone, be my guest, and include a little spinach sticking out from the edges—I mean, do that if you want to). But this plate in your head right now isn't an actual plate, it's the image of a plate, and that plate-image is really just a virtual space.

Since you do want dinner, and since dinner has to consist of something, you actively fill the plate-image with whatever other images you intend to see later, all stacked on the plate-image, as the real cooked ingredients you will eat. You hear what I'm saying? I suggest the plate, and you fill it with what you really want. Is this sounding familiar to you? Are you wondering why we would ever put our deepest secrets into the secret place someone else has constructed in our dreamworld? It's coming to that, boys and girls, because we wouldn't do that, if we could help it. But nothing is quite as hard to resist as an empty space, imagined, real, or dreamt.

You might never have thought of your dinner plate as an "imaginative space" before, but it is. The image provides an opportunity to co-ordinate the ingredients you'll have for dinner, which will require a process to change each of them from wherever they are, and whatever condition they are in, to the co-ordinated condition they will be in on your plate. So you also need to be able to specify in your imagination the steps you will go through to prepare each item, and this will normally proceed from the present situation you now inhabit, and arrive in the imagined future, with the plate-image serving as the stopping place for that story, a narrative, which ends with "and then I ate it."

That statement, "I ate it" is what Whitehead calls a "generic contrast." It's "generic" because it is more "general" than either of the contrasting terms (I and it), and this is a contrast because the food is still "the food" and I am still "myself" (in the sentence "and then I ate it"), even though the food is sating my hunger and nourishing my body—which marks the change that has occurred. Even though I and the lasagna were covariant, I varied less than did the dinner, which gives me fair claim to the nominative spot in the grammar of the contrast. The lasagna is just the object, the "it." If the lasagna should happen to eat me (as it might in a dream, after all), I'll be obliged to alter the grammar of my contrast. The point is that both my narrative about dinner and my imagined destiny for that narrative, the plate, are taken up into a higher level of generality—it's sort of a "kick," in Nolan's terms, because moving from one level of generalization to another actually involves traversing gaps in our thinking. It can be tough to follow the thread.

These sorts of imaginative spaces and narrative tales, like the tale of the lasagna and the plate and the "then I ate it," are extremely supple and elastic. You can arrange the narratives and vary the virtual spaces (in which the narratives end) almost infinitely without destroying their intelligibility and usefulness. Recognizing the relations between the narrative and the destined space, and how these are covariant, is the whole secret to thinking clearly about change, and kicking yourself from one level of generalization to another. And there is a rule: the space is always more stable than the story it co-ordinates. That's why you can so easily go back and imagine the same image a second time and use it as a touchstone for telling your story. You do it absolutely all the time, but to take control of what you're doing, like Cobb and the lucid dream-invaders (and their puppet-master Nolan), to think lucidly (while not being too much at the mercy of your habits and your memory), is part of the value of process philosophy.

Whitehead says that philosophy is more closely akin to poetry than to science, and that the practice of philosophy, the discipline it requires, is very much that of learning to create spaces and tell stories that follow, well, not the order and demands of pure expression, as poetry does, but those of possible patterns of order. If this discipline sounds a little like a Christopher Nolan movie to you, well, that's how it sounds to me too. And the kinds of order and stories that philosophy specializes in creating, in spite of our poetic proclivities, are basically mathematical. Our philosophical spaces are geometric and our narratives are algebraic. We don't just make up narratives and fanciful spaces in doing philosophy. Rather, we explore highly ordered possibilities and sets of possibilities as suggested by logical and mathematical kinds of order. It's more fun than it sounds. I'll try to prove it.

Time Won't Give Me Time

You have all probably suffered though quadratic equations—if a train leaves from Boston and another from Chicago, . . . and so on—but you might never have seen them as a sort story, or narrative, at bottom. It usually isn't a very interesting story, but that's because it's stripped down for the purposes of exhibiting some of the patterns of order implicit in all such "stories." If I were to add that Kanye West is on the Boston train and Taylor Swift is on the Chicago train, just to spice it up (and speaking of spices, sea salt and marjoram), and I expect you to tell me at what time he interrupts her, it might make the story a little more interesting, but it doesn't really change the mathematical aspects. If I say that the elapsed time from Chicago is exactly the amount of time you should bake lasagna at four hundred degrees, you would curse me for adding a second variable, wouldn't you? Even if I said that is the exact time to Toledo at the speed I'm thinking of? But there's a solution, or at least a set of possible solutions, and you know that much. Why is there a solution?

All narratives, and I mean all, exhibit algebraic order, including those written and directed by Christopher Nolan, because all temporal processes possess that kind of order. That's why we use algebra to describe the general features of covariant change. In fact, your ability to understand a story, to follow it, depends on this kind of order—it need not be explicit (fortunately, since you may suck at math), but the reason you know the difference between a story that makes sense and one that doesn't is because the algebraic order is already implicit in your own life processes, including your thinking (which is one of your life processes). In short, narrative is about time, how it passes and what you can do with it—the way time makes available to us our possibilities (variables) for action. Nolan may press the boundaries of our ability to make sense of his stories, but he does insist, as he must, on coherence in his narratives. And that is why he can't really hide the answer to the question about whether the top tumbles, as you will see if you can stay with me a little longer.

But I want to point out that Nolan's physics is consistent, because with each move to a deeper dream level, the same amount of time, the same five minutes, is dispersed over a larger total dreamspace (the city plus the hotel, plus the fortress, and so on), and that dispersal not only dilutes the effects of gravity, it also creates a geometrical progression of time expansions: five minutes become an hour, which becomes a week, which becomes a year, which becomes fifty years. If you picture those times all at once, in an image, it's geometry, but if you want to express the time-pattern, it's algebraic.

Wide Open Spaces

You've been through geometry, I'm sure, and you had to "describe" (mathematically) the necessary and invariant features of pure spatial forms—because that's what they make you do in geometry class. But you might never have considered those lovely "pure spatial forms" as imaginative places you might arrive at by telling the right kind of story, or as ways of co-ordinating all the elements of the story. (That's because you needed a more imaginative geometry teacher than you probably got.) Geometry is really about space and the ways we can think about it, but space has far more richness to it than its Euclidian structure.

Now might be a good moment for me to suggest that you check out an old story (1884) by Edwin Abbott called *Flatland*. This is the geometry teacher you wish you'd had. I should also mention that when you're rolling out your own pasta, the closer to absolute flatness you get it, the better, and the trick to that is to 1. keep the surface utterly dry and well sprinkled with flour and 2. use only fresh, room-temperature eggs and no water, and 3. don't be in a hurry.

But unlike, say, linguine, which can be cooked without drying it, the geometry of a baked lasagna depends upon drying the (very flat) pasta on a rippled board for at least a day (in dream time, that's a week); that will give it a three-dimensional geometry and creates space for things like baby spinach, feta cheese, and a very lean organic ground beef, browned in a pan for just a few minutes (keep the drippings and add those to the 4.5 ounces of tomato paste and sixteen ounces of fresh chopped tomatoes).

How rich is space? Well, it's exactly as rich as time is varied, and the reason is simple, and I am going to say this twice and then pause for a moment while you consider it—to let it rise, so to speak. Imagined space is the destiny of imagined time. Just as the plate is the destiny of your narrative about preparing dinner, any—and indeed every—space just is the destiny of some time process. Indeed, when it comes to our imaginative lives, space is frozen time. (But don't freeze your pasta, just wrap it in some Saran Wrap and let it sit for half an hour, kneading it through the wrap every five minutes or so to raise its temperature above that of the room.)

Now wait a minute. Space is frozen time? Yes, that's what I said. If you want to understand something, narrate it until you have all the elements, or all the ingredients, well described, and how they should be combined, and then consider the end result as a frozen picture in which they are all together at the same time. That last "all-together-now" is the space that was always the destiny of your narrative. The study of that space is your very own new geometry.

You're Waiting for a Train

Mathematical order, then, comes in those two forms, narrative and spatial. In my example above I asked: at what time does

Kanye interrupt Taylor? Now that's an algebraic question about an algebraic relation. I could have asked "where are they when he interrupts her?" (It's only Toledo if you're looking for the baking time). The "where" would be a geometric question about an algebraic relation, and it co-ordinates as an image everything it took to get them both there. You can sort of feel it happening—you're waiting for that train (keep your head off the tracks), and you feel those trains converging, you see the train tracks, don't you? Where are we?

You know that at any place along that track, they could meet, the Cobb and Mal of pop music, depending on their individual speeds, and now you're just waiting for me to say "Cleveland, in time for dinner" and when I do, not only will you be able to calculate how fast each train had to be travelling— that's the time issue. You are also picturing a real place, say, Cleveland (even if you haven't been there), and ignoring the fact that it was a geometric "at-the-same-timeness" that enabled you to proceed with your algebraic calculation. "At the same time" just is the meaning of space. Space comes from time and depends on time. And I must tell you that it really is Cleveland where they meet because I know the best restaurant there, on Euclid Avenue, where they have an incredible lasagna (veggie version available, but not nearly as tasty), and Kanye and Taylor definitely ought to meet there, as should Leo DiCaprio and Ellen Page, even though they'll all need a taxi from the train station (where they arrive at about 5:30, give or take).

If you want to understand something, incisively and accurately, you have to be able to tell the story that ends in and is co-ordinated by the right kind of space. When we're philosophizing, we are looking for the more variable features of the story against the backdrop of the features that vary less, and if we have chosen the best ingredients to compare, the dinner plate is filled with a most edible meal, so to speak, the intellectual lasagna of your dreams. The generic contrast is "achieved" ("and then I ate it") because the higher level of generality in which the contrasting things can co-exist is a space of some kind. What I am now prepared to offer is the thought you have been wanting to think all along, about the movie you liked well enough to read this book.

The Secret Ingredient

My man Whitehead has a lot of specialized vocabulary to describe this method of narrative and space in all of its subtleties, and his descriptions are, to his admirers, a perfect poetry of creative, reflective imagination. But we don't need all that vocabulary for now. Yet, I have to add the disclaimer that I have already created the narrative and the space in which it ends, and my choices are filled with contingencies.

With different choices at any stage along the way, the imaginative space that can be created could be similar, but not wholly consistent with what I will conclude. My conclusion, the part that says, "And then I ate it," should seem persuasive to you, at least if I compare the best factors during the narrative, and find those that interact dynamically and fruitfully. Then my story will increase the value of your life, regardless of whether you agree with it. That is what generic contrasts are. They are "accretions of value."

We think, imagine, understand, and express our ideas all for the sake of creating value. The accretion of value is the possibility that continuously lures us into action, and thinking is an action. I know you've been thinking about that damned movie. So have I. Is there an end to it? I'm aiming to bring that about. You have my promise that I'm sincere about adding to the value of your world in saying what I do say about this film. I love this film and I think it's important. Some of what I say may surprise and even provoke you, but when I'm finished, you'll be thinking about the future and you'll be trying to tell a story to yourself that puts you there in an imagined space you have created yourself.

Oh, and one last thing. Use semola for your pasta, not semolina. As my Italian cooking instructor once said "semolina is just a Toyota, semola is the Cadillac." Semola is the secret ingredient. Or so I believe. Since the pasta is time, and the cheese is just a melting dream, get time right, whatever else you do.

Mind the Gap

I love the voice on the London subway that says, oh so seductively, "Mind the gap" as you step off the train onto the platform. Nolan has devilishly concealed the answer to the main riddle, but it's there—and it's there because he's a great story-teller. His plate is full, but you have to read it as a geometry before the algebra will make sense. And there's always a clue. Follow the gaps. There are lots of gaps in this story, as there are in any story—just as when Arthur is showing Ariadne the Penrose stairs, even in a dream there will be gaps that can be concealed from those who only half-consciously consumed the lasagna you serve them. But if you're smart, you can learn to see those gaps. Three gaps will help you find your way to the truth about the spinning totem, so let me offer you three kicks to see if I can get you there.

First Kick

The first gap is a very obvious one, if you're paying attention. It's the conversation between Saito, Arthur, and Cobb—the "Don't think of an elephant" line, a conversation in which we're led to believe that "inception" is almost impossible. The reason we're given is that even though an idea is the most contagious virus there is, we can always trace the origin of an idea if it comes from outside ourselves. This provides the entire motive for attempting inception.

But it simply isn't true that we can always trace the origins of our ideas when they come from beyond ourselves. And when those ideas are reduced to archetypes, as suggested in this movie, we can't trace them in principle. Do they belong to the whole race? To life itself? We don't know. And we never will. So why, pray tell, is Nolan so quickly passing over such a knotty contradiction: ideas are super contagious, but it's devilish hard to plant one without the subject knowing it?

The truth is, as you very well know, nothing is easier to plant than an idea, and the process by which it was planted can be spread out over many experiences, and you can't always trace it, no matter how smart you are. Experience is too complex and too discontinuous. If I wanted you to be hungry for lasagna, I could even spread a recipe for it across an essay about a movie, if I had a mind to do so. And if you should find yourself wanting lasagna a year from now, long after you've forgotten reading this essay, who's to say whether I succeeded as an "inceiver," and whether you are my very own Robert Fischer?

If you find yourself thinking, next time you're in Cleveland, "What about Euclid Avenue? I heard of a place there." Well, you get the picture (and a "picture" is exactly what it is). I give my willing suspension of disbelief to Nolan when he sets up the story, but I remember thinking the first time I heard it that you can't say "an idea is the most viral thing we know" and then pretend it's nearly impossible to give one to somebody without their knowing it with perfect clarity. It's a serious gap in the story—a gap in the narrative and its believability. If we move forward with the narrative after that, it's because we accept a generic contrast: "he needs this for the story."

Second Kick

That brings us to the second gap. You know this, but you may not have seen its importance. The spinning top is not Cobb's totem. It belonged to Mal. It's never stated anywhere in the story that the top is Cobb's totem. That's an inference you probably made (and were encouraged to make) across a gap in the narrative. And you thought that the rule Cobb had made, privately, with himself, was that if it doesn't fall, he is dreaming. But no one ever says this or anything like it in the movie.

What you saw was the top falling and Cobb deciding not to shoot himself. That's all you saw. Why did you assume the top's falling was the reason Cobb took the gun down? Because you were strongly encouraged to make that jump and it was reinforced a number of times later. But that, boys and girls, is cottage cheese from the grocery store, and I am going to encourage you to hold out for feta from the Old Country, and by making it this far in my essay, you've had time to order and receive the good stuff. Hold on, because here comes the supersecret ingredient.

A gap is a gap. We're not at all forced to think that Cobb decided not to kill himself because the top fell. The spinning of the top for Cobb is a way of remembering Mal, it is a kind of mourning, not a test to see whether Cobb is dreaming. He knew he wasn't dreaming. He was just pondering whether to kill himself and didn't have the nerve. Cobb is actually a coward and he knows it, with nothing like the courage of Mal or Ariadne, or anyone else who is capable of truly trusting another human being, for that matter. I'll prove it.

The script makes it crystal clear that the top was Mal's totem. When Cobb and Mal took their long nap together, and when she built her safe in her childhood home, it was empty, as are all dreamsafes. There is no reason to believe she preferred the dreamworld to waking life. That is never said explicitly. We infer it. But Mal was an able architect. Remember, Mal and Cobb were co-architects of that amazing dreamscape, as Cobb tells Ariadne. But why did they end up laying their heads on the railroad tracks?

Something happened to Mal to plant a doubt; she could no longer rely on her totem and she could no longer distinguish the dream from reality. She doubted whether she could wake up. The reason this happened to her is because Cobb had broken the trust and had handled her totem, and he had done it while they were awake. He betrayed her. He may even have planned to trap her in the dream, she'll never know. Why was he handling her totem in the waking world? We don't know, but in any case, he was the one who wanted (at some level) the dream to last forever, so he disabled her ability to return to the real world, and then he broke into her safe, and she was completely in his power. It is an interesting kind of betrayal, and it actually poses the same uncomfortable question as *The Stepford Wives*, which is, If you could render your wife utterly subservient, would you do it?

The answer is always no, if you are an even remotely decent person, because to do that is to sacrifice all your lover's "complexities" as Cobb puts it, all her "perfections." Once Cobb had done this he saw it was a terrible mistake, but he couldn't undo it, and he couldn't set it right within the dream. So he confessed and she had to trust him—take a leap of faith—that they really were dreaming. And being an individual, an autonomous being, she didn't want to be required to trust him in that way. That's why she's afraid and he isn't when they lay their heads on the tracks. He knows they're dreaming, and she's helpless to learn whether he's telling her the truth, and he has betrayed her once already.

He had already done something that rendered her completely helpless, and a man who would do that to you has already killed you. So, to atone, he lays his head on the tracks with her. As you know, they wake up. But now the doubt has been planted, and it won't go away. The marriage is ruined and she can't go on. She loved him so much. The betrayal is too much to bear. So if Cobb won't jump with her from the hotel ledge, if he won't take the leap with her that he made her take with him, she would rather not live.

Now you know why Cobb is so deeply haunted by the moment when he spun Mal's top, while it resided in the safe of her childhood home. Cobb had no business in Mal's safe, any more than you have any business poking around in your lover's old letters (or secret recipes). Remember, even though Mal built that house in their common dream, Cobb is the one who put the top in it—or rather, he filled the safe with the very thing he most desperately desired but (perhaps) could not admit to himself, consciously. I'm giving him the benefit of the doubt here, but when he opened the safe (he is, after all, a professional thief) he saw the top because his mind wanted it to be there, as he well knew, or even worse, he put it there on purpose, but either way it's very bad news. To spin it and close the safe, well, it symbolizes his desire for total power over her. Only a coward needs that kind of power over another person.

Ariadne, by the way, immediately gets all of this, after just one shared dream (she's a quick study), and she knows exactly how damaged Cobb is and what kind of man he is. He's a man who, down deep, desires complete control over others, and especially over those who are closest to him. He is a Stepford husband. That's why Ariadne tries to walk away. That is also why Mal is so very pissed off in Cobb's subconscious; the superego is a harsh, harsh mistress. A question, Mal's question: would you make a safe for your lover to fill with whatever he or she most deeply desires, even knowing that the person you love probably can't know or admit what he would put in that safe, given the chance? Mal is a brave one, isn't she?

Last Kick

And that brings us to the final gap. I've kept you long enough. The biggest jump in the whole film is when Cobb and Saito manage to come back from Limbo all the way up to the airplane. We do not see the fifty years that pass while Cobb is searching for Saito, but I think we can safely assume he's atoning for past misdeeds. Cobb has learned his lesson about trust. That's the change that marks the meaning of the story. Being given a second chance to trust, this time with something as precious as his and Mal's children at stake, he will not make the same mistake a second time.

He chooses to take the leap of faith with Saito, because without trusting somebody, he can never have his life back. Taking the measure of Saito's character, Cobb decides Saito is an ordinary man, no saint, no villain, and ordinarily self-interested, but a man who does have wisdom. Saito's wisdom comes in his willingness to trust Cobb even though he knows very well that Cobb isn't trustworthy. (Saito does show Cobb what happens to people who betray him, as poor Nash finds out).

Cobb's dilemma is simple. Trust Saito, absolutely, or have a life that isn't worth living. Cobb chooses to trust Saito. Saito believes Cobb is self-interested enough, but also good enough, to be trusted. Saito is right. There is a crucial moment, by the way, when Cobb drops Mal's top in front of Saito, and Saito sees it but does not touch it. When Cobb washes up on the shore of Saito's mountain fortress-palace fifty (dream) years later, he has two and only two things on his person: his gun and Mal's top. These are placed before the ancient Saito, and Cobb asks him to choose, to take a leap of faith with him. The next thing we know, they wake up on the plane. That's the gap. What happened?

It's so simple it's painful. Saito didn't just spin the top. He also shot Cobb and then shot himself. (That is why Cobb woke up seconds before Saito.) This is what Cobb was asking him to do, because Cobb himself didn't have the courage to do it, but he was willing to trust Saito to follow him.

Here's your kick: The gun is Cobb's totem. He doesn't let anyone else touch it in the movie—it's heavy, unique, and so forth. Why would anyone choose a gun for a totem? It's simple. Cobb decided that if he should ever come to the point that he could not distinguish dream from reality, he would rather not go on living. Either way, if he puts the gun to his head and pulls the trigger, he ends the trouble. A safer totem cannot be imagined (unless your chemist has supercharged the serum). In the crucial moment, he gives it to Saito and trusts him to do the "right thing." And Saito doesn't disappoint him. So the gun in the first act really does go off in the third, and Nolan uses sleight-of-hand to keep you from noticing.

Does the Totem Tumble?

And finally we are at the answer to the question with which we began. Yes, the totem tumbles, but it doesn't matter. Cobb's totem is back on the airplane. Remember, Saito bought the plane to get around Australian airport security, but Cobb cannot hope to get off in LA with a gun on his person and still get through security there. He left his gun on the plane, along with his desire to commit suicide.

It actually doesn't matter whether the totem falls because it's Mal's totem, but in fact it does. It isn't a symbol of whether this is dream or reality, but rather a sign of whether Cobb has changed in the relevant way. He has learned to trust and is now fit to raise those lovely children. He is not a coward any more, the proof of which is that he lives without his own totem and walks away from Mal's without dwelling on her, or on whether the totem tumbles. He has a future. You ponder that, I'm going to get some good feta cheese. I have a lasagna to make. I do wonder what the goats of Umbria eat, but since feta requires both sheep's and goat's milk, and since it only comes from Greece, I don't need to go to Umbria. (I'm sorry about the quadratic equation on the cooking time, but you could just turn on the oven light and eyeball it—I mean, do I have to do everything for you?)

Some of Our Totems

Alber, Jan, Stefan Iversen, and Henrik Skov Nielsen. 2010. Unnatural Narratives, Unnatural Narratology beyond Mimetic Models. *Narrative* 18:2, pp. 113–136.

Anderson, John R., and Lynn Reder. 1979. Elaborative Processing Explanation of Depth Processing. In Laird. S. Cermak and Fergus M. Craik, eds., *Levels of Processing in Human Memory* (Hillsdale: Erlbaum, 2002).

Andrew, Dudley. 1984. *Concepts in Film Theory*. New York: Oxford University Press.

Antrobus, John S., and Mario Bertini, eds. 2002. *The Neuropsychology of Sleep and Dreaming*. Mahwah: Erlbaum.

Aristotle. 1983. *Physics*. Books III and IV. Oxford: Oxford University Press.

Barad, Karen. 2007. *Meeting the Universe Halfway*. Durham: Duke University Press.

Baudrillard, Jean. 2001. The Spirit of Terrorism. *Le monde* (November 2nd).

Bazin, André. 1958. *Qu'est-ce que le cinéma?* Paris: Cerf.

Beckett, Samuel. 1982. *Waiting for Godot: Tragicomedy in Two Acts*. New York: Grove Weidenfeld.

Benedikt, Michael. 1991. *Introduction to Cyberspace: First Steps*. Cambridge, Massachusetts: MIT Press.

Benjamin, Walter. 2008 [1935]. *The Work of Art in the Age of Its Technological Reproducibility, and other Writings on Media*. Boston: Belknap.

Berg, Charles Ramírez. 2006. A Taxonomy of Alternative Plots in Recent Films: Classifying the 'Tarantino Effect'. *Film Criticism* 31:1–2.

Bergson, Henri. 1922. Durée et simultanéité. Paris: Alcan.

———. 2004 [1939]. *Matière et Mémoire*. Paris: Presses Universitaires de France.

Berkeley, George. 1988. *A Treatise Concerning the Principles of Human Knowledge*. Harmondsworth: Penguin.

Bordwell, David. 2006. *The Way Hollywood Tells It: Story and Style in Modern Movies*. London: California University Press.

Borges, Jorge Luis. 1962. The Secret Miracle. In *Ficciones* (New York: Grove).

Bosnak, Robert. 2007. *Embodiment: Creative Imagination in Medicine, Art, and Travel*. Oxford: Routledge.

Botz-Bornstein, Thorsten. 2007. Dreams in Buddhism and Western Aesthetics. *Asian Philosophy* 17:1, pp. 65–81.

———. 2007. *Films and Dreams: Tarkovsky, Bergman, Sokurov, Kubrick, and Wong Kar-wai*. Lanham: Lexington.

———. 2010. Anti-Freudianism Korean Style: Kim Ki-duk's Dream. *Journal of Japanese and Korean Cinema* 2:1, pp. 51–62.

Boyer, M. Christine. 1996. *CyberCities*. New York: Princeton Architectural Press.

Branigan, Edward. 1984. *Point of View in the Cinema*. New York: Mouton.

Bulkeley, Kelly. 1994. *The Wilderness of Dreams*. Albany: SUNY Press.

Capps, Robert. 2010. Q&A: Christopher Nolan on Dreams, Architecture, and Ambiguity. *Wired* (December), <www.wired.com/magazine/2010/11/pl_inception_nolan>.

Chatman, Seymour. 1990. *Coming to Terms: The Rhetoric of Narrative in Fiction and Film*. Ithaca: Cornell University Press.

Coleridge, Samuel Taylor. 1997. *The Complete Poems*. New York: Penguin.

Davis, Mike. 2007. Sand, Fear, and Money in Dubai. In Mike Davis and Daniel Bertrand Monk, eds., *Dreamworlds of Neoliberalism: Evil Paradises* (New York: New Press).

Dawkins, Richard. 1989. *The Selfish Gene*. Oxford: Oxford University Press.

Dennett, Daniel. 1978. *Brainstorms*. Cambridge, Massachusetts: MIT Press.

Descartes, René. 1904 [1640]. *Oeuvres de Descartes*. Paris: Vrin.

———. 1996 [1641]. *Meditations on First Philosophy*. Cambridge: Cambridge University Press.

———. 2003 [1641]. *Meditations on First Philosophy*. New York: Penguin.

Dewey, John. 1938. *Experience and Education*. New York: Macmillan.

Ekman, Paul. 1985. *Telling Lies*. New York: Norton.

Elkadi, Hisham. 2006. *Cultures of Glass Architecture*. Abingdon: Ashgate.

Enders, Walter, and Todd Sandler. 2005. *The Political Economy of Terrorism*. New York: Cambridge University Press.

Epstein, Jean. 1946 [1921]. *L'Intelligence d'une machine*. Paris: Jacques Melot.

Fludernik, Monika. 1996. *Towards a 'Natural' Narratology*. London: Routledge.

Foulkes, David. 1985. *Dreaming: A Cognitive-Psychological Analysis*. Mahwah: Erlbaum.

Frampton, Daniel. 2006. *Filmosophy*. London: Wallflower.

Freud, Sigmund. 2010 [1899]. *The Interpretation of Dreams: The Complete and Definitive Text*. New York: Basic Books.

Friedman, Milton. 1970. The Social Responsibility of Business Is to Increase Its Profits. *The New York Times Magazine* (September 13th).

Fromm, Erich. 1951. *The Forgotten Language: An Introduction to the Understanding of Dreams, Fairy Tales, and Myths*. New York: Grove.

Gazzaniga, Michael S. 1998. The Split Brain Revisited. *Scientific American* 279.

Ghosh, Pallab. 2010. Dream Recording Device 'Possible', Researcher Claims. *BBC News* (October 27th).

Gino, Francesca, Michael I. Norton, and Dan Ariely. 2010. The Counterfeit Self: The Deceptive Costs of Faking It. *Psychological Science* (March), <http://pss.sagepub.com/content/early/2010/03/19/0956797610366545.full>.

Goffman, Erving. 1986. *Frame Analysis: An Essay on the Organization of Experience*. Boston: Northeastern University Press.

Grishakova, Marina. 2002. Towards the Semiotics of the Observer. *Sign System Studies* 30:2, pp. 529–553.

Grodal, Torben. 2009. *Embodied Visions: Evolution, Emotion, Culture, and Film*. Oxford: Oxford University Press.

Habermas, Jürgen. 2003. *The Future of Human Nature*. Malden: Blackwell.

Harman, Gilbert. 1977. *The Nature of Morality: An Introduction to Ethics*. New York: Oxford University Press.

Hawthorne, Christopher. 2008. Dubai Development May Be Down, but It's Not Out. *Los Angeles Times* (November 2nd).

Heidegger, Martin. 2000. ". . . dichterisch wohnet der Mensch . . ." In *Vorträge und Aufsätze* (Frankfurt: Klostermann).

———. 2002. The Origin of the Work of Art. In *Off the Beaten Track* (Cambridge: Cambridge University Press).

Heinze, Ruediger. 2008. Violations of Mimetic Epistemology in First-Person Narrative Fiction. *Narrative* 16:3.

Herman, David, Manfred Jahn, and Marie-Laure Ryan, eds. 2005. Focalization. *Routledge Encyclopedia of Narrative Theory*. New York: Routledge.

————, eds. 2005. Naturalization. *Routledge Encyclopedia of Narrative Theory*. New York: Routledge.

Hill, Thomas E. Jr. 1980. Humanity as an End in Itself. *Ethics* 91:1, pp. 84–99.

Hobson, J. Allan. 1999. The New Neurospsychology of Sleep: Implications for Psychoanalysis. *Neuropsychoanalysis* 1, pp. 157–183.

————. 2002. *Dreaming: An Introduction to the Science of Sleep*. Oxford: Oxford University Press.

————. 2005. *Thirteen Dreams Freud Never Had: The New Mind Science*. New York: Pi Press.

Hobson, J. Allan, and Robert W. McCarley. 1977. The Brain as a Dream State Generator: An Activation-Synthesis Hypothesis. *American Journal of Psychiatry* 134:13.

Hölderlin, Friedrich. 1946–52. *Sämtliche Werke*. Stuttgart: Kohlhammer and Cotta.

Hume, David. 1993. *An Enquiry Concerning Human Understanding*. Indianapolis: Hackett.

Husserl, Edmund. 1970. *The Crisis of the European Sciences*. Chicago: Northwestern University Press.

————. 1993. *Cartesian Meditations*. Dordrecht: Kluwer.

Huxley, Aldous. 1993 [1939]. *After Many a Summer Dies the Swan*. Chicago: Dee.

Jahn, Manfred. 1997. Frames, Preferences, and the Reading of Third-Person Narratives: Towards a Cognitive Narratology. *Poetics Today* 18:4.

James, William. 1950 [1890]. *The Principles of Psychology*. Two volumes. New York: Dover.

————. 1997 [1902]. *The Varieties of Religious Experience*. New York: Simon and Schuster.

Jaspers, Karl. 1998. Philosophy of Existence. In William McNeill and Karen S. Feldman, eds., *Continental Philosophy: An Anthology* (Malden: Blackwell), pp. 132–140.

Kant, Immanuel. 1996. Groundwork of the Metaphysics of Morals. In M.J. Gregor, ed., *Practical Philosophy* (New York: Cambridge University Press).

Lacan, Jacques. 2002. *Écrits I*. Paris: Seuil.

Lakoff, George. 2004. *Don't Think of an Elephant: Know Your Values and Frame the Debate*. White River Junction: Chelsea Green.

Laplace, Pierre-Simon. 1951 [1814]. *A Philosophical Essay on Probabilities*. New York: Dover.

Libet, Benjamin. 1993. *Neurophysiology of Consciousness*. Boston: Birkhauser.

Mallarmé, Stéphane. 2002. *Igitur. Divagations. Un coup de dés*. Paris: Gallimard.

Mill, John Stuart. 1993. *Utilitarianism*. New York: Bantam.

Nietzsche, Friedrich. 1956 [1887]. *The Birth of Tragedy and On the Genealogy of Morals*. New York: Anchor.

———. 1990 [1886]. *Beyond Good and Evil: Prelude to a Philosophy of the Future*. London: Penguin.

Nolan, Christopher, and Jonah Nolan. 2010. *Inception: The Shooting Script*. St. Rafael: Insight.

Nozick, Robert. 1974. *Anarchy, State, and Utopia*. New York: Basic Books.

Peirce, Charles Sanders. 1996. How to Make Our Ideas Clear. In Max H. Fisch and Nathan Houser, eds., *Classic American Philosophers: Peirce, James, Royce, Santayana, Dewey, Whitehead* (New York: Fordham University Press).

Penfield, Wilder. 1975. *The Mystery of Mind*. Princeton: Princeton University Press.

Plato. 1991. *The Republic of Plato*. New York: Basic Books.

Prince, Stephen. 2000. The Aesthetic of Slow-Motion Violence in the Films of Sam Peckinpah. In Stephen Prince, ed., *Screening Violence* (New Brunswick: Rutgers University Press), pp.175–201.

Ramirez, Carlos. 1997. Schemata, Frames, and Dynamic Memory Structures <http://kar.kent.ac.uk/21537/>.

Rawls, John. 1999. *A Theory of Justice*. Cambridge: Harvard University Press.

Ro, Tony. 2008. Unconscious Vision in Action. *Neuropsychologia* 46.

Rock, Andrea. 2004. *The Mind at Night: The New Science of How and Why We Dream*. New York: Basic Books.

Rupprecht, Carol S., ed. 1993. *The Dream and the Text: Essays on Literature and Language*. New York: SUNY Press.

Searle, John R. 1995. *The Construction of Social Reality*. New York: Simon and Schuster.

Sheehan, Paul. 2002. *Modernism, Narrative, and Humanism*. Cambridge: Cambridge University Press.

Shklovsky, Viktor. 1965 [1919]. Art as Technique. In *Russian Formalist Criticism: Four Essays* (Lincoln: University of Nebraska Press).

Simons, Jan. 2008. Complex Narratives. *New Review of Film and Television Studies* 6:2 (August).

Singer, Peter. 1993. *Practical Ethics*. New York: Cambridge University Press.

Skinner, Burrhus Frederic. 1971. *Beyond Freedom and Dignity*. Indianapolis: Hackett.

Small, Edward S. 1994. *Direct Theory*. Carbondale: Southern Illinois University Press.

Smith, Adam. 2003 [1776]. *The Wealth of Nations*. New York: Random House.

Smith, David Woodruff. 2009. Phenomenology. In Edward N. Zalta, ed., *The Stanford Encyclopedia of Philosophy* <http://plato.stanford.edu/archives/sum2009/entries/phenomenology>.

Solms, Mark. 1997. *The Neuropsychology of Dreams: A Clinico-Anatomical Study*. Mahwah: Erlbaum.

————. 2005. The Interpretation of Dreams and the Neurosciences. Paper presented on April 19th, <www.psychoanalysis.org.uk/solms4.htm>.

Stepaniants, Marietta. 2002. *Introduction to Eastern Thought*. Lanham: AltaMira.

Strindberg, August. 1973. *A Dream Play and Four Chamber Plays*. Washington: University of Washington Press.

Swann, William B., Jr. 1983. Self-Verification: Bringing Social Reality into Harmony with the Self. In Jerry Suls and Anthony G. Greenwald, eds., *Psychological Perspectives on the Self* (Hillsdale: Erlbaum).

Taylor, Kathleen. 2004. *Brainwashing: The Science of Thought Control*. New York: Oxford University Press.

Tierney, John. 2007. Our Lives Controlled from Some Guy's Couch. *New York Times* (August 14th).

Valéry, Paul. 1929. Questions du rêve. In *Cahiers Paul Valéry* III (Paris: Gallimard).

————. 2007. *Poésies*. Paris: Gallimard.

Wittgenstein, Ludwig. 2003 [1969]. *On Certainty*. Oxford: Blackwell.

Just Projections of Someone's Subconscious

NATHAN ANDERSEN is never quite sure he's not dreaming, but tries not to think about it much. At 6'9" (2.05m), he may not be the tallest living philosopher, but is almost certainly the tallest living Hegel scholar who is also the co-director of an eclectic environmental film festival and a "top 100" Amazon reviewer in his spare time. His tastes in film range from beautifully shot but depressing and angsty existential explorations to big-budget science-fiction extravaganzas. He is an Associate Professor of Philosophy at Eckerd College in Saint Petersburg, Florida.

RANDALL E. AUXIER lives in a dream and dreams he teaches philosophy at Southern Illinois University in Carbondale, where forests and streams make a labyrinth from which few want to return. He has actually only been there about five minutes, but to him it seems like a dozen years or so, and he wonders if, somewhere somewhen, a spinning top refuses to tumble.

THORSTEN BOTZ-BORNSTEIN is a German philosopher attempting to be slightly funnier than Kant. Currently he is trying to incept philosophical ideas as an Assistant Professor in the minds of students of the Gulf University for Science and Technology. Being attracted by everything that is virtual, playful, and dreamlike he has found much of the desired dreamlike atmosphere in classical Japanese and Chinese philosophy but has also elaborated on profound parallels between the design of the new Mini Cooper and Japanese pottery. His current research takes place in a setting that some might classify as utterly unreal: Kuwait.

BERIT BROGAARD is an Associate Professor of Philosophy and Psychology at the University of Missouri, St. Louis, and a neuroscience geek who likes to browse twentieth-century medical journals to make sure no brilliant idea was overlooked merely because it wasn't resilient or highly contagious. She also likes to do experiments on humans, and while she hasn't yet hacked into anyone's dreams, she is hoping she will soon be able to use transcranial magnetic stimulation to temporarily zap localized regions of people's brains. When she doesn't do experiments or read dusty medical journals, she publishes articles and books, talks to synesthetic savants and plants ideas in her students' minds without them even noticing.

MATTHEW BROPHY bides his time by teaching philosophy as an assistant professor at High Point University, while he waits for the "kick" —whereupon he'll wake up as a dashingly handsome spy on the trail of danger, intrigue, fame, and fortune. Until then, he patiently resides with his beautiful wife and above-average child in Greensboro, North Carolina. So far, he's resisted succumbing to the temptations of gaming dreamscapes like *World of Warcraft*. As you can imagine, his wife helps.

HIU M. CHAN is a dreamer. She dreams as she writes. Without separating dream and reality, she graduated with a BA Film Studies degree from Oxford Brookes University. She was then realistically accepted by UCL to continue her MA in Film Studies. Hiu has recently submitted her PhD application to different institutions around the globe. As well as academic writing, her dreamy status also enables her to be involved in creative writing. She is only awake when she dreams.

EMILIE DIONNE often dreams of buildings with multiple staircases and mysterious hidden passages that challenge *known* physics, and it is always with a sense of wonder that she awakes in the morning and finds *reality* by her side. She longs to *incept* the idea in her mind that dreams are like a reflection in a looking-glass through which she can step, for a moment, and peek through time. Maybe she would learn more about herself than in reality. But if she manages to walk through walls and travel without jet-lag in her dreams, reality tells us that she received a master degree in Political Studies from the University of Ottawa and is currently a doctorate candidate in Social and Political Thought at York University, Ontario, Canada. Her work involves applications of feminist and post-structuralist critiques to popular culture. Her aim is to expose the dreams of our culture in the harsh realities of its fallaciously fixed categories.

NICOLAS FLOURY attempted psychoanalysis when he was very young, once switching to science where he did not find the truths he was looking for. He then headed towards philosophy and started working on PhD at the University of Nanterre. But sooner or later he realized that nothing can be said about truth in any way, at least not as long as you are trying to say something true about it. He became a psychologist and would soon enjoy listening to other people's ever unique life stories. He found that *Inception* was a perfect attempt at deciphering life, similar to what he is doing every day.

INDALECIO GARCÍA could appropriate one of Cobb's lines, albeit slightly modified: "Resilient, highly contagious. Once a question's taken hold in the brain it's almost impossible to eradicate." In his case, that question is 'What is time?' —an issue as resilient as 'What is reality?' Because of this question alone, Indalecio studied philosophy at the Universidad Nacional de Colombia, and is now developing his PhD research on the concept of time in Aristotle's philosophy.

JOSEPH GARVIN is a once-and-future philosophy student, currently taking a years break between his masters degree, from University College Dublin, and his doctorate, from somewhere yet to be determined. Since starting this article, his dreams have been particularly odd, and particularly vivid, and he's wondering if someone is practicing inception on him . . . and if it would be ethical to do so. If you asked him what his dream was, right now it's just to sit back down in a seminar room and have a lecture, as he's really missing that.

JASON J. HOWARD is an Associate Professor of Philosophy at Viterbo University. In addition to publishing in the areas of moral psychology, ethics, and Hegel, he continues to work part-time as a stunt double on some of Nolan's films. He took it hard when he was passed over as the double for DiCaprio in *Inception*. As a way of making it up to him Nolan tried to recognize Jason's efforts by acknowledging him in one of the last scenes of the movie, the scene where DiCaprio exits the airport terminal. Unfortunately he got the name wrong on the welcome sign—it's J. Howard and not T. Howard. Nice try Chris!

VALENTIN HUSSON is a PhD student at the University of Strasbourg, France. Convinced that to live in a world means to build one, he hardly sees any difference between dream and reality. This is also why he can't objectify the end of *Inception*. Whether the spinning top falls or not—why would this matter? Dream or reality? If we have doubts about it, this shows that we are already building this real or dreamlike world and that we dwell and live in it.

THOMAS KAPPER earned a doctorate that combined philosophy, law, and economics from the University of Wisconsin at Madison. He is director of the firm, Peregrine Aesthetics Group, which is concerned with the valuation of the environment and real estate. Dr. Kapper tends to watch too many movies and ask too many questions. He has practiced Zen for over a decade seeking a swift kick, and will gladly tip you over backward in your chair if it will help you to wake up.

DANIEL P. MALLOY is an adjunct assistant professor of philosophy at Appalachian State University in Boone, North Carolina. When he is not teaching, he does research on the practical side of philosophy, primarily dealing with issues in ethics and political philosophy. He has published numerous chapters on the intersection of popular culture and philosophy, particularly dealing with ethical issues. In his spare time, Daniel works as a corporate spy for publishing houses—invading the dreams of editors to steal book ideas and sell them to the highest bidder.

ORA C. MCWILLIAMS reads too many comic books and really needs to work on his dissertation as a Ph.D. student in the Department of American Studies at the University of Kansas. That experience is probably a dream within a dream, within a dream. He can never *really* tell but embraces the regress, nevertheless. His totem is a sun-bleached 1997 Marvel Comics Thanos figure with the Infinity Gauntlet painted on his hand . . . but perhaps he's said too much.

MICHAEL RENNETT is a PhD candidate in Media Studies at the University of Texas, Austin. He graduated from CSU Northridge in 2004 with a BA degree in Media Theory and Criticism and a minor in Jewish Studies. He received his Master's degree from Chapman University in the field of Film Studies in 2006. He has contributed to *The Journal of Popular Culture, The International Journal of Baudrillard Studies,* and *The Journal of Religion and Film* as well as volumes on *Lost* and Pedro Almodóvar. He's currently dreaming that he's taking a long walk by a snowy mountain fortress, but wishes that he was on a beach.

In this layer of the dream, **JOSHUA RICHARDSON** is a student of film and media studies and American studies at the University of Kansas. His interests include horror film, fan culture, and new media. The weirdest dream he ever had involved animate chess pieces.

CHRISTOPHE D. RINGER is a doctoral candidate in Vanderbilt University's Department of Religion. Christophe is an aspiring dream architect who can't remember where he left his totem.

MARCUS SCHULZKE is a PhD candidate in political science at the State University of New York at Albany. His primary research interests are political theory and comparative politics, with special attention to contemporary political theory and political violence. He has published work on military ethics, information ethics, counterinsurgency, political associations, political activism, and digital media. He is currently working on a dissertation about how soldiers make moral decisions in combat. After school, he plans to open the world's first dream defense firm and expects it to have a perfect success record until someone invents extraction.

After years of teaching physics, world history, psychology and statistics in Florida and New Hampshire **JANET TESTERMAN** has finally accepted that she is being manipulated by forces outside her control and happily embraces the conclusion "It is not my fault." She has masterfully implanted the following inception in her students of writing where she is an assistant professor at Gulf University of Science and Technology in Kuwait: Do not allow anyone access to your dreams.

SYLVIA WENMACKERS became a fan of science fiction through Asimov's *Foundation* series and *Star Trek*. The ideas in these series proved to be very resilient and motivated her to study science. In 2008, she obtained a PhD in Physics at the Institute for Materials Research of Hasselt University (Belgium) for a study dealing with synthetic diamond and its application to biosensors: science fiction for real! As much as she loves science fiction, she hates open endings: they make her stay up all night to figure out what they mean. Physics can tell you why a top always stops spinning, but not what it signifies . . . In 2011, she obtained a second PhD at the Philosophy Department of Groningen University (The Netherlands). Her current research focuses on the philosophy of probability. Now she can prove that there is a non-zero probability that life is just a dream.

Architectural Code